STUDENT GUIDEBOOK

YOUR STEP BY STEP RESOURCE FOR AN INFORMED FUTURE

Authors: Jayda Batchelder & Courtney Fadley

10th EDITION PUBLISHED AND DISTRIBUTED BY
Education Opens Doors

Education Opens Doors is a nonprofit organization whose mission is to activate all students to determine and pursue an informed future. To learn more or inquire about partnership, please contact us directly at info@educationopensdoors.org.

www.educationopensdoors.org

10th Edition

Copyright © 2012, 2013, 2014, 2015, 2016, 2017, 2018, 2019 by Jayda Batchelder

Education Opens Doors, Inc.

All rights reserved. No part of this book may be reproduced or utilized in any form or by any means, electronic or mechanical, including photocopying, recording, or by any information storage and retrieval system, without permission in writing from the publisher.

Readers should be aware the Internet Web sites offered as citations and/or sources for further information may have changed or disappeared between the time this was written and when it is read.

Limit of Liability/Disclaimer of Warranty: While the publisher and author have used their best efforts in preparing this book, they make no representations or warranties with the respect to the accuracy or completeness of the contents of this book and specifically disclaim any implied warranties of merchantability or fitness for a particular purpose. No warranty may be created or extended by sales representatives or written sales materials. e advice and strategies contained herein may not be suitable for your situation. You should consult with a professional where appropriate. Neither the publisher nor author shall be liable for any loss of profit or any other commercial damages, including but not limited to special, incidental, consequential, or other damages.

Cover Design by Addison Den Hartog; addisondenhartog.com

Page design by Lyndsay Wright David; www.lyndsaywrightdesign.com

Printed in the United States of America by Hill Print Solutions, Ltd.

ISBN 978-0-692-90372-8

For more information visit: www.educationopensdoors.org

Starting in 2009, every student who left my classroom stated, "Education Opens Doors!" as they passed through the doorway. Today, through this guidebook, the legacy lives on in you. Education does open doors. Which door will it open for you?

– Jayda Batchelder, author

I have dreams of graduation ceremonies filled with faces I've never seen and families I've never met. It's your graduation ceremony—yours and those of thousands of students who use the Education Opens Doors Student Guidebook to boldly pursue a goal-filled future!

– Courtney Fadley, author

This project would not have been possible without the dedication of the Education Opens Doors team, past and present, who have significantly contributed to the continued improvement of this manual. In addition, we have immense gratitude for the students, community members, and especially educators in Dallas, Texas, who have inspired, supported, and uplifted us for years.

Table of Contents

UNIT 1: EXPLORING MY CHARACTER AND MINDSET 9
- Unit 1 Vocabulary 10
- How to Use This Guidebook 11
- Grade Level Checklist 15
- Building Character for College and Career 23
- Analyzing My Mindset 27
- The Impact of Education 31
- Unit 1 Summary: Exploring My Character & Mindset 36

UNIT 2: MAKING CHOICES FOR MY FUTURE 37
- Unit 2 Vocabulary 38
- Grade Point Average (GPA) and Class Rank 42
- Time Management 47
- Study Habits 50
- Types of High Schools 53
- High School Fit 60
- Extending My Learning: Researching Local High Schools 63
- Credit Hours and Graduation Plans 65
- Meet with Your Guidance Counselor 67
- Understanding Course Credits 69
- Advanced and Unique Courses 73
- Life Outside of the Classroom 79
- Community Service 80
- Extracurricular Activities 81
- Jobs and Internships 85
- Choosing a Healthy Lifestyle 89
- Unit 2 Summary: Making Choices for My Future 94

UNIT 3: PROFESSIONALISM: SHOWING UP AS MY BEST SELF 95
- Unit 3 Vocabulary 96
- Professionalism 97
- Networking 99
- Virtual Identity 102
- Personal Statement 105
- Cover Letter 107
- Recommendation Letters 113
- Writing a Thank You Note 116
- Résumé Building Blocks 122
- Preparing for an Interview 137
- Unit 3 Summary: Professionalism: Showing Up As My Best Self 158

UNIT 4: KNOWING MY OPTIONS AFTER HIGH SCHOOL 159
- Unit 4 Vocabulary 160
- Options After High School 162
- Understanding My Why 171
- Exploring the Career for Me 175
- Soft Skills 177
- Understanding Career Pathways 179
- Degrees and Certification Programs 183
- Education Pays: Lifetime Earnings 190
- Choosing a Course of Study 193
- Playing a Sport While in College 203
- Unit 4 Summary: Knowing My Options After High School 208

UNIT 5: UNDERSTANDING MY FINANCES AFTER HIGH SCHOOL 209
- Unit 5 Vocabulary 210
- Calculating the Cost of Continuing My Education 212
- Understanding Financial Aid 219
- Financial Aid: The FAFSA 234
- Comparing Financial Aid Packages 240
- Financial Literacy 245
- Establishing Financial Goals 246
- How to Build a Budget 248
- Making Your Money Work for You 251
- Unit 5 Summary: Understanding My Finances After High School 258

UNIT 6: COMPLETING MY APPLICATIONS 259
- Unit 6 Vocabulary 260
- College Rankings and Selectivity 261
- Types of College Admission 264
- Choosing A School 267
- Extending My Learning: My Top College Research 272
- The College Application Process 273
- About the SAT and the ACT 276
- Application Essay 281
- Application Tracker 290
- Practice College Application 291
- Unit 6 Summary: Completing My Applications 296

APPENDIX 297
- Helpful Web Searching Techniques 298
- Resources for Students in Foster Care and Students Who Are Homeless 299
- Resources for Students Who Are Parents 301
- Resources for Students with Learning Disabilities 303
- Resources for Students Who Are Undocumented 305
- Resources for Students Who Are Economically Disadvantaged 307
- Resources for Students Preparing for Nontraditional Training and Employment 309
- Resources for Students with Limited English Proficiency 311
- Resources for Students Who Identify as LGBTQ+ 313
- Resources for Students with Physical Disabilities 315
- Glossary of Terms 319
- Guidebook Review 330
- Transition to College Timeline 332
- Extras 333
- Certificate of Completion 347

UNIT 1
EXPLORING MY CHARACTER AND MINDSET

DIRECTIONS: Read the topics of this unit. Draw a picture of your emotions about this content.

What is the impact of continuing my education after high school?

▶ **Unit 1 Vocabulary** page 10

How to Use This Guidebook page 11

Grade Level Checklist page 15

Building Character for College and Career page 23

Analyzing My Mindset page 27

The Impact of Education page 31

Unit 1 Summary page 36

How am I unique and why are my unique contributions important to my community?

What goals do I have for my future?

Unit 1 Vocabulary

DIRECTIONS:

1. DEFINE each word using the glossary in this book or a dictionary.
2. ANSWER the questions listed below for each word.

Vocabulary Word	Definition	Have you ever heard/seen this word before?	Explain how you have heard this word used before. If you've never heard or seen it, what other word (in any language) does it look like to you?
Freshman		Y N	
Sophomore		Y N	
Junior		Y N	
Senior		Y N	
Character Strengths		Y N	
Mindset		Y N	
Income		Y N	
Expenses		Y N	

Additional words to complete on notebook paper: _____
_____
_____

How to Use This Guidebook

This guidebook is designed for YOU! Read this page to understand the layout and how to interact with the information most effectively.

How to Use The Margins

On most pages, the margins (the blank space on the side of each page) have been left blank for you to write in. We encourage you to make this guidebook yours.

- Take notes.
- Add comments.
- Highlight important information that you want to remember later.
- Do whatever works for you!

Formatting Used Throughout This Guidebook

Pink boldface is used throughout this manual to emphasize vocabulary.

Italics are used throughout this manual for special notes or disclaimers.

Red boldface is used for web addresses in order to help you easily find and refer to them later.

How the Education Opens Doors Guidebook is Organized

UNIT 1	Exploring My Character and Mindset
UNIT 2	Making Choices For My Future
UNIT 3	Professionalism: Showing Up As My Best Self
UNIT 4	Knowing My Options After High School
UNIT 5	Understanding My Finances After High School
UNIT 6	Completing My Applications
APPENDIX	Extra Resources

Icons Used in This Guidebook

TIP
Yellow Tip boxes identify helpful tips and warns you of commonly made mistakes to watch out for.

BIG IDEA
Green Big Idea boxes give a summary of important information found in that section.

Vocabulary
Pink Vocabulary boxes provide quick definitions of helpful terms.

Activity
Orange boxes and/or **orange text** indicate that you have an activity to complete.

Message to Students

Dear Student,

Your future isn't written yet. What will your story say?

You are capable of extraordinary accomplishments and truly changing the world. This manual is one tool you can use on your journey to make the world a more incredible place.

Below is some advice from the creators:

- Surround yourself with a positive circle of support.
- Know that you have the right to live a choice filled life.
- Use the resources available to you.
- Speak up for yourself.
- Explore all of your options.
- Ask questions.
- Keep this manual and use it as a guide!

The journey starts with you! Now is the time to explore the pathways that will lead to your ideal future.

All our best,

The Education Opens Doors team
www.educationopensdoors.org

Follow us for updates: @educationopensdoors

Pick a Path

Based on this letter, describe two ways that this guidebook can be a guide as you work to achieve your goals.

_____
_____
_____
_____
_____
_____
_____

My Commitment

DIRECTIONS: You are the owner of your educational journey. Complete and sign the document below as a commitment to yourself.

On this _____ **day of** _____, **20**_____,

I, _____ (print name),

a/an _____ (grade level) **student at** _____

_____ (name of school)

know that I am capable of extraordinary things and can one day truly change the world. I will speak up for myself, explore options available, and ask questions. I commit myself to setting goals based on my own life choices and to using this guidebook as a resource on my journey to pursue an informed and goal-filled future, beginning with my high school graduation in year 20____.

Signed, _____

BIG IDEA

I am the owner of my educational journey and using the resources available to me will help guide my path.

Unit 1: My Character & Mindset

www.educationopensdoors.org

My Personal Shield

DIRECTIONS:

1. Write your name in the banner running across the shield.
2. Answer the questions in each quadrant of your shield using words or drawings.
3. Decorate your shield.

What is something that makes you feel proud?

What is something you are grateful for?

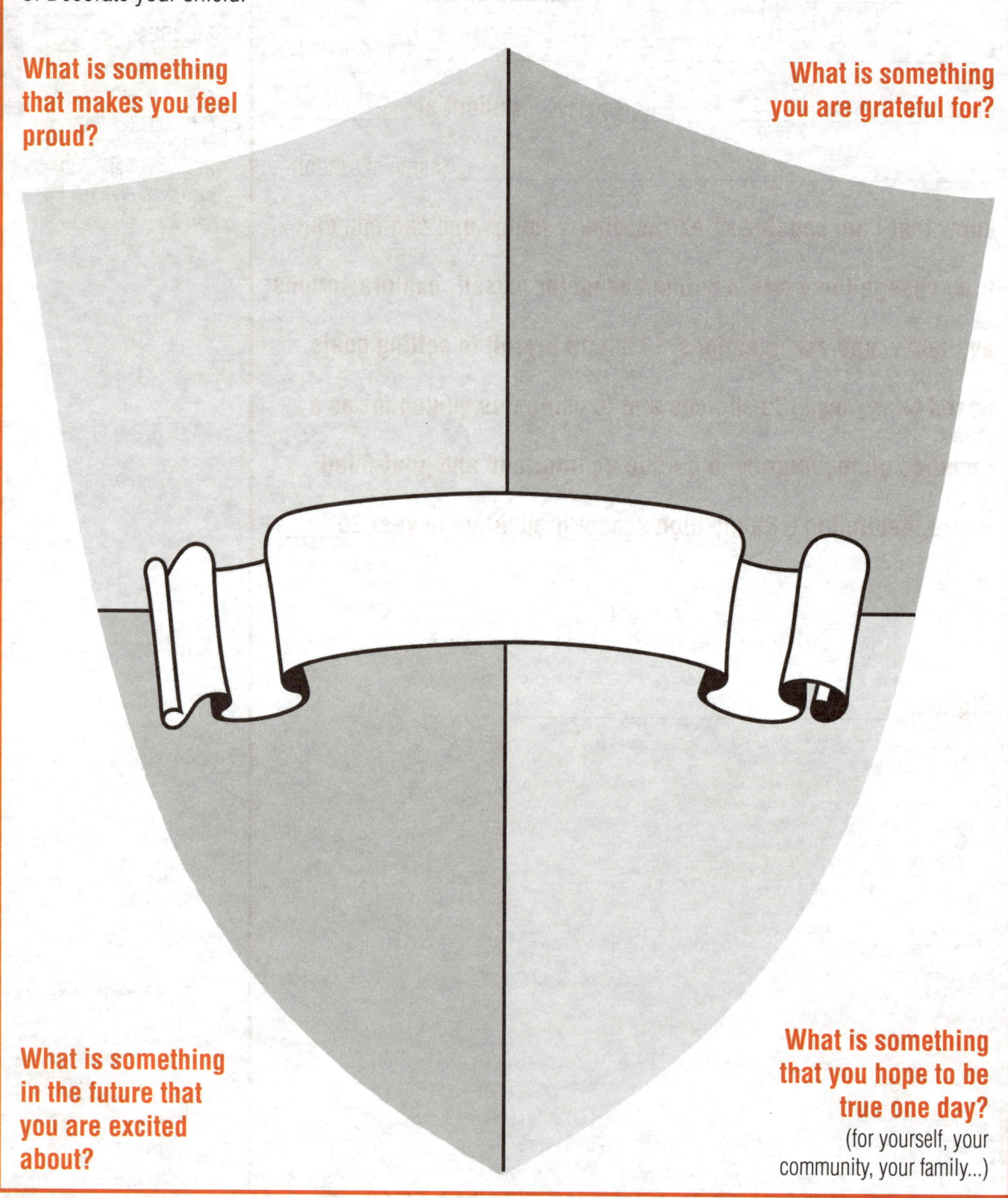

What is something in the future that you are excited about?

What is something that you hope to be true one day?
(for yourself, your community, your family...)

Grade Level Checklist

BIG IDEA
Using this grade level checklist will help keep me on the path to attaining my educational goals.

6th Grade

Inside the Classroom

- ☐ Calculate your own GPA at the end of each grading period (such as Six Weeks, Quarter, or Semester).
- ☐ Do your best on state, national and district tests. High school admission to a school of choice can depend upon your 6th and 7th grade scores.
- ☐ Practice and develop strong reading and writing skills.
- ☐ Talk to your teachers and guidance counselor about Pre-AP or advanced courses, especially in math.

Outside the Classroom

- ☐ Write 3 goals you have for your future and share them with someone you trust to support you.
- ☐ Determine your personal learning style. Ask yourself if you learn better by seeing, doing, or listening. You can take a learning styles quiz online to help determine the answer. Search: "learning style quiz."
- ☐ Take a career/interest inventory. These are surveys that help to match your interests to possible career choices.
- ☐ Participate in school extracurricular activities like clubs, fine arts, and sports.
- ☐ If you are traveling, research colleges in that area and ask if you can drive to see 1 or 2 of them.
- ☐ Draw or journal about 3 things you want to know more about. Then ask someone you trust to support you if they know of ways you can learn more about each of your interests.

Not A 6th Grader?
Even if you are in a higher grade, look through all of the lists to make sure that you have completed everything.

Writers Are Readers Too
The strongest writers often read more than they write! Picking up a book can improve your writing skills.

7th Grade

First, review the 6th grade checklist. Place a check next to tasks already completed. Any that are not complete, add them as tasks you need to do this year in addition to the 7th grade checklist.

Inside the Classroom

- ☐ Meet with your school counselor and decide which classes you need to take as you prepare for high school; especially ask for classes that earn high school credit.

Outside the Classroom

- ☐ Stay involved in extracurricular activities and pursue leadership roles.
- ☐ Determine if you may benefit from tutoring. Attend review and tutoring sessions made available by your teachers.

> **Orientation**
> *See if your high school offers a summer orientation program that you can attend!*

8th Grade

First, review the 6th and 7th grade checklists. Place a check next to tasks already completed. Any that are not complete, add them as tasks you need to do this year in addition to the 8th grade checklist.

Inside the Classroom

- ☐ Ask your math teacher and guidance counselor about classes that earn you high school credit and if you should enroll.
- ☐ Consider taking a foreign language class, even if you already know multiple languages.
- ☐ Ask your guidance counselors what national tests are available to students at your school and what resources are available for preparation (examples: ACT and SAT).
- ☐ Ask your teachers what major content tests you have this year (state, district, or national level) and how to best prepare for them.
- ☐ Ask your guidance counselor and teachers about your options for high school and what the admission requirements are.
- ☐ Locate contact information for the guidance counselor at the high school you plan to attend and ask them about graduation plans and when to register for classes.

Outside the Classroom

- ☐ Ask your counselor when and where high school fairs are happening near you. Attend these events to learn more about your high school options.
- ☐ Begin researching colleges that you are interested in and what majors they have available.
- ☐ See if your high school will offer a summer orientation program that you can attend.

9th and 10th Grades

Unit 1: My Character & Mindset

In high school, preparation for options after graduation become more specific. Use the checklists for each category to keep on track.

Academics

- ☐ Use the "My Plan for High School" template in Unit 2 to create a 4-year high school plan.
- ☐ Set up a meeting with your guidance counselor to ask the following questions: What graduation plans are available at this school? What classes do I need to take now in order to be set up for advanced or dual credit classes later?
- ☐ Set a goal to maintain a 3.0 or higher GPA.
- ☐ Determine your personal learning style. Ask yourself if you learn better by seeing, doing, or listening. You can take a learning styles quiz online to help determine the answer. Search: "learning style quiz."
- ☐ Consider taking a foreign language class, even if you already know multiple languages.
- ☐ Calculate your own GPA each time you get a report card.
- ☐ Ask your teachers what major content tests you have this year (state, district or national level) and how to best prepare for them.
- ☐ Consider summer school classes if they are available at your school.
- ☐ Seek feedback and advice from your teachers about taking advanced coursework next year, including AP, IB, and dual credit.
- ☐ Visit a local community college and a university in your city or a nearby city. Search "colleges in my area."

Freshman (9th)
Sophomore (10th)
Junior (11th)
Senior (12th)

A name referring to which year a student is in during high school or college.

NMSQT

The NMSQT is the National Merit Scholarship Qualifying Test which can lead to scholarship money or recognition.

www.educationopensdoors.org **17**

9th and 10th Grades

Extracurriculars and Wellness

- ☐ Join clubs, sports, fine arts, service organizations, or any other extracurricular activities at your school or in your local community.
- ☐ Explore opportunities for summer jobs and internships.
- ☐ Write 3 goals you have for your future and share them with someone you trust to support you.
- ☐ Draw or journal about 3 things you want to know more about. Then ask someone you trust to support you if they know of ways you can learn more about each of your interests.
- ☐ Document awards, honors, and certificates you receive in preparation for writing a résumé. Use the "Brainstorming for a Résumé" template in Unit 3.

Testing

- ☐ Ask your guidance counselors what national tests/entrance exams are available to students at your school and what resources are available for preparation (examples: PSAT, ACT and SAT).
- ☐ Ask your teachers what major content tests you have this year (state, district, or national level) and how to best prepare for them.
- ☐ Search "free ACT test prep course" or "Free SAT test prep course" to locate test prep resources online.

Preparing for Postsecondary

- ☐ Write down 3 goals you have for your life after high school. Meet with a guidance counselor, mentor, coach, teacher, or someone else you trust to support you and share your goals. Ask for feedback and advice on ways to work towards those goals.
- ☐ If you are traveling, research colleges in that area and ask if you can drive to see 1 or 2 of them.
- ☐ Take a career/interest inventory. These are surveys that help to match your interests to possible career choices.
- ☐ Begin researching colleges that you are interested in and what majors they have available.
- ☐ Research jobs available in your community and apply to any that are interesting to you.
- ☐ Ask your counselor about college fairs in your community.
- ☐ Identify 3 factors that are important to you in choosing an education option after high school.
- ☐ Document work experience, service opportunities, internships, etc. on your résumé.
- ☐ If you would like to attend a military academy, request a precandidate questionnaire by searching "_____(military branch) pre-candidate questionnaire"

Financial Aid

- ☐ Put money aside for your education. Every little bit helps.
- ☐ Determine what national standardized tests you can take and find out what scores you need to receive in order to be eligible for scholarships.
- ☐ Search "Federal Student Aid" to learn about your financial aid options. Any sites ending in ".gov" are reliable sources of information (examples: www.student.ed.gov, www.fafsa4caster.gov, www.fafsa.gov, etc.).
- ☐ Start saving money for the future.

11th Grade

Academics	☐	Focus on your GPA; 11th grade GPA is a highlight on your college applications.
	☐	With your guidance counselor, finalize your senior class schedule and determine any remaining requirements for your graduation plan.
	☐	Check in with your guidance counselor to compare your class schedule with your desired graduation plan to ensure you are on track.
Extracurriculars and Wellness	☐	Pursue leadership roles and document them on your résumé.
	☐	If you plan to play sports in college, in order to be eligible, you must complete the NCAA clearinghouse application. Do so by searching "NCAA clearinghouse"
	☐	Write 3 goals you have for your future and share them with someone you trust to support you.
	☐	Update your résumé with all leadership, community involvement, work experiences, and other accomplishments.
	☐	Locate an internship or work experience aligned with your career goals.

11th Grade

Testing

- [ ] Take the PSAT if you have not already (or take it again if you want to raise your score!). Only students who take the PSAT by their junior year will qualify for certain scholarships like the National Merit Scholarship.
- [ ] Locate prep books for the SAT and ACT at a local book store or online by searching "SAT or ACT test preparation" to take practice tests and read about tips for each test.
- [ ] Sign up for the early administrations of the SAT and ACT. Ask your school guidance counselor about fee waivers.
- [ ] Register for AP exams for AP courses you are enrolled in. Ask your teacher and guidance counselor about fee waivers.
- [ ] Ask your teachers what major content tests you have this year (state, district, or national level) and how to best prepare for them.
- [ ] Ask your school counselor to help you complete waiver applications for standardized tests if needed.
- [ ] Take the ACT, SAT, or any other entrance exam, depending upon your Top 10 List admission requirements.
- [ ] If you have already taken the ACT and SAT but want to improve your scores, sign up to retake them.
- [ ] Take AP exams; scores 3 and higher often earn college credit.

Preparing for Postsecondary

- [ ] Make a Top 10 List of schools you would like to attend that offer degree plans you are interested in.
- [ ] Sign up for newsletters from your Top 10 List schools.
- [ ] Determine if the schools on your Top 10 List require the SAT, ACT, both, or neither for admission.
- [ ] If schools on your Top 10 List are nearby, visit them with someone who has supported you in your education.
- [ ] If you are traveling to a city with a school in your Top 10, call their admissions office and schedule a visit.
- [ ] Practice writing college application essays by searching "college application essay prompts" and asking your English teacher to review it.
- [ ] Develop a calendar of deadlines to keep track of when you need to submit application materials (application itself, essays, recommendation letters, transcripts, deposits, and application fees). See Unit 6 for more information on applying to college.
- [ ] Consider who you would like to write you a recommendation letter. Often schools require a recommendation letter from at least 1 core content teacher. Refer to the Recommendation Letter section in Unit 3.
- [ ] If a military academy is in your Top 10, begin the ROTC scholarship application if available to you.
- [ ] Do research to find more college fairs and attend so your college list can become more specific.

11th Grade	Financial Aid		
		☐	The tax forms parents complete this tax season will be used to determine your college financial aid package. Ask your parents for a copy of their tax return or transcript to use next year.
		☐	You, and at least 1 parent, create your FSAID and password at **studentaid.gov/fsaid**.
		☐	Research scholarship opportunities and document their application requirements and deadlines using the scholarship organizer in Unit 5.
		☐	Troubleshoot any unique FAFSA situations with your guidance counselor. See the FAFSA section in Unit 5 for more information.

12th Grade

Refer to Unit 6 for a detailed timeline of the Fall and Spring semesters.

12th Grade	Academics		
		☐	Check in with your counselor to ensure you have met all requirements for your graduation plan.
		☐	Request official transcripts to be sent to schools as you apply.
	Extracurriculars and Wellness	☐	When you turn 18, one of the most important things you can do for your community is registering to vote and voting on issues you care about.
		☐	Research student health requirements for your Top 10 and determine if you are required to receive any immunizations before attending.
		☐	Refine your résumé with all leadership experiences, work, or extracurriculars as well as community involvement.
		☐	Write thank you notes to anyone who has helped you on your journey - especially those who wrote recommendation letters.
	Testing	☐	If you have not taken the ACT, SAT, or other entrance exams, or want to take them again, take them as soon as possible. Check with your guidance counselor for available fee waivers.
		☐	Ask your teachers what major content tests you have this year (state, district, or national level) and how to best prepare for them.
		☐	Take AP exams; scores 3 and higher often earn college credit.

12th Grade

Preparing for Postsecondary

- [ ] Refine your Top 10 List to ensure all schools still align with your goals and desires.
- [ ] Sign up for application notifications from your Top 10 List schools, if available.
- [ ] Use the application tracker in Unit 6 to track application requirements and deadlines for your Top 10 List. Make a goal to complete all applications by December 1st.
- [ ] Organize your Top 10 List by school selectivity. See Unit 6 for more information.
- [ ] Determine which schools are Foundation, which are Target, and which are Reach. See Unit 6 for more information.
- [ ] Rank your Top 10 schools based upon your preference. Number 1 is your top choice.
- [ ] Consider applying early decision to your reach schools, as applying early increases your odds of admission. Many early decision deadlines are in November.
- [ ] At least 1 month before you need them returned, ask teachers and school leaders to complete recommendation letters.
- [ ] Draft content you would like to include in your application essay and seek feedback from someone willing to edit your work.
- [ ] **SUBMIT YOUR APPLICATIONS!**
- [ ] After submission, call or email admission offices at your top schools to confirm they received all necessary documents for your application.
- [ ] Receive admission letters! Based upon your letters (accepted or waitlisted) and the criteria most important to you, narrow choice down to your top 2. See the Choosing a School section in Unit 6 for more information.
- [ ] Once you feel confident and comfortable with your choice, narrow down to your top 1 and finalize all of your admission paperwork.

Financial Aid

- [ ] If you are a male, within 30 days of turning 18, you must register with the selective service in order to receive federal financial aid. Go to **www.sss.gov** to register.
- [ ] Ask leaders at your school and in your community about local scholarship opportunities.
- [ ] Starting October 1st, complete the FAFSA at **fafsa.gov**. Apply early to maximize your financial aid award.
- [ ] Check the Financial Aid websites at your Top 10 schools for recommended scholarship opportunities.
- [ ] Search "CSS/Financial Aid profile" and complete your profile and application. This is an application for non-federal financial aid from colleges and scholarships.
- [ ] If you submitted the CSS/Financial Aid Profile, check on your account to ensure all information is correct and no documents are missing. If you need to make revisions, contact the financial aid office at each school directly.
- [ ] Once you receive your Student Aid Report from FAFSA, send it to any schools on your Top 10 that weren't originally included.
- [ ] Contact schools directly if you have any questions about your financial aid package.

Building Character for College and Career

NEW STUDENT   **YOU**

If a new student was simply standing next to you, could you identify their character strengths?

What would they need to do in order for you to be able to determine a character strength of theirs?

We see a character strength in someone by the way they show up or exist in the world. We cannot know a person's character strengths if they are just standing; there must be something produced out of that person in order for a character strength to be recognized: words, actions, facial expressions, body language, etc.

BIG IDEA
A character strength is a positive quality a person has and is able to share with others and their community.

A **character strength** is an internal positive quality a person has and can share with those around them. Everyone has several character strengths. Just because you have character strengths does not mean you show them all of the time.

Identifying My Character Strengths

DIRECTIONS: Write your name in the box below, and then follow along with the directions throughout part 1 and part 2.

PART 1

NAME _____

Look at the cover of your student guidebook for a moment. Based upon what you see on the outside of the book, what 3 words can you use to describe the cover?

- _____
- _____
- _____

Does the cover tell you EVERYTHING about the inside? Why or why not?

_____
_____
_____
_____
_____

Unit 1: My Character & Mindset

www.educationopensdoors.org

Identifying My Character Strengths

PART 2

DIRECTIONS: Now think of yourself as a book. Based upon what you see on the outside, what 3 positive words can people use to describe you? Write your responses in the book graphic below.

In other words, what could a new student identify about you by simply standing next to you?

NEW STUDENT   YOU

What internal positive strengths do you have that you can share with others? On the inside of the book below, write words that describe your character strengths.

NEW STUDENT   YOU

BIG IDEA
My identity shapes my experiences.

Why are these character strengths important to you?
_____
_____

Who is someone you admire who exhibits one or all of these character strengths?
_____

© 2019 Education Opens Doors, Inc.

Connecting Character Strengths to Experiences

DIRECTIONS: Identify your number one character strength. Write a story of an experience from your life that shows how you shared your character strength with others.

MY TOP STRENGTH _____

_____
_____
_____
_____
_____
_____
_____
_____
_____
_____
_____
_____
_____
_____
_____

Can you think of a career that would utilize your top character strength?

_____
_____

Would you be excited to pursue that career? Why or why not?

_____
_____
_____

Unit 1: My Character & Mindset

Extending My Learning: Character Strengths Assessment

DIRECTIONS: Search "character strengths test" online and locate an assessment to take. There are assessments for young people as well as grown-ups. Identify one test to take and document your results below.

NOTES

Are you surprised by your results? If so, why are they surprising?

_____
_____
_____
_____
_____

What are 3 ways you can use this information in the future?

- _____
- _____
- _____

Analyzing My Mindset

What is Growth Mindset?

A *mindset* is a way of thinking. Growth mindset is your way of thinking about a challenge or setback and how you respond by reflecting on the language you use and the way you choose to think about the challenge in a new way.

Let's consider the following student, Jackie, and how they use growth mindset. Jackie is training for an athletic competition. They are not performing well this week because they have been up late studying.

> **BIG IDEA**
>
> *A person with a growth mindset knows that all abilities can be developed through effort and persistence.*

GROWTH MINDSET LOOKS LIKE…	GROWTH MINDSET FEELS LIKE…	GROWTH MINDSET SOUNDS LIKE…
If Jackie practices their growth mindset, then… • They might ask their teammate for feedback on particular skills. • They would find additional practice time in their schedule.	If Jackie practices their growth mindset, then… • They might believe that they can ultimately be successful. • They can reflect on the small improvements they have been able to make. • They would feel proud of how well they did on their test.	If Jackie practices their growth mindset, then they might say, • "This gives me an opportunity to focus on how to train when I am tired." • "This helps me understand that some weeks I may train better than others, but overall I am improving."

Mindsets Change

What is an example of a time that you demonstrated growth mindset like Jackie?
_____

What is an example of a time that you could have demonstrated growth mindset?
_____

Understanding Failure

Imagine a baby is learning to walk. If the baby falls, has it failed? Consider the last time you tried to learn a new skill. If you stumbled as you learned, do you believe you failed?

What are some skills you have tried to learn?
_____

How did you demonstrate your success?
_____

If you were not successful, how did you feel?
_____

Practicing Growth Mindset

DIRECTIONS: Read each scenario below. Brainstorm what growth mindset might look like, feel like, and sound like in the table.

	WHAT GROWTH MINDSET LOOKS LIKE…	WHAT GROWTH MINDSET FEELS LIKE…	WHAT GROWTH MINDSET SOUNDS LIKE…
Charlie applied to an Arts Magnet School. They spent the summer creating a portfolio, but it was rejected in August.			
A teacher notices that their class always talks during independent reading time. They remind students of expectations, but students continue to ignore them.			

Understanding Accountability

BIG IDEA

I can make choices to demonstrate growth mindset.

Write one goal that you want to accomplish this year.

_____

_____

When you are working on a goal, it could be helpful to identify a person who can hold you accountable. The person who holds you accountable to your goal would ensure that you were responsible for meeting it and help you monitor your progress.

Write the names of five people you are closest to.

- _____
- _____
- _____
- _____
- _____

Then circle the name of the person above who you believe will hold you accountable to one of your goals this year.

Extending My Learning: Make a Plan

DIRECTIONS: Consider what skills you would like to improve this school year. They could be related to academics, athletics, soft skills, etc. Write a list here:

- _____
- _____
- _____
- _____
- _____

Choose one skill from above and break it into smaller tasks.

Create a 14 day plan to demonstrate how you hope to improve your chosen skill by scheduling the smaller tasks below.

> **BIG IDEA**
> *The best way to grow in intelligence is to challenge myself with difficult tasks throughout my life.*

DAY 1	DAY 2	DAY 3	DAY 4	DAY 5	DAY 6	DAY 7
DAY 8	DAY 9	DAY 10	DAY 11	DAY 12	DAY 13	DAY 14

Unit 1: My Character & Mindset

Notes

The Impact of Education

How much money do you think it takes to pay all of the bills each month?

Monthly Expenses versus Monthly Income

DIRECTIONS: Add up the total monthly expenses, then answer the question below.

Monthly Expenses

Apartment or house	$ 1,000
Utilities (gas, electric, cable/internet)	$ 130
Car	$ 350
Gas	$ 150
Car Insurance	$ 150
Health Insurance	$ 300
Cell Phone (on family plan)	$ 40
Groceries and food	$ 300
Entertainment (sports, movies, shopping, etc.)	$ 100
Donations to charitable, religious, or non-profit organizations	$ ____
Other	$ ____
TOTAL per month	$ _____

Expenses
Money spent on personal needs and desires. (housing, food, transportation, etc.)

Don't Forget Taxes…
Taxes are money that the government (Federal, State, and Local) collects each year to pay for public services (e.g. police, schools, and firefighters). The amount you owe is based on how much money you make and spend each year.

Can you think of any additional monthly expenses that should be added to this list?

EXPENSE	AVERAGE COST
_____	$ ____
_____	$ ____

Monthly Income

Income
Money gained through employment and investment returns.

Let's take a look at 3 different households and their income for each month.

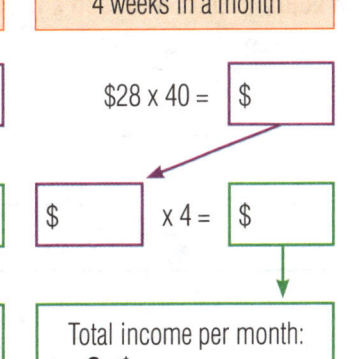

A	B	C
$12 per hour	$17 per hour	$28 per hour
40 hours per week	40 hours per week	40 hours per week
4 weeks in a month	4 weeks in a month	4 weeks in a month

$12 x 40 = $ ____ $17 x 40 = $ ____ $28 x 40 = $ ____

$ ____ x 4 = $ ____ $ ____ x 4 = $ ____ $ ____ x 4 = $ ____

Total income per month: A $ ____
Total income per month: B $ ____
Total income per month: C $ ____

www.educationopensdoors.org

Monthly Expenses versus Monthly Income

Monthly Difference

Look back at the total monthly expenses number and write it in the first box. Determine the difference between the cost of monthly expenses and the amount of monthly income for each household. Then pretend you are a part of that household. How would you answer the questions below?

> **BIG IDEA**
> *The choices I make have an impact on my educational outcomes.*

Total monthly expenses:
$

	A: Total income per month: $	B: Total income per month: $	C: Total income per month: $
−	Total monthly expenses: $	Total monthly expenses: $	Total monthly expenses: $
	How much money will you owe or have left at the end of the month? $	How much money will you owe or have left at the end of the month? $	How much money will you owe or have left at the end of the month? $
	What expense would you choose to give up each month to be able to pay all of your bills?	**What would you add to your monthly expenses with the extra money each month?**	**If you know you will have extra income each month, what would you adjust about your monthly expenses?**

Identify at least 5 factors that could impact a person's monthly income.

_____
_____
_____
_____

Visualizing Yourself as an Adult

DIRECTIONS: Draw or write a demonstration of how you imagine your life to look as an adult. Include information about your education level, career, income, and family life.

Making Choices and Building Supports

Between now and your adult life, you will make millions of choices.

BIG IDEA

As the level of my education increases, so does the potential for increased income.

What is one choice that can impact your high school graduation?
_____

What is one choice that could impact your completion of a job training certificate or college degree?
_____

Who is in your life now or can you seek out to help you achieve the life you visualize for yourself?
_____

In what ways can you ask them to help you?
_____

What resources are available to you to help you achieve the life you imagine?
_____

Unit 1: My Character & Mindset

Extending My Learning: The Impact of Education

DIRECTIONS: Ask your parents or caretakers to help you understand the finances for your household. What are recurring expenses your family pays for? If they feel comfortable sharing, fill in the chart with real numbers. If not, fill in some numbers using your best estimations and ask if they seem realistic.

EXPENSE	AVERAGE COST
_____	$ _____
_____	$ _____
_____	$ _____
_____	$ _____
_____	$ _____
_____	$ _____
_____	$ _____
_____	$ _____
_____	$ _____

As an adult, how would you manage your finances differently? How will you manage them the same? Write your reflection in the space below.

Notes

Unit 1 Summary: Exploring My Character and Mindset

You have the opportunity to shape your own future by setting goals of what success looks like in your life. Every person has unique strengths and skills which are important contributions to the community where you live.

Setting goals is a crucial step in the process of mapping your journey. Your Education Opens Doors Student Guidebook can help guide you on the path you create.

Checklist Check-In

1. Consider where you are in your educational journey. Circle it below.
   - ☐ 6th Grade
   - ☐ 7th Grade
   - ☐ 8th Grade
   - ☐ 9th Grade
   - ☐ 10th Grade
   - ☐ 11th Grade
   - ☐ 12th Grade
   - ☐ High School Graduate
   - ☐ GED Recipient

2. Turn to the "Grade Level Checklist" at the beginning of Unit 1. Locate your current grade level. **Review what you checked off at the beginning of the program and check off any other activities you have completed.**

Unit Review Opportunities

1. Go back to the "Extend Your Learning" pages in this unit. Research, ask questions, and locate resources to complete those activities.
2. Complete any remaining vocabulary tasks for this unit's vocabulary and use each word in a sentence this week.
3. Answer the questions on the unit cover page, and complete the directions in the white box.

Moving Forward…

Select one of the colors from the triangle to describe how you feel about new understandings gained from this unit. Justify your answer in at least 3 sentences.

_____
_____
_____
_____
_____
_____
_____

UNIT 2
MAKING CHOICES FOR MY FUTURE

DIRECTIONS: Read the topics of this unit. Draw a picture of your emotions about this content.

- Time Management — page 47
- Grade Point Average (GPA) and Class Rank — page 42
- Unit 2 Vocabulary — page 38
- Study Habits — page 50
- Types of High Schools — page 53
- High School Fit — page 60
- Researching Local High Schools — page 63
- Credit Hours and Graduation Plans — page 65
- Meet with Your Guidance Counselor — page 67
- Understanding Course Credits — page 69
- Advanced and Unique Courses — page 73
- Life Outside of the Classroom — page 79
- Community Service — page 80
- Extracurricular Activities — page 81
- Jobs and Internships — page 85
- Choosing a Healthy Lifestyle — page 89
- Unit 2 Summary — page 94

Why is community involvement important?

Which high school is the right fit for me?

What classes should I take?

What is GPA, and does it matter?

What is an internship?

Unit 2 Vocabulary

DIRECTIONS:

1. DEFINE each word using the glossary in this book or a dictionary.
2. ANSWER the questions listed below for each word.

Vocabulary Word	Definition	Have you ever heard/seen this word before?	Explain how you have heard this word used before. If you've never heard or seen it, what other word (in any language) does it look like to you?
Grade Point Average (GPA)		Y N	
Class Rank		Y N	
Percentile		Y N	
Semester		Y N	
Study Group		Y N	
Syllabus		Y N	
Early College		Y N	
High School Application Requirements		Y N	
Attendance Zones		Y N	
Course Credit		Y N	
College Admission Requirements		Y N	

Vocabulary Word	Definition	Have you ever heard/seen this word before?	Explain how you have heard this word used before. If you've never heard or seen it, what other word (in any language) does it look like to you?
High School Graduation Plan		Y N	
Academic Advisor/ Guidance Counselor		Y N	
International Baccalaureate		Y N	
Dual Credit		Y N	
Advanced Placement		Y N	
Community Service		Y N	
Extracurricular Activities		Y N	
Internship		Y N	
Variety (food)		Y N	
Whole Foods		Y N	
Hydrate		Y N	

Additional words to complete on notebook paper: _____
_____
_____

Unit 2: My Choices

www.educationopensdoors.org

Calculating Point Values

DIRECTIONS: In basketball, different shots earn different point values. The more difficult the shot, the more points you earn. Place the correct point values on the diagram below.

1 POINT   2 POINTS   3 POINTS

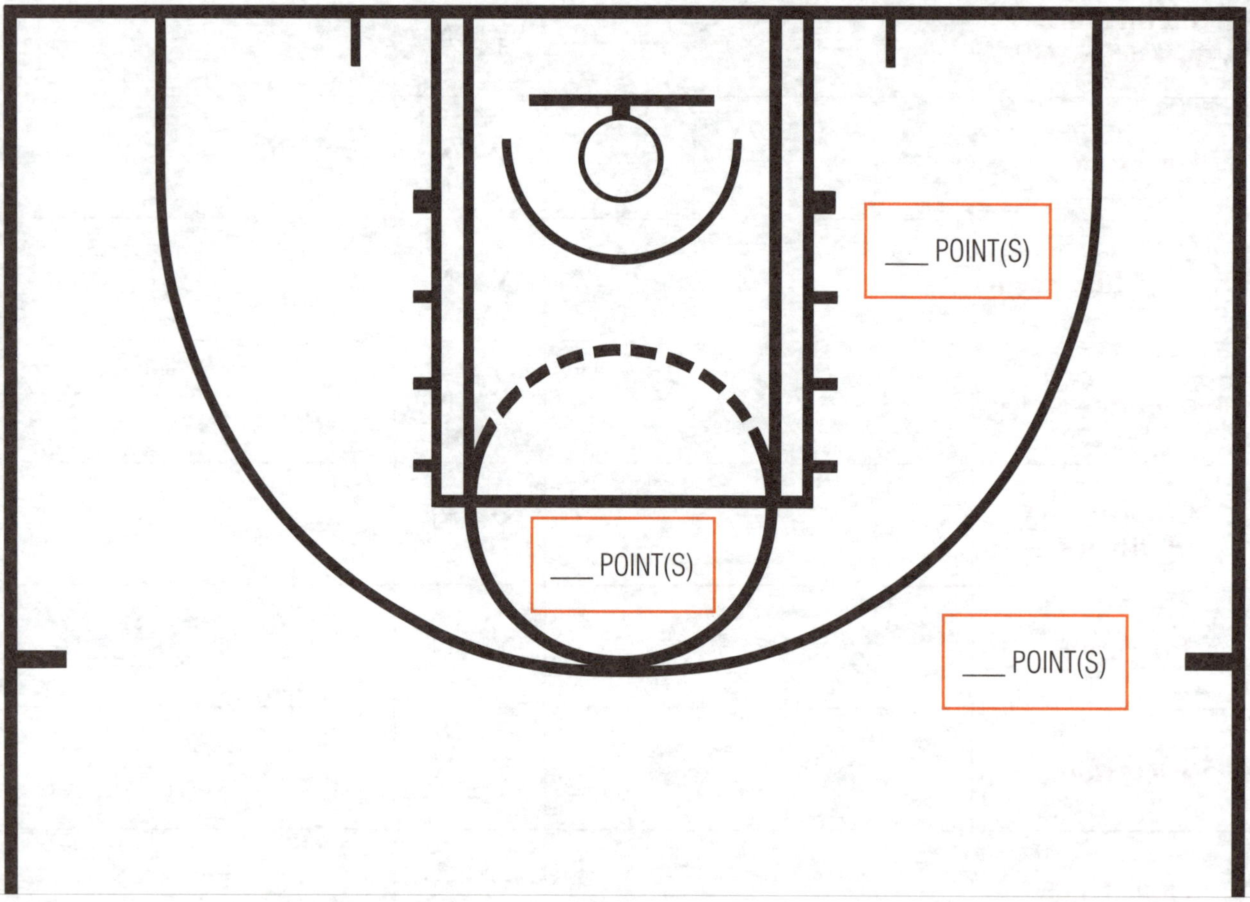

___ POINT(S)

___ POINT(S)

___ POINT(S)

Let's Play a GPA Game!

GAME Point Average

1. Pretend 3 people are playing basketball. Each takes 3 shots.
2. Indicate where player 1 took their 3 shots from by adding three 1's anywhere on the basketball court diagram. Do the same for players 2 and 3.
3. Did they make or miss the shot? Circle all shots that were made. You can decide!
4. Complete the chart below to determine each player's game point average.
    *Remember, if they missed the shot, the point value is 0.

Player	Shot 1	Shot 2	Shot 3	Total Number of Game Points	Game Point Average
1	Make or Miss? Game Point Value: ☐	Make or Miss? Game Point Value: ☐	Make or Miss? Game Point Value: ☐	☐ + ☐ + ☐ = ☐ (Shot 1, Shot 2, Shot 3)	☐ Total Points ÷ 3 — ☐ Average
2	Make or Miss? Game Point Value: ☐	Make or Miss? Game Point Value: ☐	Make or Miss? Game Point Value: ☐	☐ + ☐ + ☐ = ☐ (Shot 1, Shot 2, Shot 3)	☐ Total Points ÷ 3 — ☐ Average
3	Make or Miss? Game Point Value: ☐	Make or Miss? Game Point Value: ☐	Make or Miss? Game Point Value: ☐	☐ + ☐ + ☐ = ☐ (Shot 1, Shot 2, Shot 3)	☐ Total Points ÷ 3 — ☐ Average

Which player has the highest GAME point average?

_____

In school, there is something called a GRADE point average (GPA). What do you think could be used to determine a student's GRADE point average?

_____

Unit 2: My Choices

Grade Point Average (GPA) and Class Rank

What is a "Grade Point Average?"

Grade Point Average (GPA)

Grade point average (GPA) is an average of all of your grades from your freshman year through your senior year of high school. Note that high school level courses taken in middle school count in your final GPA.

Your **grade point average (GPA)** is the average of all of your grades. It is calculated by adding the point value of all of your grades and then dividing that by the total number of credits or classes taken. Usually, points are calculated on a 4.0 scale and some schools give plus/minus grade points. *Not all schools use the same number scale for calculating GPA.*

Regardless of the scale used at your school, the higher your GPA, the better.

Sample +/- GPA Scale		
Letter Grade	Percent Grade	4.0 Scale
A+	97-100	4.0
A	93-96	4.0
A-	90-92	3.7
B+	87-89	3.3
B	83-86	3.0
B-	80-82	2.7
C+	77-79	2.3
C	73-76	2.0
C-	70-72	1.7
D+	67-69	1.3
D	65-66	1.0
E/F	Below 65	0.0

Semester

A semester is a half-year term in a school or college, typically lasting 15 to 18 weeks.

Semester GPA vs. Cumulative GPA

On your report card, you will typically see two types of GPAs – semester and cumulative. A semester GPA calculates your grade point average from the current semester only. Your cumulative GPA calculates your grade point average from all of your classes since the beginning of high school. Your cumulative GPA is what colleges and potential employers will be looking at when you apply.

BIG IDEA

Every grade I earn can be assigned a point value, and advanced courses have a weighted GPA that goes above 4.0.

Weighted GPA and Unweighted GPA

A 4.0 GPA scale is considered "unweighted." Many schools offer advanced courses. Since these classes are more difficult than regular courses, schools assign a different point system to the harder classes. To weight the GPA, the semester grade in each course is added to the course weight. All weighted courses are totaled and divided by the total number of courses to get the weighted GPA.

> **BIG IDEA**
> *Weighted GPA goes beyond a 4-point scale as a result of taking accelerated or advanced courses.*

4.0 SCALE
UNWEIGHTED GPA
(regular classes)

Letter Grade	Point Value	%
A	4.0	100-90
B	3.0	89-80
C	2.0	79-70
D	1.0	69-60
F	0	59-0

5.0 SCALE
WEIGHTED GPA
(advanced classes)

Letter Grade	Point Value
A	5.0
B	4.0
C	3.0
D	2.0
F	0

For example, a student earns an A in Dr. Blackwell's AP Chemistry class. This student's points will be calculated using a weighted GPA since it is an advanced course. Think of it as earning an additional point because you are in an advanced course. So instead of earning a 4.0 for an "A," this student would receive a 5.0.

Check with your guidance counselor to learn more about which advanced classes are available at your school. Taking advanced classes and doing well in them can help to raise your GPA. Your transcript will most likely show both your weighted GPA on a 5.0 scale and your unweighted GPA on a 4.0 scale.

What is "Class Rank?"

Your **class rank** measures your GPA compared to others in your class. For example, if you have a GPA of a 3.7 and your friend has a GPA of 3.6, you will rank higher than your friend. Class rank may be used as a number or as a **percentile**. Admission officers for colleges and scholarships usually look at both your GPA and class rank together, so it is just as important to have a high class rank as well as a high GPA. A "really good" class rank is typically considered to be in the top 25% of your class and to be in the top 10% is considered "highly competitive" or "excellent." Think of it as a friendly competition between you and all of your classmates.

> **BIG IDEA**
> *Class rank compares your weighted GPA to other students at your school.*

> **Top 10%**
> *Some states offer <u>automatic</u> acceptance in college for ranking in the top 7-10% of your class.*

Unit 2: My Choices

www.educationopensdoors.org 43

How to Calculate GPA

Practice Calculating GPA

To calculate your GPA, remember to ADD all of your grades together and DIVIDE by the total number of classes. Round to the nearest hundredth. For example:

$$\frac{A+A+B+B+C+A+B}{7} = \frac{4.0+4.0+3.0+3.0+2.0+4.0+3.0}{7} = \frac{23}{7} = \mathbf{3.28}$$

DIRECTIONS: Sandra's report card is missing some information! Follow the 4 steps to help her calculate her GPA. Use the example below for help!

Sample +/- GPA Scale

Letter Grade	Percent Grade	4.0 Scale
A+	97-100	4.0
A	93-96	4.0
A-	90-92	3.7
B+	87-89	3.3
B	83-86	3.0
B-	80-82	2.7
C+	77-79	2.3
C	73-76	2.0
C-	70-72	1.7
D+	67-69	1.3
D	65-66	1.0
E/F	Below 65	0.0

EXAMPLE

STEP 1: Change letter grades to grade points.

Subject	Letter Grade	Grade Points
English	A	4.0
History	A-	3.7
Math	B+	3.3
Science	B	3.0

STEP 2: Add up all of the grade points.

4.0 + 3.7 + 3.3 + 3.0 = **14 Grade Points**

STEP 3: Count the number of classes.

English + History + Math + Science = **4 Classes**

STEP 4: Divide the Total Grade Points (TGP) by the Number of Classes (NC).

$$\frac{TGP}{NC} = GPA \quad \frac{14}{4} = 3.5$$

STEP 1: Change Sandra's letter grades to grade points.

Skyrise High School
Sandra Medina
Semester 1

Subject	Letter Grade	Grade Points
Algebra II	A	4.0
English II	A	4.0
World History	B-	2.7
Art I	B	
Biology I	A	
Team Sports	B+	
Newspaper	A	

STEP 2: Add up all of Sandra's grade points.

STEP 3: Count the number of classes Sandra has.

STEP 4: Divide Sandra's grade points by number of classes.

What is Sandra's GPA? _____

More Practice Calculating GPA

DIRECTIONS: Now, look at Darrion's report card. Follow the steps to calculate his GPA.

Cityview High School
Darrion Maher
Semester 2

Subject	Letter Grade	Grade Points
Yearbook	A-	3.7
Choir	A	4.0
Geography	B	3.0
Algebra II	B+	
Chemistry	A	
English II	C+	

STEP 1: Change letter grades to grade points.

STEP 2: Add the total grade points:

STEP 3: Count the total number of classes:

STEP 4: Divide the total grade points by the total number of classes:

What is Darrion's GPA? _____

> **BIG IDEA**
>
> *GPA is a number that is used to determine scholarships and admission to degree and certification programs.*

Extending My Learning: Calculating My GPA

What's My GPA?

DIRECTIONS: After speaking with your guidance counselor, fill in the chart below:

What numerical value does your school assign for each of the following grades (just in case it's different from the previous page)?

A+ =	B+ =	C+ =	D+ =
A =	B =	C =	D =
A- =	B- =	C- =	D- =

GPA
Calculate your GPA every time you receive your report card.

Use this specific scale and your report cards to calculate your own GPA and make sure you are staying on track! To practice, fill in the chart below with each of your classes and the grade you earned from last semester.

Class	Letter Grade Earned	Numerical Value
Example: Math	B	3.0

STEP 1: Change letter grades to grade points!

STEP 2: Add total grade points:

STEP 3: Count total # of classes:

STEP 4: Divide grade points by # of classes:

My Calculated GPA = _____

Types of High Schools

Where do you plan to go to high school?

_____

> **BIG IDEA**
> *Every type of high school has benefits and limitations; choosing the best fit for me is what's important.*

> **Attendance Zone**
> *The boundaries a city has established for which neighborhoods attend which schools.*

There are several different types of high schools. This section will help you compare across the types of schools your city might have to offer.

Public High School

Public schools get their funding from local, state, and federal government funds. Public schools are free to attend. Teachers must abide by state and district guidelines for curriculum (what they teach) and testing. Traditional public schools do not have an application process because they are open to any student who lives in the attendance zone.

In your opinion, what is an advantage to attending this type of school?	In your opinion, what is a disadvantage to attending this type of school?

Private High School

Private schools receive funding from student tuition and donations. Because there is a cost to attend, private schools offer scholarships to families who qualify. Private schools may require interviews, essays, résumés, and testing as a part of their admission process. Any student can apply. Many private schools have small class sizes and as a result, an ability to focus a lot of time and attention on each student's learning progress. Since private schools are not funded by the government, students are not required to take state assessments. Instead, private schools set their own curriculum and testing practices best suited for their student population.

In your opinion, what is an advantage to attending this type of school?	In your opinion, what is a disadvantage to attending this type of school?

Magnet High School

Magnet schools are public schools with specialized classes to prepare students for a career. Since they are public, they are free to attend. Common magnet school programs are: health care, automotive or aeronautic mechanics, performing arts,

Unit 2: My Choices

> **BIG IDEA**
> *I have an opportunity to attend a high school with unique learning experiences even if it is outside of my attendance zone.*

culinary, cosmetology, engineering, and many more! These schools are called "magnet" because they attract students from all over the city based upon their specialty curriculum. They do not have attendance boundaries.

Students need to apply to magnet schools by completing application forms, writing essays, taking admissions tests, going to an interview, and possibly participating in auditions. Magnet high schools often request to see a student's 7th and 8th grade GPA and test scores.

In your opinion, what is an advantage to attending this type of school?	In your opinion, what is a disadvantage to attending this type of school?

Home School

Home school is sometimes called "interest-motivated education" or "self-motivated education" because students set their own pacing through content and can also focus time on topics that really interest them. Home school students are required to learn the same curriculum as students in a traditional school setting. The biggest difference is the learning environment– students learn at home and their teacher is a parent or guardian. Teachers must apply to become the teacher of record for their student(s) and are responsible for purchasing instructional and testing materials.

In your opinion, what is an advantage to attending this type of school?	In your opinion, what is a disadvantage to attending this type of school?

Early College High School

Early college high schools give students the opportunity to be enrolled in high school and college at the same time. Graduates receive a high school diploma and an Associate's Degree at the same time through dual credit classes. They are a type of public high school and are free to attend. To enroll in Early College students must complete the application process, which often includes an essay, letters of recommendation, portfolio, GPA and test scores from middle school, and sometimes a family interview.

In your opinion, what is an advantage to attending this type of school?	In your opinion, what is a disadvantage to attending this type of school?

Charter High School

Charter schools are a type of public school, which means they are free to attend. Students at charter schools are required to take the same state level tests as traditional public schools, but there is more flexibility in what curriculum is taught because the districts are often small. Any student can apply to a charter school; there are no application requirements. All applicants are put into a lottery, which means if a student is picked at random, they are admitted.

In your opinion, what is an advantage to attending this type of school?	In your opinion, what is a disadvantage to attending this type of school?

Status Check

DIRECTIONS: Complete the following sentence stem. Then write a brief paragraph explaining your choice.

I feel I will fit in best at a _____ type of high school because…

_____
_____
_____
_____
_____
_____
_____
_____
_____
_____

Unit 2: My Choices

Types of High Schools Scavenger Hunt!

DIRECTIONS: Below is a table that summarizes the differences between the various types of high schools that students can attend. Using the information in the surrounding boxes as clues, search for the correct answers to complete each box. Hint: hunt for the correct information in the previous pages and/or by using your outside knowledge.

	Public	Private	Charter	Magnet	Early College
Expenses	Public schools get money from the state so they are free for students to attend.	Private schools receive no money from the state so students are required to pay to attend.	Charter schools receive money from the state, so they are free for students to attend.	_____ _____ _____	_____ _____ _____
Application Requirements	No application is required.	_____ _____ _____	_____ _____ _____	_____ _____ _____	Applications are required. These require an essay, academic history, and letters of recommendation.
Attendance Zoning	As long as you live in the boundaries of that particular school zone, you have a right to attend public school.	_____ _____ _____	_____ _____ _____	_____ _____ _____	If you apply and are accepted, you are, of course, allowed to attend!
High School Examples In My Community	Research local examples _____ _____	Research local examples _____ _____	Research local examples _____ _____	Research local examples _____ _____	Research local examples _____ _____

Public Service Announcement!

DIRECTIONS:

1. CREATE a public service announcement (PSA) to inform other students about the advantages of each type of school. Your PSA can be a song, skit, flyer, or anything else you can think of to share your knowledge.
2. Use the space below to DRAFT out your PSA, including any script or talking points.
3. SHARE your PSA with other students.

Unit 2: My Choices

Extending My Learning: Types of High Schools

DIRECTIONS: Using the types of high schools listed here, research a list of 10 or more high schools in your community. Include the type in the chart below.

	School Name	School Type	I am interested in learning more information about this school.	
1			YES	NO
2			YES	NO
3			YES	NO
4			YES	NO
5			YES	NO
6			YES	NO
7			YES	NO
8			YES	NO
9			YES	NO
10			YES	NO
11			YES	NO
12			YES	NO
13			YES	NO
14			YES	NO
15			YES	NO

Does the Perfect High School Exist?

DIRECTIONS:

STEP 1: In the center box, draw a picture to represent the perfect school. It can be a view from the outside or the inside.

STEP 2: Answer the following questions in text or pictures around your center image.

- How many students are in each grade level?
- How does the class schedule work? (i.e. how many classes per day, lunch schedule, etc.)
- What is the school's main focus?
- What are the demographics of the students?
- What are the application requirements? (i.e. fees, GPA minimum, exam scores, interview, etc.)
- What extracurricular activities are available?
- How close is the school to your home?

Unit 2: My Choices

High School Fit

High School Application Requirements
The specific requirements needed to gain admission to a magnet or private high school, which can include a minimum GPA, strong recommendations, advanced coursework, etc.

Consider all of your options! There are many factors to consider if you plan to apply to a high school. All schools are different. **Note:** *To the best of our knowledge, we have used "yes" or "no" statements. There are always exceptions as legislation varies by state. Check school websites and call the school directly to confirm details.*

What is one question you have about the high school application process?

_____
_____
_____

High School Fit

DIRECTIONS: Review all of the chart titles (factors to consider) and questions in the charts. In the "More Info" box, put a STAR next to the any of the questions that you would like to seek more information on.

Application/Registration Timeline	Local Public	Charter	Early College	Private	Magnet	More Info
Do I need to complete an application?	No, but enrollment is required.	Yes, but applications are not merit based.	Yes	Yes	Yes	

Application Fees	Local Public	Charter	Early College	Private	Magnet	More Info
Is there an application fee?	No	No	No, as long as you are a resident within the district.	Yes, but there are often waivers available.	No, as long as you are a resident within the district.	

Entrance Exam	Local Public	Charter	Early College	Private	Magnet	More Info
Do they look at my test scores?	No	No	Yes	Yes	Yes	

GPA Requirements	Local Public	Charter	Early College	Private	Magnet	More Info
Is there a minimum GPA requirement?	No	No	Yes	Yes	Yes	

Interview Requirements	Local Public	Charter	Early College	Private	Magnet	More Info
Will I be asked to interview?	No	No	Yes	Yes	Yes	

Typical Dress Code	Local Public	Charter	Early College	Private	Magnet	More Info
What is the typical dress code?	Varies, check the school website.	Varies, check the school website.	Varies, check the school website.	Usually requires a uniform.	Usually requires a uniform.	

Subject Area Focus	Local Public	Charter	Early College	Private	Magnet	More Info
If I like a particular subject area, can the school have a focus on it?	Some local public schools have a subject of focus, but it is not as common as charter or magnet schools.	Yes. Charter schools are founded on a particular "charter" or emphasis.	Early College schools focus on dual credit across all subjects.	Yes, many private schools have an emphasis on religious courses and/or college prep.	Yes, magnet schools have a program or content focus.	

Extracurriculars	Local Public	Charter	Early College	Private	Magnet	More Info
Are there sports and activities to get involved in?	Yes	Varies	No	Varies	No	

Proximity to Home	Local Public	Charter	Early College	Private	Magnet	More Info
Can I attend if the school is not in my neighborhood?	Varies	Yes	Yes	Yes	Yes	

Which option is right for me?

There is no right or wrong option – it is all about finding the best option for YOU.

TIP

All students have options for high school outside of their neighborhood public school. Applying to other schools can offer unique learning opportunities.

www.educationopensdoors.org

High School Fit Debrief

DIRECTIONS: Answer the following questions.

What questions do you still need answers to in order to decide your high school choice?

- _____
  _____
  _____

- _____
  _____
  _____

- _____
  _____
  _____

- _____
  _____
  _____

- _____
  _____
  _____

Who will you ask to help answer these questions?

_____
_____
_____

Extending My Learning: Researching Local High Schools

DIRECTIONS: Write the names and types of school of 5 high schools in your city.

Name of School	Type of School (e.g.: magnet, charter, public, etc.)

TIP
Remember to talk to your guidance counselor to gather more information.

Identify 3 schools you want to know more about, and circle them on your chart. Use this list of questions to research the 3 schools you circled. Include any additional questions in the space provided.

How far is the school from your home? What are the transportation options available?
- School 1: _____
- School 2: _____
- School 3: _____

What types of advanced or unique programs are available to students?
- School 1: _____
- School 2: _____
- School 3: _____

What are the steps to take in order to apply?
- School 1: _____
- School 2: _____
- School 3: _____

What is the school website and phone number?
- School 1: _____
- School 2: _____
- School 3: _____

What are the application deadlines?
- School 1: _____
- School 2: _____
- School 3: _____

Unit 2: My Choices

Extending My Learning: Researching Local High Schools

What are the fees/tuition/costs to students?
- School 1: _____
- School 2: _____
- School 3: _____

Graduation Rate
The number of students who graduate based upon how many students started at the school freshman year, or in some cases, the beginning of senior year.

Are there scholarships available?
- School 1: _____
- School 2: _____
- School 3: _____

What is the graduation rate?
- School 1: _____
- School 2: _____
- School 3: _____

What are the average SAT and ACT scores of seniors?
- School 1: _____
- School 2: _____
- School 3: _____

College Acceptance Rate
High schools often publish the number of graduating students who are accepted to college. This is called the college acceptance rate.

What is the college acceptance rate?
- School 1: _____
- School 2: _____
- School 3: _____

Which extracurricular activities are available?
- School 1: _____
- School 2: _____
- School 3: _____

Are trade, vocational, and technical courses available?
- School 1: _____
- School 2: _____
- School 3: _____

Is there a program/partnership for students to engage with a local business or organization?
- School 1: _____
- School 2: _____
- School 3: _____

Additional Question: _____?
- School 1: _____
- School 2: _____
- School 3: _____

Credit Hours and Graduation Plans

Credit Hours

Each class you take has a credit hour, or **course credit** attached to it which links to your GPA. Generally, the number of credit hours for a class relates to the amount of time spent in that class.

In middle school and high school, 1 credit hour is usually assigned to a yearlong class. In college, the number of credit hours depends upon the number of hours spent in the classroom per week.

Middle School and High School	**1 Year (2 Semesters) of Algebra 2** Attended for 50 minutes on Monday - Friday for 2 semesters	1 Credit Hour
College	**1 Semester of College Algebra** Attended for 50 minutes on Mondays, Wednesday, and Fridays for 1 semester	3 Credit Hours

High School Graduation Plans

In order to earn a high school diploma, a student must earn a set number of credit hours based upon their **high school graduation plan**. Some schools have multiple graduation plans. Below is a sample of graduation plans from a fictional high school. Ask your guidance counselor for the graduation plans available at your school, or future school.

	Foundations (minimum) Graduation Plan	**Endorsement Graduation Plan**	**Distinguished Achievement Graduation Plan**
Total Credits	22 (5.5 credits per year)	26 (6.5 credits per year)	26 (6.5 credits per year)
Unique Factors	• No endorsement required • 3 math and science credits	• 4 endorsement credits and 2 advanced classes • 4 math and science credits	• 4 endorsement credits and 3 advanced classes, including Algebra II • 4 math and science credits • Service learning project

BIG IDEA
My high school graduation plan may be different than the admission requirements at my school of choice.

TIP
Search "High school graduation requirements for _____ (your state)" for a list of the minimum requirements to receive a high school diploma in your state.

Unit 2: My Choices

www.educationopensdoors.org

BIG IDEA
It is important to be in communication with my guidance counselor about classes offered at my school.

Before choosing a graduation plan, think about your goals. Some graduation plans do not align with **admission requirements**. This means students on the minimum plan may not be eligible to apply for certification programs or **college**. Search "admission requirements" for the certification or degree program you hope to pursue and see if the course requirements match up with your degree plan.

Planning for College Admission Requirements

DIRECTIONS: Kia is a senior in high school and is scheduled to graduate on time. They want to apply to Achieve College. Answer the following questions based upon what you know about graduation plans and admission requirements.

Admission Requirements for Achieve College	Graduation Plan Requirements for Kia's High School
• 4 English credits • 4 Math credits, including Pre-Calculus • 2 credits of the same foreign language* • 4 Science credits • 3 History credits • 1 credit of visual or performing arts	• 4 English credits • 4 Math credits • 2 computer programming credits, taken in place of foreign language* • 3 Science credits • 2 History credits • 1 Fine Arts credit • 1 P.E. credit • 5 Elective credits

*The term "foreign language" represents all languages other than English. Although the US does not have an official language, schools often use this term.

Can Kia apply to Achieve College? _____

Why or why not?
_____
_____

If you were in the same situation, what would you have done differently?
_____
_____

Why is it important to pay close attention to the classes you select in high school?
_____
_____

Based upon your education goal, how will your time in high school affect whether or not you are able to reach your goal?
_____
_____

Meet with Your Guidance Counselor

Credit Hours

A **guidance counselor** is someone who helps students enroll in the best classes for them, troubleshoots scheduling hurdles, and connects students to resources.

Who is your guidance counselor? _____

What is their e-mail address? _____

Helpful topics to address with your guidance counselor:

- Taking all of the classes you need to graduate on time
- Taking the types of classes that line up with your goals after graduation
- Locating help to do your best in all of your classes
- Aligning classes with your interests as well as goals

Tips to keep in mind when meeting with your guidance counselor:

- Determine what topics you want to address
- Schedule a time to meet (begin at the beginning of the school year)
- Tell them the objectives for your meeting

> **BIG IDEA**
> *I can choose the classes to fill my school schedule with and it's my responsibility to make sure they align with graduation and admission requirements for my education goals.*

Unit 2: My Choices

Ask Your Guidance Counselor

DIRECTIONS: Circle each of the questions you would like answers to. Then schedule a time to meet with your guidance counselor and fill in responses to these questions together.

What Graduation Plans are available at our school?

Name of Plan: _____	Name of Plan: _____	Name of Plan: _____	Name of Plan: _____
PROS	PROS	PROS	PROS
CONS	CONS	CONS	CONS
Number of Credit Hours Required for Graduation?	Number of Credit Hours Required for Graduation?	Number of Credit Hours Required for Graduation?	Number of Credit Hours Required for Graduation?
Are there unique course requirements for this plan?	Are there unique course requirements for this plan?	Are there unique course requirements for this plan?	Are there unique course requirements for this plan?

www.educationopensdoors.org

Social and Emotional Counselor

A type of counselor who promotes skills and practices to help students make decisions, build relationships, develop coping skills to process difficult emotions, and mature through self-awareness.

Academic Advisor

In college, a guidance counselor is often called an academic advisor. Their role is the same as a guidance counselor.

What advanced and unique courses are available at our school?

_____
_____
_____
_____

Are there opportunities to earn course credit while working off campus through trade or certification programs?

_____
_____
_____
_____

If I choose to participate in athletics or fine arts, which can take a significant number of credit hours, will that impact my graduation plan?

_____
_____
_____
_____

Can we schedule a meeting every semester to evaluate my progress to graduation?

_____
_____
_____
_____

Understanding Course Credits

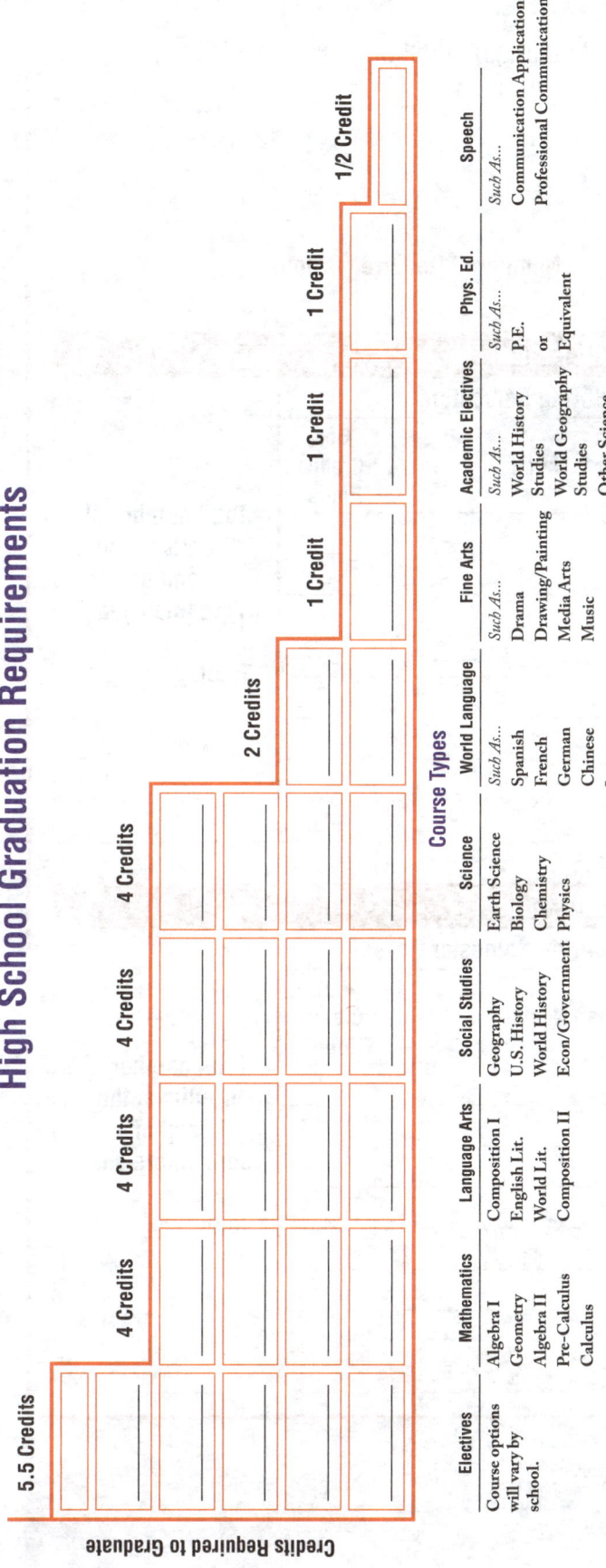

DIRECTIONS: Using the course names listed on this page, draft a copy of your ideal course schedule by writing each course name in the blocks.

Notes:
*1 credit = 1 year of class in certain subject
* Ask your guidance counselor for the actual graduation requirements at your local high school. These are a representative of what is most common.

Common Electives

- Visual Arts
- Drawing
- Sculpture
- Painting
- Photography
- Film Studies
- Art History
- Performing Arts
- Choir
- Drama
- Band
- Orchestra
- Dance
- Guitar
- Vocational Education
- Woodworking
- Metalworking
- Computer-aided Drafting
- Automobile Repair
- Agriculture
- Cosmetology
- FFA
- Sewing
- Computer Science
- Word Processing
- Programming
- Graphic Design
- Web Design
- Web Programming
- Video Game Design
- Music Production
- Journalism/Publishing
- School Newspaper
- Yearbook
- TV Production
- Foreign Languages
- American Sign Language
- Business Education
- Accounting
- Data Processing
- Management
- Culinary Arts
- Childhood Development
- Nutrition
- Weight Training

5 Years of Math?

Many high schools only require 4 years of math to graduate, BUT many colleges require completion of all 5 math courses for admission.

How can you adapt your schedule to include all 5 math courses?

_____
_____
_____
_____

Unit 2: My Choices

www.educationopensdoors.org 69

Extending My Learning: My Plan for High School

DIRECTIONS:

1. After meeting with your guidance counselor(s), and obtaining graduation requirements for your school, complete the chart below.
2. List the classes you will take each year.
3. List credit hours for that course.

My Graduation Plan: _____   **Number of Required Credits:** _____

Freshman Year (9th Grade)

Fall Semester		Spring Semester		
Course Name	# of Credit Hours	Course Name	# of Credit Hours	**Total number of Credits at the end of Freshman year** Total: _____
Total		**Total**		

Sophomore Year (10th Grade)

Fall Semester		Spring Semester		
Course Name	# of Credit Hours	Course Name	# of Credit Hours	**Total number of Credits at the end of Sophomore year** Total: _____
Total		**Total**		

Junior Year (11th Grade)

Fall Semester		Spring Semester		Total number of Credits at the end of Junior year
Course Name	**# of Credit Hours**	**Course Name**	**# of Credit Hours**	
				Total: _____
Total		**Total**		

Senior Year (12th Grade)

Fall Semester		Spring Semester		Total number of Credits at the end of Senior year
Course Name	**# of Credit Hours**	**Course Name**	**# of Credit Hours**	
				Total: _____
Total		**Total**		

Total Credits Towards Graduation: _____

Important notes:

- High school graduation requirements vary from school to school and often change.
- You can only receive credit for a class 1 time.
    - If you do not pass a class, you do not receive credit.
    - If you are enrolled in a class more than once, you will only receive credit for the first time you took the class.
- In order to participate in a sport or fine art for all 4 years you will need to use elective credits or possibly receive 0 credits once you reach your maximum P.E. or fine art credit limit.

Notes

Advanced and Unique Courses

You get to choose the classes you are enrolled in once in high school. Why not choose ones that that challenge you and align with your interests? Although there are more than 3, we are going to focus on the 3 main types of advanced and unique courses: dual credit (DC), advanced placement (AP), and international baccalaureate (IB). The end of this section has a list of benefits as well as a list of questions you can take to your guidance counselor to learn about all the options at your school or local community schools.

BIG IDEA
There are benefits to participating in Dual credit, AP, and IB courses.

What are the benefits of advanced and unique coursework?

- Diverse course availability to match my interests.
- Opportunity to earn college credit while in high school.
- High learning expectations.
- GPA benefit with weighted GPA given for challenging courses.

Dual Credit

Dual credit (DC) courses provide students an opportunity to earn course credits towards two programs at the same time. For example, a student is in a class called "Construction Technology" at their high school and is also enrolled in a construction management certification program at the local community college. After successful completion of the class, they will receive 1 credit towards their high school diploma, and 1 credit towards their certificate in construction management.

College Credit
There are ways to receive college credit while you are in high school. Ask your counselor for more information.

There are two types of dual credit programs: Technical Dual Credit and Academic Dual Credit. **Special note:** *If your dual credit course has "Applied" in the title, it likely will not transfer to a degree program, only a certificate program.*

Technical Dual Credit	Academic Dual Credit
All credits count towards a certificate program and may also transfer to credits towards an associate's degree if your college accepts them.	These credits can be transferred to an associate's or bachelor's degree program if your college accepts them.

> **BIG IDEA**
> *In order to enroll in advanced and unique coursework, I need to make a plan with my guidance counselor.*

Advanced Placement (AP)

Advanced Placement (AP) courses are college level courses you can take in high school. You receive college credit based upon your score on the AP exam at the end of the class. The AP exam is scored on a scale from 1 to 5. Usually, colleges will accept a score of 3 or higher for course credit. Schools offer a select number of AP classes based upon funding and teacher availability. Search "College Board AP" to find the website to see a list of all courses available and ask your guidance counselor about options on your campus.

If AP is not an option at your school, ask about Pre-AP or other advanced courses.

International Baccalaureate (IB) Diploma Program (DP)

The **International Baccalaureate (IB)** programme provides a unique type of advanced coursework designed to "develop inquiring, knowledgeable, and caring young people who help to create a better and more peaceful world though intercultural understanding and respect." Students who graduate with a diploma from an IB world school have several scholarship and admission opportunities opened for them in addition to college credit. You can learn about IB programs in your community by searching "international baccalaureate schools near me."

Consider the Options

DIRECTIONS: Record at least 1 question you have about each type of program you read about and any additional questions below.

Dual Credit (DC)	Advanced Placement (AP)	Int'l Baccalaureate (IB)

Additional Questions

Case Study

DIRECTIONS: Pretend you are Courtney's guidance counselor. Courtney is trying to decide which advanced classes to take. The school offers: **5 AP classes, 3 DC classes, AND the IB program in additional to all regular classes**. Courtney cannot enroll in all of them.

Courtney has a few options:

- Take some of the AP/DC classes offered.
- Take none of the AP/DC classes offered.
- Enroll in the IB Program.
- Take all of the AP/DC classes offered.

As Courtney's guidance counselor, develop a pro and con for each option.

	Some AP/DC	No AP/DC	IB Program	All AP/DC
PRO				
CON				

Based on the PRO/CON list, which option would you advise Courtney to take? Why?
_____
_____

As a guidance counselor, what questions could you ask Courtney to inform your advice?
_____
_____
_____

Now imagine you are in Courtney's spot. What questions do you need to ask your guidance counselor in order to decide?
_____
_____

What are my next steps?

STEP 1: Determine what advanced coursework options are available to you.

Ask your guidance counselor about all of the options available at your school and at schools in your community (e.g., local community college).

Meet with Guidance Counselor

DIRECTIONS: Tear this page out and fill in the worksheet below with your guidance counselor.

Student Name: _____ Counselor Name: _____

What AP, Dual Credit, IB or other unique courses are available at our school?
_____
_____

Are there pre-requisites for any of these courses?
_____
_____

How are students identified to be a part of these class options? _____

Which advanced or unique class options am I currently eligible for?
_____
_____

What steps do I need to take in order to enroll in these classes?
_____
_____

If I am not eligible today, what steps do I need to take in order to become eligible?
_____
_____

Are the dual credit classes technical DC or academic DC?
_____

Of the dual credit options available, what will my course credit apply towards after successfully completing the course?
_____
_____

Are there other advanced or unique courses available at a local community college?
_____

Additional questions:
_____
_____
_____

STEP 2: Anticipate possible obstacles and identify solutions.

Take time to anticipate possible obstacles and identify solutions before enrolling. Some common obstacles for students who choose advanced and unique classes are:

- Time to study and practice
- Time and transportation available to travel to a local college
- Resources for exam fees
- Scheduling conflicts with extracurricular activities

Anticipate Obstacles and Identify Solutions

DIRECTIONS: Answer the questions below.

What, if any, are some potential obstacles that you can anticipate facing?

_____
_____
_____
_____

What are some possible solutions? Write them below.

_____
_____
_____
_____

In addition to the solutions you wrote, consider these…

1
CREATE STUDY GROUPS
Make a study group with your friends and support each other when you take advanced classes together.

2
OFFICE HOURS
If your teacher or professor keeps office hours, make sure to visit them with questions about your class.

3
SEEK OUT FREE TEST PREP
If you plan to take AP exams, seek out tutoring sessions with your teacher and online study materials!

4
TEST FEE WAIVERS
AP exams cost money; meet with your guidance counselor to see if you would qualify for free test waivers.

STEP 3: Enroll in classes and do your best!

Unit 2: My Choices

Extending My Learning: Meeting with Guidance Counselor Again

DIRECTIONS: Meet with your guidance counselor again to register for the classes you've selected. Use the questions and worksheet available to you in this section. Take notes in the space below.

Guidance Counselor Name: _____ **Date of Meeting:** _____

Advanced and Unique Courses I have questions about…
- _____
- _____
- _____

Notes
_____
_____
_____
_____
_____
_____
_____
_____
_____

Next Steps and Follow Up:
- _____
- _____
- _____
- _____
- _____

Life Outside of the Classroom

Your "in school" life is not all that defines you. Experiences outside of the classroom, gained through jobs, internships, extracurricular activities, and being involved in your community help you stand out and help in the pursuit of your goals after high school.

So many options are available! The sooner you start looking, the better. Seek a job, camp, internship, or community service experience to do in the summertime.

While you're looking for extracurricular activities to set you apart, ensure it's also something that you enjoy. Remember that summer jobs, extracurricular activities, and community service activities ultimately help develop you as a person and provide life skills that you'll need after high school.

In the following pages, you will find examples and websites you can explore to find the perfect fit for you and your community.

TIP
Professional and volunteer activities provide opportunities to use your skills to help others, work in teams, gain leadership experience, and effectively manage your time outside of the classroom.

Volunteer Hours
Many schools require students to complete volunteer hours to graduate. Stretch your hours out, starting freshman year.

Unit 2: My Choices

What Does Community Mean?

DIRECTIONS: Words can have several definitions. You can define a word with your own context. Below are two definitions of the word community. In the last box, draft your own definition.

Community can be a group of people living in the same place or having a particular characteristic in common.	Community can be a feeling of fellowship with others, as a result of sharing common attitudes, interests, and goals.	To me, community is…

BIG IDEA
Community can have different meanings and it is valuable for me to understand the communities I belong to.

Since this is your book, you get to establish a definition from your perspective. Turn to the **glossary** in the back of the book and write your definition of community in the space provided.

What 3 communities are you a member of?
- _____
- _____
- _____

Glossary
A section, usually at the end of a book, with an alphabetical list of vocabulary words and definitions related to the content in the book.

www.educationopensdoors.org

Community Service

Community Service is a way to help others and to make sure that the causes and initiatives you care about are prioritized. Volunteering shows you care about the world around you and that you are willing to take action for your passions or beliefs. Just as jobs and internships do, community service helps develop skills and interests that can inform your future career.

Examples of Community Service

DIRECTIONS: Do you know of organizations serving each of these communities? Write your examples in the boxes under the chart.

If you do not know of specific organizations, write an example of something YOU can do to positively impact one or more of these communities.

Global	National	City	School	Neighborhood	Home

Community Service

Community service may include any experiences you have giving back to your classmates, school, or community. Activities such as tutoring a classmate, walking your neighbor's dog, or reading to the kids at your sibling's daycare may all be considered community service!

TIP

When you join a club, listen for when leadership positions open up or elections are being held.

Reflecting on My Community

What is one way your community can be improved?
_____
_____

How can you support this improvement?
_____
_____

Circle any of the options in this list of common places to volunteer that sound interesting to you.

- Soup kitchens
- Food banks
- Churches
- Retirement homes/communities
- Political campaigns
- Schools
- Animal shelters
- Homeless shelters

Extracurricular Activities

When you are considering which extracurricular activities fit you, keep the following tips in mind.

1. **Follow your intuition.** Don't worry about what other people may be participating in. Make a choice that is right for you.
2. **Explore different options.** Take advantage of many different opportunities! Get out of your comfort zone and try something new.
3. **Be a leader.** Leaders influence people. Think about how you can influence others to achieve a goal.
4. **Don't take on too much.** Take on everything that interests you, but ensure you're able to maintain a good GPA at the same time. Choose activities that you can commit to and where you might desire a leadership role at some point.
5. **Innovate.** If something you're interested in or passionate about doesn't exist at your school, start a club or organization. Find a teacher, counselor, or parent who will help you.

> **Extracurricular Activities**
> *Non-classroom activities that students can get involved in at school or in their community.*

> **BIG IDEA**
> *Volunteer and extracurricular activities provide opportunities for me to develop new skills and gain leadership experience.*

Unit 2: My Choices

Get Involved

DIRECTIONS: Below is a list of clubs, sports and volunteer opportunities outside of the classroom.

1. Circle activities you are currently involved in.
2. Draw a box around activities you are excited to get involved with or want to know more about.

Sports

Football	Tennis	Cross Country	Golf
Basketball	Soccer	Wrestling	Swimming
Volleyball	Track and Field	Baseball	Drill/Dance Team
		Softball	Cheerleading

Clubs

Student Council	Jr. ROTC	Speech and Debate	DECA – International Association of Marketing Students
National Honor Society	Newspaper	UIL – Academic Competition	
National Jr. Honor Society	FCA – Fellowship of Christian Athletes	Yearbook	Men and Ladies of Distinction
Language Clubs		Choir	Book Club
Dance	Mock Trial	Band	

Off-Campus Extracurriculars

Big Brothers Big Sisters	Boy and Girl Scouts	Music Lessons	Young Life
Vacation Bible School	Piano	Dance Lessons	Boys and Girls Club
Church Choir	Select Sports Teams	Steppers' Groups	YMCA Youth Leadership

What club or organization would you like to start at your school?

_____

_____

_____

www.educationopensdoors.org

Write a Letter to Your Principal

Innovate and Advocate

DIRECTIONS: Describe a club you would like to create at your school. Use the table below to draft your ideas.

1. What is one reason your club would benefit your school community?	
2. What is one skill you would gain from creating this club or participating in this club?	
3. What is one way your club would help your school reach one of its goals?	

DIRECTIONS: DRAFT a letter to your principal using the table you created.

_____ (date)

Dear _____ (principal name)**,**

I hope this letter finds you in good spirits. I am writing to share an idea I had during _____ (teacher's name) **class.**

I believe that our school community would benefit from _____ _____ (club name)**.**

> **Write your response to question 1 in a complete sentence.**

> **Write your response to question 2 in a complete sentence.**

> **Write your response to question 3 in a complete sentence.**

I would like to know what additional steps I might need to take in order to start this club. Would you be willing to meet to discuss my idea?

Sincerely,

_____ (your name)

Unit 2: My Choices

Extending My Learning: Research

DIRECTIONS:

1. Refer back to the activities you placed a square around on the "Get Involved!" section.
2. Search each of them online to get basic information.
3. Write a description of each in the space below.
4. Ask others in your community about opportunities to participate.

Name of sport, club, or activity: _____

Description: _____
_____
_____

Who can I contact to learn about opportunities to participate in my community?
_____
_____

Name of sport, club, or activity: _____

Description: _____
_____
_____

Who can I contact to learn about opportunities to participate in my community?
_____
_____

Name of sport, club, or activity: _____

Description: _____
_____
_____

Who can I contact to learn about opportunities to participate in my community?
_____
_____

Jobs and Internships

What is a job?

What is an internship?

An *internship* is a temporary job (usually 2-3 months) that allows you to experience a work environment for a specific career. Internships can help you narrow down what career you want to pursue in the future. Sometimes internships are not paid positions.

Advantages of Having a Job or Internship

1. **…improve your resume**
   Applying for future jobs and/ or certificate or degree programs will be easier if you have previous work experience on your resume.

2. **…benefits**
   Jobs and internships can come with benefits; you may receive specialized training, discounts, free tickets, and other exciting perks.

3. **…responsibility**
   Demonstrating that you kept a job shows that you are dependable and motivated.

4. **…pay**
   Jobs and most internships will pay you for your time.

> **Internships**
> *Internships are short-term jobs that help you explore career paths and gain "hands-on" experience, and can be paid or unpaid.*

> **Be Flexible**
> *Being flexible and having availability in your schedule will help you secure a job.*

Comparing Similarities and Differences

DIRECTIONS: Complete the Venn Diagram by writing similarities and differences between jobs and internships.

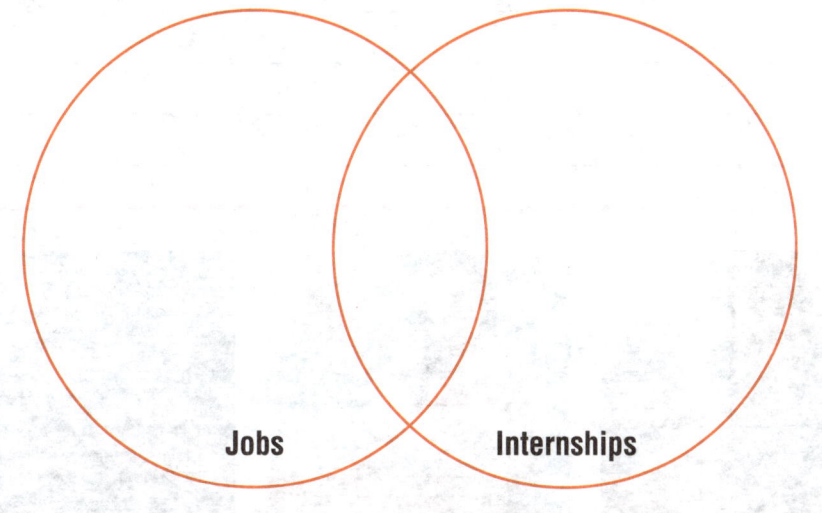

Jobs | Internships

Job and Internship Opportunities for Teens

BIG IDEA
There are differences between jobs and internships and advantages to both of them.

Be Prepared
Be prepared in case you are interviewed on the spot when you drop off your application.

Advantages of Timing

DIRECTIONS: Identify 2 advantages for each question below.

What are 2 advantages of looking for a job/internship as an adult?	What are 2 advantages of looking for a job/internship as a teenager?

What Are My Next Steps?

DIRECTIONS: Pretend you are a senior in high school and want to get an internship for the summer. What would be the first step you would take? Think about the people who you know or people within your network that would be able to connect you to individuals in the industry that you're interested in.

_____
_____
_____
_____
_____
_____
_____

Where Can Teens Search for Jobs or Internships?

DIRECTIONS: Read the categories of jobs below as well as the examples. Then fill in additional ideas you have for each category.

Food Service	grocery store			
Retail	shops at a mall			
Health Services and Public Safety	chart filing			
Arts, Entertainment, and Recreation	theater performer			
Education	day care teacher's aide			
Manufacturing and Logistics	package delivery			
Construction	building construction			
Business	mail delivery			
Technology	hardware recycling			
Government	student advisory committee			

Unit 2: My Choices

Extending My Learning: Steps to Prepare

DIRECTIONS: Although jobs and internships are not exactly the same, the steps to prepare for them are similar. Answer the following questions to help get the process started.

STEP 1: Determine your needs and desires.

What do you hope to learn or what skills do you hope to gain from the opportunity?
_____

When will you be available to work? _____

What will your transportation to and from work be? _____

What skills do you have to offer to an employer?
_____
_____

What type of work environment are you hoping to be a part of?
_____
_____

What amount of pay do you require for the opportunity? _____

STEP 2: Research.

Which category of jobs/internships sounds interesting to you?
_____

Which adults in your network can you ask about job or internship opportunities that align with your career goals?
_____

What resources can you use to search for jobs and internships?
_____

STEP 3: Develop a Résumé.   (*Note: Writing résumés is covered in Unit 3)

How can you share your skills and interests with a potential employer?
_____
_____
_____

STEP 4: APPLY!

Choosing a Healthy Lifestyle

If someone has a healthy lifestyle, what are some of the things that they do?
_____
_____

> **BIG IDEA**
> *Choosing a healthy lifestyle is important, and I have the opportunity to make healthy choices for myself.*

Lifestyle Assessment

DIRECTIONS: Read the boxes below and color in the activities you did yesterday.

You had a home cooked meal.	You did one relaxing activity.	You did 30 minutes of physical activity.	You ate vegetables.
You drank 8 glasses of water.	You ate breakfast.	You got a full night's sleep.	You wrote in your journal.

Factors to Consider for a Healthy Lifestyle

1. Intake (food and water)
2. Output (sleep, exercise, mindfulness)

Food Intake

DIRECTIONS: Imagine a meal you would like to eat right now. Draw it in the space below. Label the different components.

> **BIG IDEA**
> *There are several elements to consider when creating a meal.*

When you are putting together a meal, you may want to consider the following factors:

- **Eating a Rainbow – of fresh ingredients!** The makeup of foods creates their colors. Different types of foods are different colors and all have different nutrients. The more colors you eat in a meal, the more variety in food and thus nutrients you are taking in. Keep in mind, this is referring to naturally occurring colors – not foods with artificial coloring.
- **Portion Size.** The size of your meal depends on your height, weight, and physical activity.
- **Variety – of food groups.** Meals should include a mix of vegetables, protein, and some grains.
- **Quantity of fresh foods.** Processed food has more sugar and less nutrients than fresh foods, also known as **whole foods**.

Unit 2: My Choices

Water Intake

DIRECTIONS: Below are 8- 8 oz glasses of water. Color in the number of glasses of water that you had yesterday. Then determine your necessary daily intake.

An easy way to know how much water you should drink (being **hydrated**) is to divide your body weight in half and drink that many ounces of water.

Quick Math:

☐ ÷ 2 = ☐

Your Body Weight　　　Ounces of Water

Pay Attention to Your Body

Your body gives you signs to let you know if it needs you to change a behavior. You want to pay attention to any changes in your body, especially the following:

- Headaches
- Blurred Vision
- Stomach Bloating
- Bowel Movement Regularity
- Urine Color
- Cracked Lips
- Skin Blemishes

If you notice any of these changes, tell a trusted adult and ask yourself the following questions:

- Have I had enough water?
- Have I slept 7-8 hours regularly?
- Have I eaten enough fresh fruits and vegetables?
- Have I exercised for at least 20 minutes every day?

Case Studies

DIRECTIONS: Review the case studies below and develop three recommendations for each child based on the questions listed.

Case Study 1: New Video Game

Taylor received a new video game for their birthday! They have been so excited about it that they have come straight home every day and played for 3-4 hours before going to bed. By Friday, Taylor fell asleep during second period and felt irritable for the rest of the day.	Consider the following: • Taylor's food consumption • Taylor's water consumption • Taylor's sleep schedule • Taylor's exercise schedule • Taylor's relaxing activities	Your recommendations: • • • • •

Case Study 2: Late for School

Jesse was late to school today and left without their backpack! They missed breakfast in the classroom, but ate a slice of pizza and a fruit cup for lunch. They have a headache at the end of the day and their lips are starting to crack.	Consider the following: • Jesse's food consumption • Jesse's water consumption • Jesse's sleep schedule • Jesse's exercise schedule • Jesse's relaxing activities	Your recommendations: • • • • •

Case Study 3: Busy, Busy, Busy

Vic is taking 3 Pre-AP classes this year, is on the soccer team, and committed to volunteering 5 hours a week at the local animal shelter. They get home late from soccer practice and volunteering, so Vic has been waking up at 3:45 AM to work on homework. In order to stay awake, Vic drinks a soda every day during lunch. Recently their coach noticed that Vic is not moving as quickly during practice.	Consider the following: • Vic's food consumption • Vic's water consumption • Vic's sleep schedule • Vic's exercise schedule • Vic's relaxing activities	Your recommendations: • • • • •

Unit 2: My Choices

Extending My Learning: Practicing Mindfulness

Research has shown huge benefits to practicing mindfulness, including a decrease in stress and an increase in joy.

Ways to Be Mindful

- Journal about your daily life or talk about your experiences with someone you trust
- Take deep breaths
- Stretch
- Prayer or mediation
- Search "mindfulness exercises" online to find more ways to practice.

DIRECTIONS: Follow the steps below to go through a simple mindfulness practice. Read through the steps first and then complete the practice after you learn the steps.

1. Sit at the edge of a chair with your feet flat on the floor in front of you.
2. Rest your hands on top of your legs.
3. Roll your shoulders back.
4. Make your back straight as if a string is pulling you up from the top of your head.
5. Pull your tailbone in under your body.
6. Close your eyes or lower your eyelids.
7. Relax your muscles, especially in your face. Be sure you're not squinting your eyes or clenching your jaw.
8. Slowly take 3 full deep breaths in filling your lungs completely. Let each breath out slowly until your lungs are empty.
9. At the end of your 3rd breath, slowly begin counting down from 50. If a thought interrupts your countdown, start over.
10. Once your countdown successfully gets to 0, open your eyes and stand to walk around.

Meditation Space

DIRECTIONS: Think of a space that is peaceful to you. Draw or describe it below, and then use that space to practice the meditation activity above.

Notes

Unit 2 Summary: Making Choices for My Future

High school is a launching point for your future. Choose the plan that challenges you and aligns with the types of colleges you would like to enroll in.

Since high school is so important, you have many options to consider when you are in middle school. Choose the high school that will best prepare you for the field of study you wish to pursue in the future.

The number of experiences that you can pursue are almost limitless. The most important thing is to take the initiative in starting the search. Your life is destined for success, make sure you take the steps to enjoy it!

Checklist Check-In

1. Consider where you are in your educational journey. Check the corresponding box below.
   - ☐ 6th Grade
   - ☐ 7th Grade
   - ☐ 8th Grade
   - ☐ 9th Grade
   - ☐ 10th Grade
   - ☐ 11th Grade
   - ☐ 12th Grade
   - ☐ High School Graduate
   - ☐ GED Recipient

2. Turn to the "Grade Level Checklist" at the beginning of Unit 1. Locate your current grade level. **Review what you checked off at the beginning of the program and check off any other activities you have completed.**

Unit Review Opportunities

1. Go back to the "Extend Your Learning" pages in this unit. Research, ask questions, and locate resources to complete those activities.
2. Complete any remaining vocabulary tasks for this unit's vocabulary and use each word in a sentence this week.
3. Answer the questions on the unit cover page, and complete the directions in the white box.

Moving Forward…

Select one of the colors from the triangle to describe how you feel about new understandings gained from this unit. Justify your answer in at least 3 sentences.

_____
_____
_____
_____
_____
_____

UNIT 3

PROFESSIONALISM: SHOWING UP AS MY BEST SELF

What is a résumé? Why is it important?

How can I prepare for an interview?

How is building relationships important for my network?

- **Virtual Identity** — page 102
- **Personal Statement** — page 105
- **Cover Letter** — page 107
- **Recommendation Letters** — page 113
- **Writing a Thank You Note** — page 116
- **Résumé Building Blocks** — page 122
- **Preparing for an Interview** — page 137
- **Unit 3 Summary** — page 158
- **Networking** — page 99
- **Professionalism** — page 97
- **Unit 3 Vocabulary** — page 96

DIRECTIONS: Read the topics of this unit. Draw a picture of your emotions about this content.

Unit 3 Vocabulary

DIRECTIONS:

1. DEFINE each word using the glossary in this book or a dictionary.
2. ANSWER the questions listed below for each word.

Vocabulary Word	Definition	Have you ever heard/seen this word before?	Explain how you have heard this word used before. If you've never heard or seen it, what other word (in any language) does it look like to you?
Professionalism		Y N	
Networking		Y N	
First Impression		Y N	
Cover Letter		Y N	
Personal Statement		Y N	
Recommendation Letter		Y N	
Résumé		Y N	
References		Y N	
Interview		Y N	
Business Professional		Y N	
Business Casual		Y N	
Mock Interview		Y N	

Networking

> **BIG IDEA**
> *Building relationships with others is an essential part of developing myself.*

Networking is building relationships, both personally and professionally. Relationship building is meeting people, interacting with them, and developing connections.

How can networking help you? Connections to other people can open doors to opportunities, whether it is needing help with an immediate need like fixing a flat tire or needing help locating a job for the future. Every opportunity to meet someone is an opportunity to build a relationship and establish your network.

Think of someone you have a close relationship with. Your relationship today looks different than when you first met. What caused that relationship to change?

_____
_____
_____

Building Relationships

Relationships exist in different settings: a classroom, at home, in a professional setting. What all settings have in common is how relationships build over time and usually involve developing trust and mutual respect, as well as sharing interests and passions. Read the tips below for building positive relationships in a professional and personal setting.

Develop Trust. To build rapport with someone, start with giving full attention to what the speaker is saying.

Demonstrate Interest. Ask questions throughout the conversation. Also, more than half of our communication is nonverbal. Have awareness of the message your body language and facial expressions share during a conversation.

Foster Mutual Respect. Keep the conversation 2-sided so that both people are able to share thoughts. Follow up after the meeting with a call or note. Arrive to meetings on time.

Share Passions. Talk openly about your convictions and beliefs.

How can you use these tips to build your network in a professional setting?

_____
_____
_____

How can you use these tips to build your network in a personal setting?

_____
_____
_____

Unit 3: My Professionalism

How Networking Works

Imagine your sibling is looking for a job.

PHASE 1

They visit 4 of their teachers to share their career goals and ask for advice.

PHASE 2

After meeting with teachers, your sibling was given contact information for 4 local business leaders who are hiring students.

PHASE 3

They completed the application requirements for all 4 businesses and are excitedly awaiting reply!

Personal Statement

Personal statements are an opportunity for you to showcase either your personal background or your opinion on a particular topic. The purpose of the personal statement is to:

- Grab the readers' attention and demonstrate your academic potential.
- Explain how you persevered in a unique circumstance or hardship.
- Highlight your achievements.

> **BIG IDEA**
> *The purpose of a personal statement is to demonstrate your desire and passion for applying to a high school or college.*

Personal statements are a type of application essay. Below are 6 steps to take when starting to write any essay, including a personal statement. Let's break down the steps together!

1. **Find a place to write.**
   Find a place where you can focus on your essay for at least 1 to 2 hours and get all of your necessary tools in one place.

2. **Determine if you are writing a new essay or rewriting an essay you have previously written.**
   Many scholarship essays have similar prompts. If you have already written an essay for a different application and it is a strong essay, then you can rewrite the essay with similar ideas and concepts.

3. **Brainstorm about yourself.**
   Process your strengths, goals, and other elements that make you unique.

4. **Create your personal brand statement.**
   A personal brand statement defines you as a unique applicant. It often goes at the end of the opening paragraph.

5. **Outline your essay.**
   - Choose a hook that will grab your audience's attention by using a quote, action, or describing a scene.
   - Organize your thoughts in a logical way in order to outline important points.
   - As you are writing, make sure you are following the directions that were laid out for you by the prompt.

6. **Begin writing essay.**
   - Turn your outline into a flowing narrative (not a list).
   - Keep the details simple.
   - Focus on grammar, syntax, and paragraph structures.
   - Search "sample personal statements" online to see how others have formatted their essays.

7. **Gather feedback and edits, and revise.**
   Ask others to read your work and recommend edits.

Public Service Announcement!

DIRECTIONS: Use the prompting questions below to brainstorm for your personal statement. Write or draw your ideas below.

- What are you especially good at?
- What are the things you struggle with?
- What are the things you are interested in?
- What extracurricular activities have you participated in?
- What are your character strengths?
- When have you demonstrated leadership abilities?
- Describe your work experience.
- What are your goals and dreams?

Cover Letter

What is the purpose of a book cover?

_____

Much like the cover of a book gives an introduction to the content inside the book, a **cover letter** introduces you as the applicant.

Often, jobs and sometimes schools will require a cover letter as part of the application. A cover letter and a personal statement have the same purpose, but are different.

> **BIG IDEA**
> *The purpose of a cover letter is to introduce yourself and encourage follow up from a school or employer.*

BOTH

Personal Statement

Format = essay

Utilized in school applications usually

Purpose:
- Grab the readers' attention.
- Showcase your knowledge and skills.
- Explain how you persevered in a unique or difficult circumstance.
- Highlight your achievements.

Cover Letter

Format = letter

Utilized in job applications usually

Writing a Letter

Because of the way letters are sent, they require information from the sender and recipient to be included. They also have a very specific formatting.

DIRECTIONS: Circle all of the elements listed below that you think should be included in a letter. Then check your work using the sample and the formatting activity on the next two pages.

E-mail address	Body, introduction, and closing paragraphs
High school name	Phone number
Address of sender	Salutation (Dear…)
Address of recipient	Date
Signature	Closing
GPA	Social media handles

Unit 3: My Professionalism

Sample Cover Letter

123 Rocks Street
Dallas, TX 75211

November 20, 2016

Ashley Flores, Child Life Intern Program
Children's Medical Center
341 Medical District Drive
Dallas, TX 12345

Dear Ms. Flores:

After speaking with my high school counselor about volunteer opportunities, I learned about your Child Life Internship Program at Children's Medical Center. As someone who hopes to attend medical school in the future, I would love the opportunity to volunteer and serve others through your program.

My younger sister was a patient at Children's Medical Center as a baby. During that experience, I realized I wanted to be a pediatrician and provide the same loving care for young people as my sister received. I have worked hard towards that goal ever since. I currently hold a 3.83 GPA at Sunrise High School. Last summer, I was a Public Relations intern with The Birthday Party Project. During my internship, I had the opportunity to translate documents for Spanish-speaking residents. In addition, I learned so much about the importance of virtual security and privacy, while sharing the joy of birthdays with hundreds of homeless youth.

Children's Medical Center's commitment to its patients and reputation for excellence are compelling reasons for joining your Child Life Intern program. I believe that my work ethic and commitment to service are values shared by your staff. Joining the Child Life Internship program would be an outstanding way to serve others and work towards my own goal of someday becoming a pediatrician. That said, I would love to interview with you in person and have enclosed my résumé. You may reach me at (123) 456-7890 or alma@education.eod. Thank you for your consideration.

Sincerely,

Alma Rodriguez

Alma Rodriguez

Matching Cover Letter Format and Contents

DIRECTIONS: Match each content description in **orange** to its correct format location in the **blue** cover letter template in by drawing lines.

Template (blue):
- My Address
- Date
- Recipient Address
- Salutation: Dear _____,
- Opening Paragraph or Introduction
- Body Paragraph
- Closing Paragraph
- Signature Line

Content descriptions (orange):

- This paragraph states why you are interested in the position, organization, or school and captures the reader's attention.
- Name of Person and Title
  Company/Organization
  Their Street Address
  Their City, State and ZIP Code
- This paragraph is devoted to explaining your qualifications for the job and why you are a perfect match for the role and company or organization.
- List your contact information so that they know when and how to reach you.
- This paragraph summarizes your key strengths as a future employee, re-emphasizes your excitement of joining the organization, and shares gratitude for considering you as an applicant.
- Write the letter to a specific person.
- Today, 20XX
- Sincerely,
  Sign your name
  Type your name
- Your Street
  Your City, State and ZIP Code

Unit 3: My Professionalism

BIG IDEA

A cover letter should have an introduction, body and closing, be tailored to your passion for that job, and be addressed to the specific group of people offering the job.

www.educationopensdoors.org 109

Practice Outlining a Cover Letter

DIRECTIONS: The Mayor of your city needs your help! Answer the following questions, read the prompt, brainstorm some ideas, and practice outlining a cover letter on the next page.

HELP WANTED!

Describe one thing you love about your community.
_____
_____

How can you share that with all communities in your city?
_____
_____

Dear Applicant,

Included in this letter is a brief job description for the position of Special Project Intern. This opportunity could be beneficial to your community as you consider the ways you want to share your community's strengths with the rest of our city. *You will need to submit a formal cover letter to be considered.*

As the Special Project Intern, you will have the opportunity to meet many elected officials and share your great ideas with them. You will also develop and execute a plan to make your idea come to life.

I will want to know what strengths and experiences make you the most qualified applicant, as well as what you hope to learn from the experience.

I am also looking for bilingual applicants. If you are able to write this letter in a language other than English, please do so.

In our city, we need young people like you to continue to make our city wonderful for everyone.

Sincerely,
Mayor

Brainstorm Your Cover Letter

Outlining a Cover Letter

DIRECTIONS: Create an outline of your cover letter.

_____

_____

_____

Mayor's Council
Special Project Department
123 Busy Street
Busy Town, TX 12345

Dear Mr./Ms. _____:

Introduction

_____
_____
_____

Body

_____
_____
_____
_____

Closing

_____
_____
_____

Sincerely,

_____

_____

I've Written My Outline - What's Next?

1. Write a draft of your cover letter
2. Ask multiple people to read your draft and provide feedback
3. Proofread and revise

Unit 3: My Professionalism

Extending My Learning: Practice Writing

Proofread!
Proofread your letters for errors and avoid using the word "I" too much.

DIRECTIONS: Use the space below to write a personal statement for a school application or a cover letter for a job application. Once you have written it here, type it on a computer and save it. Ask a grown up to read it for feedback, then revise as needed.

Recommendation Letters

What is a recommendation letter?

A recommendation letter is a letter about you. It specifically highlights your skills, accomplishments, leadership experience, academic successes, extracurricular involvement, ambition, and goals. **Recommendation letters** are a part of the application process for colleges and universities as well as many jobs and internships.

Who should I ask to write me a recommendation letter?

An adult who knows you well but isn't family should write your letter(s) of recommendation. This person should be someone who can easily write about your skills, accomplishments, leadership experience, academic successes, extracurricular involvement, ambition, and goals.

Some applications require recommendation letters from specific people. Check the instructions in your application packet, on their website, or by asking a representative from their location for details. For example, military academies require a nomination from an elected official. Some colleges require a recommendation letter from a core content teacher or your principal.

> **BIG IDEA**
> *A letter of recommendation is usually written by a teacher or other adult who knows your academic and leadership strengths.*

> **Build Relationships!**
> *Start building positive relationships with potential recommenders early. The more genuine your relationship, the better!*

Brainstorm Recommenders

DIRECTIONS: Complete the chart below.

Who should I ask to write me a recommendation letter?

Name of person	Person's role or title	Person's relationship to you
Example: Coach Jaime	Former head coach	Coach Jaime was my mentor and coach for three years

When should I ask someone to write my recommendation letter?

Request a letter of recommendation at least 1 month prior to your application deadline.

TIP

Schools often prefer confidential letters from recommenders which means the letter is sealed so you cannot read it. This ensures the recommender feels they can be fully honest in their recommendation.

Say Thank You!

Send the person who wrote your letter a handwritten thank you card.

How do I request a letter of recommendation?

Ask in person, over the phone, via e-mail, or in a physical letter. Tell the recommender why you need a letter of recommendation and why you have selected them to write it. Share why you appreciate that person being a part of your life and something you have learned from them.

Practice Asking a Recommender

DIRECTIONS: Write a draft of an e-mail to your recommender.

Dear _____,

_____

_____

_____

_____

With Gratitude,

_____

What information do I need to provide to the person recommending me?

Some schools and employment opportunities have specific formatting requirements for recommendation letters. Check instructions for each individual opportunity in your application packet, by asking a representative at their location, or by looking on their website.

Providing a copy of your résumé or an activity list like the one you completed in the résumé lesson (pictured here) is helpful.

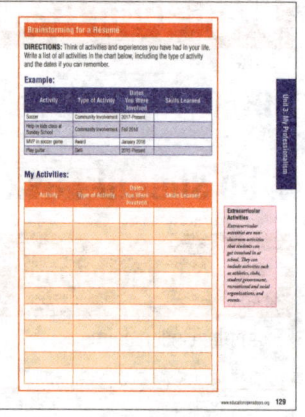

Review: 5 Steps for Getting a Great Recommendation Letter

1 BRAINSTORM
Who am I going to ask?

2 GATHER DOCUMENTS
Create a written document highlighting your skills and any directions given by the opportunity.

3 ASK
Ask recommender verbally, via email or mail.

4 FOLLOW UP
Make sure you letter is submitted on time.

5 THANK
Show appreciation for recommender in writing.

Recommendation Reflections

DIRECTIONS: Write your responses to each question below.

What do you think your teachers, or employers, would say about you in a recommendation letter?

_____
_____
_____
_____
_____

How do you feel about that response?

_____
_____
_____
_____
_____

Think about 1 adult you want to ask to write a recommendation letter. How did you build a relationship with them?

_____
_____
_____
_____

What are steps you can take to build a relationship with another adult?

_____
_____
_____
_____
_____
_____
_____
_____

> **BIG IDEA**
> *The purpose of a recommendation letter is to provide a school or employer with a mentor's perspective of you as a student or employee.*

Unit 3: My Professionalism

Writing a Thank You Note

BIG IDEA
Sending a hand written thank you note is a great way to show gratitude to someone who helped you in some way.

A Special "Thank You"
Write your notes on card stock or stationery.

Sending a thank you note is a simple way to show gratitude. Some people believe that sending thank you notes is old fashioned, but it shows the recipient how truly grateful you are for them and their help.

Follow these simple steps to send a great thank you note.

1. **Address Your Note (Salutation)** – "Dear _____,"
2. **Start With Gratitude** – Begin with thanking them.
3. **Share Thoughtful Specifics** – Add concrete details of how their contributions impacted you.
4. **Closing** – Phrases such as "Sincerely," or "Thank you," are good.
5. **Signature** – Print your name at the bottom of the note so they know who sent it.

Sample Thank You Note

DIRECTIONS: Read the sample thank you note below. Identify one phrase you would change if you were Alex.

> Dear Ms. Fadley,
>
> Thank you so much for writing a college recommendation letter for me. Your words and confidence in me continue to be encouraging as I complete the application process. I hope to one day join you as a "Horned-Frog" alum of TCU. Again, thank you so much for your help. You will be the first to know when I hear back!
>
> Sincerely,
> Alex

Write your new sentence here:

_____
_____
_____
_____
_____

Draft Your Thank You Note

DIRECTIONS: In the space provided, write a draft of a thank you note to someone special. Once you are happy with the phrasing, tear out the thank you card on the next page, re-write your note and deliver the card.

Unit 3: My Professionalism

Extending My Learning: Practicing Gratitude

Research has proven that practicing gratitude can reduce negative feelings like frustration, depression, anger, stress, resentment, physical pain, and many more. The same research also shows that practicing gratitude can increase positive emotions like happiness, empathy, and self-esteem. Practicing gratitude is as simple as thinking about who or what we are thankful for every day.

What Am I Grateful For?

DIRECTIONS: Using the prompts below, write things you are grateful for in your life. If you feel encouraged to do so, share your gratefulness with others.

I am grateful for who I am because…
_____
_____
_____
_____
_____

I am grateful for friendship with _____ because…
_____
_____
_____

I am grateful for this good thing that happened this week…
_____
_____
_____

I am grateful for this person _____ because…
_____
_____
_____

I am grateful for this thing _____ because…
_____
_____
_____

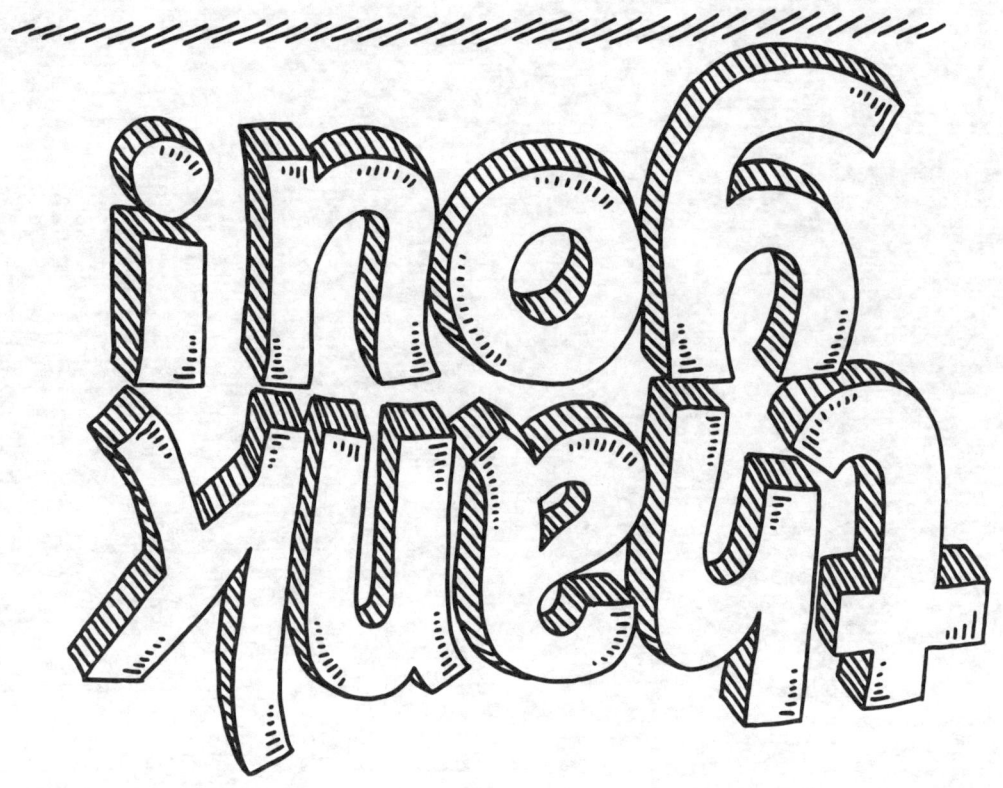

Notes

Résumé Building Blocks

BIG IDEA
The purpose of my résumé is to highlight my education, work and academic experiences, community involvement, awards and honors as well as skills in a brief way.

Top 3 GPAs

DIRECTIONS: Rank the following GPAs in order from highest to lowest: 3.0, 2.8, 4.0, 2.5, 3.7.

_____

_____

_____

_____

_____

GPA is a number. It reflects all of your grades combined into an average. However, applicants are more than a number. Other than GPA, what else would you want a college or hiring committee to know about you? Possibly your skills, your achievements, your community involvement? Submitting a résumé solves that problem! A **résumé** is a one-page summary of your experiences, awards, and skills.

More Than A Number

DIRECTIONS: Pretend you are on the admissions committee at Pursuit School of Achievement. You have 5 applicants and only have space for 3. Read the highlight from their résumés listed below. Combined with their GPA, which ones would you choose to admit? Circle 3.

APPLICANT 1	APPLICANT 2	APPLICANT 3	APPLICANT 4	APPLICANT 5
GPA: 3.0	GPA: 2.8	GPA: 4.0	GPA: 2.5	GPA: 3.7
Selected to attend an enriching summer program.	Competed in and won first place in an all-region athletic competition.	Participated in a community service project.	Planned and led a community wide service project.	Directs the varsity choir.

Did you choose the ones with the top 3 GPAs? Why or why not?

_____

_____

Résumé Building Blocks

Colleges and universities do not always choose applicants with the highest GPA. Work and academic experiences, community involvement, awards, honors, and skills are a part of the selection process.

Starting today, what aspect of your future application can you focus on improving? Circle it below and write a goal to pursue this school year.

GPA	Work/Academic Experiences	Community Involvement	Awards and Honors	Skills

My Goal:

_____
_____
_____
_____

NOTES:

Unit 3: My Professionalism

www.educationopensdoors.org

Middle School Résumé

Alma Rodriguez

456 Happy Way, Boulder, TX 75211 | alma@education.eod | 123.456.7890

EDUCATION

Centennial Middle School, Boulder Valley School District	2013-2015

Cumulative GPA: 3.4
Advanced and Unique Courses:
- Advanced Math, Language Arts, and U.S. History
- Education Opens Doors College Prep Class

WORK AND ACADEMIC EXPERIENCES

- Played as catcher on baseball team — 2013-2015
- Engineering Camp at Boulder Community College — Summer 2014
- Served 2 terms as president of the Spanish Club — 2014-2015
- Competed in the Knowledge Bowl Competition — 2014
- Participated on the Math Team for 1 competition — 2015

COMMUNITY INVOLVEMENT

- Tutored elementary students in After School Club program — 2014-2015
- Volunteered at the annual Thanksgiving Canned Food Drive — 2014
- Read to toddlers at Sunshine Day Care — 2015

AWARDS AND HONORS

- Most Valuable Player, baseball team — 2013
- Most improved Math Student Award — 2013
- Junior Zoo Keeper Certificate, Dallas Zoo — 2014
- 3rd Place in Knowledge Bowl Competition — 2014

SKILLS

- Bilingual, fluent in speaking, reading, and writing English and Spanish

REFERENCES

Kristen Watkins
English Teacher and Knowledge Bowl Teacher Sponsor
Phone: 123.456.7891
E-mail: Kristen.watkins@education.eod

Andy Lovley
Baseball Coach and Math Teacher
Phone: 123.456.7892
E-mail: andy.lovley@education.eod

Please Note: Image is not to scale. Real résumé files are printed on an 8.5" x 11" sheet of paper.

Building A Résumé

The purpose of a **résumé** is to highlight your education and experiences in a concise way. Résumés change over time as you gain more experience. Throughout this section, notice the changes in Alma's résumé as the résumé transitions from middle school to high school and into a professional version.

What is included in a résumé?

- Name and Contact Information
- Education
- Work and Academic Experience
- Community Involvement
- Awards and Honors
- Skills
- References

> **Ordering Your Information**
> *When listing your activities, do so in reverse chronological order. More recent events should come first.*

Name and Contact Information

When someone first looks at your résumé, make it easy for them to find your name and contact information. Place this information at the top of your résumé and make your name the largest font (don't go larger than 16-point font). Use a permanent mailing address, phone number, and professional email address. A professional email address typically includes your first and last name.

Education

This section follows your personal contact information. Here is where you put the name of the high school you are graduating from. Always include your GPA if it is above a 3.0. (to find your GPA, check your high school transcript or talk to your counselor). Including "advanced and unique coursework" is optional. Consider including this if you have taken courses that are related to what you are applying for. For example, if you took AP US History and are applying to a history program, you would definitely want to mention it.

Work and Academic Experience

If you have had any previous experience that was paid or non-paid, this is where to include those responsibilities and accomplishments. One way to organize this information is to include the exact title of your position, the name of the company/organization, and how long you held this position on one line. Under this information, bullet point your responsibilities and accomplishments to help recruiters understand what you did in this role. If you reference more than one experience, list it in reverse chronological order, most recent first.

> **Review!**
> *Revisit Unit 2 to refresh on internships, jobs, community service, and extracurricular activities for examples.*

> **References**
> *A reference is someone who can comment positively on your personal character and work ethic.*

Community Involvement

Community can be defined many ways. Think about how you have been involved in any communities you are a part of. If you are involved in both extracurricular activities and community service organizations, it is okay to have separate sections for each. If you held leadership positions in these activities, don't forget to include them here too. This can be an optional section if you included this information in the experience section.

Awards and Honors

If you did not include your awards and honors in the experience section, make sure to list them here. It is always helpful to include a short description of the award/honor and when you received it.

Skills

If you are fluent in speaking, reading, and/or writing a language other than English, include it here. This is the place for you to list specific skills that are relevant to what you are applying for. For example, if you are applying for computer jobs, include the programs you are proficient (skilled) in (such as MS Word, Excel, and PowerPoint, Adobe Illustrator and Photoshop). This can be an optional section.

References

Create a **reference** list of three to five people who know you in a professional setting and would be willing to talk about you. A reference may be contacted before or after an interview. This can be on a separate page from your résumé. Title the page, "References for _____". If you have had a job before, use your supervisor or boss as a reference. Other references could include teachers, coaches, or extracurricular sponsors who know you. Do not include family members or friends. When you list your references, include their full name, title, work address, phone number, and email address. Ask your references for permission before you list them, and let them know what you are interviewing for. After the interview, send them a thank you card for being a reference.

High School Résumé

Alma Rodriguez
456 Happy Way, Boulder, TX 75211 | alma@education.eod | 123.456.7890

EDUCATION
Sunrise High School, Boulder Valley School District — 2016-2020
Cumulative GPA: 3.83   Rank: 15/367
SAT Score: 1340   ACT Score: 31

WORK AND ACADEMIC EXPERIENCES
Student Council — 2017-2020
Community Liaison
- Served as communication between school and local organizations
- Raised over $10,000 for the school in the form of donations from the community
- Created a list of local organizations hiring teens for students to locate internships

Sunrise High School Volleyball Team, Defense — 2016-2020
Varsity Co-Captain — 2019-2020
JV Most Valuable Player — 2016

COMMUNITY INVOLVEMENT
Children's Medical Center, Pediatric Oncology Department — Summer 2017
Child Life Intern
- Assisted in planning and facilitation of 2 activities in the hospital playroom per week
- Delivered joy to patients with flowers and gifts

The Birthday Party Project — Summer 2016
Public Relations Intern
- Assisted PR Coordinator in creating a 6-month social media content schedule
- Collected and organized media release for all images and quotes from families

AWARDS AND HONORS
Who's Who at Sunrise High School — 2020
- Recognized as one of 30 seniors for outstanding service and leadership

Most Likely to Change the World — 2019
- Awarded as the student most likely to make a difference in the community

"A" Honor Roll — 2019
- Earned straight A's during junior year

SKILLS
- Fluent in Spanish (reading, writing, and speaking)
- Adept in graphic editing using Photoshop and Illustrator

REFERENCES

Dr. Meghan Coates
Science Teacher and Student Council Advisor
Phone: 123.456.7890
E-mail: meghan.coates@education.eod

Chelsea Johnson
Public Relations Coordinator at The Birthday Party Project
Phone: 123.456.7891
E-mail: Chelsea.johnson@tbp.eod

Please Note: Image is not to scale. Real résumé files are printed on an 8.5" x 11" sheet of paper.

Unit 3: My Professionalism

Formatting a Résumé

Research states that most employers will initially spend about 10 seconds looking at a résumé. Below are tips for résumé formatting to ensure it is easy to read quickly and highlights the most important elements.

Find the Format

DIRECTIONS: Read the formatting tips in the list below and point to where you see the tips being utilized in Alma's résumé.

TIPS

- It is okay to have white space on your résumé as long as the page is balanced
- Align dates on the right side of the page
- Leave 1-inch margins
- Print your resume on white or off-white paper, size 8.5 x 11
- Only include pictures if requested to do so
- Use reverse chronological order
- Avoid using the pronoun "I"
- Begin each description with an action verb
- Always type your résumé rather than hand writing

BIG IDEA

Résumés have very specific structure and formatting, including being 1-2 pages, listing experiences in reverse chronological order, and avoiding the pronoun "I".

Alma Rodriguez
456 Happy Way, Boulder, TX 75211 | alma@education.eod | 123.456.7890

EDUCATION
Sunrise High School, Boulder Valley School District 2016-2020
Cumulative GPA: 3.83 Rank: 15/367
SAT Score: 1340 ACT Score: 31

WORK AND ACADEMIC EXPERIENCES
Student Council 2017-2020
Community Liaison
- Served as communication between school and local organizations
- Raised over $10,000 for the school in the form of donations from the community
- Created a list of local organizations hiring teens for students to locate internships

Sunrise High School Volleyball Team, Defense 2016-2020
Varsity Co-Captain 2019-2020
JV Most Valuable Player 2016

COMMUNITY INVOLVEMENT
Children's Medical Center, Pediatric Oncology Department Summer 2017
Child Life Intern
- Assisted in planning and facilitation of 2 activities in the hospital playroom per week
- Delivered joy to patients with flowers and gifts

The Birthday Party Project Summer 2016
Public Relations Intern
- Assisted PR Coordinator in creating a 6-month social media content schedule
- Collected and organized media release for all images and quotes from families

AWARDS AND HONORS
Who's Who at Sunrise High School 2020
- Recognized as one of 30 seniors for outstanding service and leadership

Most Likely to Change the World 2019
- Awarded as the student most likely to make a difference in the community

"A" Honor Roll 2019
- Earned straight A's during junior year

SKILLS
- Fluent in Spanish (reading, writing, and speaking)
- Adept in graphic editing using Photoshop and Illustrator

Brainstorming for a Résumé

DIRECTIONS: Think of activities and experiences you have had in your life. Write a list of all activities in the chart below, including the type of activity and the dates if you can remember.

Example:

Activity	Type of Activity	Dates You Were Involved	Skills Learned
Soccer	Community Involvement	2017-Present	
Help in kids class at Sunday School	Community Involvement	Fall 2018	
MVP in soccer game	Award	January 2018	
Play guitar	Skill	2015-Present	

My Activities:

Activity	Type of Activity	Dates You Were Involved	Skills Learned

Extracurricular Activities

Extracurricular activities are non-classroom activities that students can get involved in at school. They can include activities such as athletics, clubs, student government, recreational and social organizations, and events.

Unit 3: My Professionalism

Extending My Learning: Building a Résumé

DIRECTIONS: Create a draft of a résumé using an online template to practice formatting.

STEP 1: Search "résumé template" online to locate a template you can edit on a computer.

STEP 2: Begin to input information into the template using the brainstorming page and the résumé formatting page.

STEP 3: Analyze the formatting of the document to establish if it is utilizing correct résumé formatting or not.

STEP 4: Send your draft to a friend or adult to ask for feedback.

Spacing
Pay careful attention to the spacing of your résumé and make sure it appears clean and consistent.

Formatting
Dates should be right aligned throughout your entire résumé.

NOTES:

Sample Professional Résumé

Alma Rodriguez
456 Happy Way, Boulder, TX 75211 | alma@education.eod | 123.456.7890

EDUCATION

Pursuit School of Achievement | School of Social Welfare — Berkeley, CA
Masters in Social Welfare, Concentration in Management and Planning — May 2030

Pursuit School of Achievement | College of Letters and Sciences — Berkeley, CA
Bachelor of Arts in Sociology and Mass Communications — May 2024

WORK EXPERIENCE

The Counsel Project | Hill High School — El Cerrito, CA
Individual and Group Counselor, MSW Intern — 2029
- Facilitated 15 weeks of curriculum for a group of immigrant youth to explore identity, culture, and future aspirations
- Built rapport, consulted, and partnered with students, staff, teachers, and school administrators to design and execute a student-centered needs assessment for immigrant youth
- Counseled high school students in weekly sessions utilizing youth-centered narrative therapy practices

Community Health Organization — Oakland, CA
Bilingual Community Engagement Coordinator — 2028
- Led and executed data collection project administering health surveys and interviewing nail salon workers to identify workplace issues
- Conducted over 25 nail salon visits and trained owners/workers in green energy efficiency and water conservation practices in salons
- Co-created and facilitated community building events between immigrant nail salon workers and clients

African American Studies, Pursuit School of Achievement — Berkeley, CA
Research Assistant — 2027
- Independently planned and implemented all logistics for a 7-day research trip across Louisiana, visited 9 plantation and museum sites, and conducted 15 interviews with site staff on the preservation of slave cabins and the representation of (or lack of) slave stories
- Executed data collection projects on the representation of race, history, and the formation of collective memory

California Energy Center — Berkeley, CA
Program Planning and Evaluation Assistant, Intern — 2026-2027
- Managed, collected, and analyzed data for a young adult needs assessment to drive program planning, operational efficiency, and impact
- Conducted environmental landscape and program analysis to identify best practices for young adult college and job training programs

COMMUNITY INVOLVEMENT

Social Welfare Graduate Assembly | School of Social Welfare — Berkeley, CA
Co-Chair of Operations and Chair of Equity and Inclusion — 2029-2030
- Served as student representative for Masters in Social Welfare student body in administrative meetings with the School of Social Welfare dean, faculty, and staff regarding changes in curriculum, faculty, and the direction of the school
- Planned and implemented anti-oppression workshops for incoming first year students

AWARDS AND HONORS
- Excellence in Leadership Block Grant Award
- School of Social Welfare Department Award

SKILLS
- Fluent Spanish speaker with reading and writing skills
- Proficient in Microsoft Office Suite and Google Suite
- Adept in Adobe InDesign, Salesforce, Asana Task Management System, SmartSheet, and Remark
- Conversational in Vietnamese

REFERENCES

Courtnee Benford, LCP The Counsel Project, Licensed Counselor
Phone: 123.456.7891   E-mail: courntee.benford@eduation.eod

Sandra Godina, Professor of Social Work Policy, Pursuit School of Achievement
Phone: 123.456.7891   E-mail: Sandra.godina@education.eod

*Please Note: Image is not to scale. Real résumé files are printed on an 8.5" x 11" sheet of paper.

Action Verbs

On a resume, use action verbs to describe your work experiences, community involvement, awards, honors, and skills. Statements describing each of your experiences start with action verbs. Use past tense for previously held positions and organizations. Use present tense to describe any experiences you are currently involved in.

Using Action Verbs

Verb Tense
Pay careful attention to the verb tense you use when describing past and present positions.

DIRECTIONS: Read the action verbs listed below. In the space under the list, write 6 additional action verbs. Hint: Use Alma's professional résumé. Then, use a word(s) from the list to describe what is happening in the image.

Administered	Counseled	Improved	Raised
Advised	Created	Improvised	Recognized
Allocated	Delegated	Increased	Recruited
Analyzed	Developed	Influenced	Reduced
Appraised	Delivered	Invented	Referred
Assigned	Directed	Led	Represented
Assisted	Drafted	Maintained	Researched
Awarded	Earned	Managed	Scheduled
Budgeted	Edited	Marketed	Served
Built	Educated	Motivated	Shaped
Calculated	Established	Obtained	Solved
Clarified	Evaluated	Organized	Supervised
Collaborated	Examined	Oversaw	Supported
Collected	Executed	Planned	Trained
Conducted	Facilitated	Prepared	Upgraded
Contracted	Financed	Prioritized	Wrote
Consolidated	Founded	Produced	
Coordinated	Guided	Projected	

Can you think of 6 additional action verbs?

_____   _____   _____

_____   _____   _____

Which action verbs from the list above best describe what's happening in this image?

_____

_____

132   © 2019 Education Opens Doors, Inc.

Reverse Chronological Order

Chronological order means experiences are listed with the most recent at the bottom.

For example, if you were asked to place the numbers below in chronological order, it would look like this…

> 6 months old
> 7 years old
> 12 years old

The most recent number falls at the bottom of the list. This is chronological order. When we link an experience to a date, it makes more sense to list them in reverse chronological order, with the most recent experience at the top.

For example, if you were visiting the dentist and they asked you to share the milestones of your dental history, you would share the most recent event first…

> When I was 12 years old, my 2 front teeth came in.
> When I was 7 years old, I lost my first tooth.
> When I was 6 months old, I got my first baby tooth.

Recall how long an employer looks at a résumé? Approximately 10 seconds. In order to have your most recent experiences highlighted, it's important to list them first. To do so, use reverse chronological order on a résumé.

Practice Reverse Chronological Order

DIRECTIONS: Place the following dates in reverse chronological order using the table on the right.

- SUMMER 2017
- FALL 2018
- SPRING 2020
- FALL 2019
- SUMMER 2020

Résumé Fill-In Template

Practice Writing a Résumé

DIRECTIONS: Use the following two pages as an outline to begin building your résumé. Fill in as many lines as possible and continue to update.

CONTACT INFORMATION

Full Name: _____
Street Address: _____
City, State ZIP: _____
Reliable Phone Number: _____
Appropriate Email Address: _____

EDUCATION

School: _____   **Dates of Attendance:** _____
GPA: _____ on a 4.0 scale
Class Rank: _____ / _____
Highest SAT Score: _____ (_____ Verbal, _____ Math, _____ Writing)
Highest ACT Score: _____

WORK AND ACADEMIC EXPERIENCES

List Advanced and Unique Coursework.

Course: _____
Course: _____
Course: _____
Course: _____

List special academic programs you've attended (i.e. Engineering Camp, Science Club for Girls)

Name of Program: _____   **Year(s):** _____
Name of Program: _____   **Year(s):** _____

List both academic (i.e. Math Team) and non-academic (i.e. sports, volunteer activities).

- **Organization:** _____   **Year(s):** _____
  Title: _____   **Role Description:** _____
- **Organization:** _____   **Year(s):** _____
  Title: _____   **Role Description:** _____
- **Organization:** _____   **Year(s):** _____
  Title: _____   **Role Description:** _____
- **Organization:** _____   **Year(s):** _____
  Title: _____   **Role Description:** _____
- **Organization:** _____   **Year(s):** _____
  Title: _____   **Role Description:** _____

COMMUNITY INVOLVEMENT

List any work (i.e. dog walking, babysitting) or volunteer experience (i.e. reading at the day care, helping at the animal shelter).

- **Organization:** _____ **Year(s):** _____
  Title: _____ **Role Description:** _____
- **Organization:** _____ **Year(s):** _____
  Title: _____ **Role Description:** _____
- **Organization:** _____ **Year(s):** _____
  Title: _____ **Role Description:** _____
- **Organization:** _____ **Year(s):** _____
  Title: _____ **Role Description:** _____

HONORS AND AWARDS

List any awards or honors you have received (i.e. Perfect Attendance, Outstanding Student of the Month, Outstanding Student in Math).

- **Award:** _____ **Year(s):** _____
  Short Description: _____
- **Award:** _____ **Year(s):** _____
  Short Description: _____
- **Award:** _____ **Year(s):** _____
  Short Description: _____

SKILLS

Include special skills you have (i.e. language fluency, computer skills).

- **Skill:** _____
- **Skill:** _____
- **Skill:** _____
- **Skill:** _____
- **Skill:** _____

REFERENCES

Brainstorm teachers, counselors, coaches, and mentors who you would like to list as a reference. Be sure to get their permission to list them as a reference as well as their contact information.

- **Full Name:** _____ **Job Title:** _____
  Phone Number: _____
  Email Address: _____
- **Full Name:** _____ **Job Title:** _____
  Phone Number: _____
  Email Address: _____
- **Full Name:** _____ **Job Title:** _____
  Phone Number: _____
  Email Address: _____

Unit 3: My Professionalism

Extending My Learning: Résumé Review Worksheet

DIRECTIONS: Meet with an adult you trust and who knows you well. Ask them the following questions to help build your résumé.

What stands out about me that I should include in my résumé?
_____
_____
_____
_____
_____
_____
_____

Have I demonstrated any skills to you that I should include in my résumé?
_____
_____
_____
_____
_____
_____
_____
_____
_____

May I list you as a reference on my résumé?
_____
_____

If so, what contact information and job title should I include?
_____
_____
_____
_____

Would you be willing to review my resume for feedback once I'm finished?
_____
_____

Preparing for an Interview

An **interview** is a scheduled meeting of two or more people that can occur in person, on the phone, or via video conference. The purpose of an interview is to build relationships and gather information through questions and responses. A job, school admission, or scholarship interview provides an opportunity for both the interviewee (applicant) and the interviewer (employer/selection committee) to ask questions about the applicant's skills and experiences to determine if they are a good fit for the opportunity.

STEP 1: Research

Research the company, organization, or school ahead of time. Before going into an interview, take time to search online, ask friends and family, or read published content about the opportunity you are applying for. You can also call or e-mail the school, company, or organization to ask questions about the opportunity

Asking Questions

DIRECTIONS: Below are some common questions to ask employers or an admission committee to help you learn about an opening. Consider contacting the school or place of employment either through e-mail or by phone. Read these questions and include 2 more for each category.

Questions to ask a school before your interview	Questions to ask an employer before your job interview
How do you define success for each individual student?	What are the day to day responsibilities of this role?
What do you think students would say their favorite thing about this school is?	What do you enjoy most about your role?
What is the participation rate for extracurricular activities?	What 3 words would you use to describe the relationship you have with your boss?

BIG IDEA

An interview is an opportunity to make my best first impression wearing business professional or business casual clothing and carrying myself with confidence.

Informational Interviews

When you contact someone in the field you are interested in to hear about their experience and seek advice, you are conducting an informational interview. Don't forget to prepare questions.

Unit 3: My Professionalism

BIG IDEA
I can prepare for an interview by researching the company or organization, using professional communication, and planning ahead.

STEP 2: Use Professional Communication

E-mail Best Practices

Creating an e-mail address

Do you have an e-mail account that you access regularly? _____

What is your current e-mail address?
_____

Does your e-mail address represent a positive first impression of you? _____

If not, what could you change your e-mail address to be?
_____

Writing an Email

In the interview process, you might email the admission committee or employer. Here are some tips to frame your communication via e-mail.

- Use a meaningful description in the subject line. Use something that is a brief description of the content of the email.
- Just like a letter, start the e-mail by addressing the person you're sending it to. For example, "Dear Dr. Jon Salazar".
- Use sentence case (some capital letters, some lowercase).
- Type out full words; in other words, don't use abbreviations or shorthand text.
- Write a concise message.
- Double check spelling, grammar and punctuation.
- Re-read the note before sending.

Practice Writing an Email

DIRECTIONS: Write an email draft using the best practices you read about.

_____
_____
_____
_____
_____
_____
_____
_____

STEP 3: Plan Ahead

Social Media

Do you have a social media account? _____

If so, what platforms do you use?
_____
_____

> **TIP**
> *Some social media platforms are specifically designed for professional settings, while others are designed for personal use.*

Often, when employers and admission committees review applications, they will look at the applicant's online profiles.

Transportation

If your interview is in person, plan how you will get there and what time you need to leave your home in order to arrive early. Keep in mind that traffic can change depending upon the time of day you are traveling. A best practice is to make a trip to the location on a different day so that the location is familiar on the day you go for your interview.

How would you get to an interview if it were tomorrow?
_____
_____

www.educationopensdoors.org

Outfit

An interview is often the first time you meet an employer or admission committee, and thus an opportunity to make a first impression that represents you well. Usually interviews require a specific type of dress code called business professional or business casual. If the dress code is not shared, assume it is business professional.

Business Professional attire can be identified with the following outfit choices:

- Neutral colors (black, brown, gray, beige, tan, blue)
- Suit jacket
- Simple accessories or a necktie
- Clothes that are well fitting, clean, and wrinkle free
- Closed-toe dress shoes
- No denim or athletic clothing
- Logos and graphics are small or not visible

Business Casual attire can be identified with many of the same outfit choices, with some minor differences:

- Neutral colors (black, brown, gray, beige, tan, blue)
- Simple accessories
- Clothes that are well fitting, clean, and wrinkle free
- Closed-toe dress shoes
- No denim or athletic clothing
- Logos and graphics are small or not visible

How's My Wardrobe?

DIRECTIONS: Think about the clothes you have or would like to borrow or purchase. In the space below, explain or draw an outfit that you would like to wear to an interview.

Extending My Learning: Preparing for an Interview

STEP 4: Practice

DIRECTIONS: Ask a person you trust if they are willing to help you practice your interview skills by holding a **mock interview**. In a mock interview, someone else asks you questions and pretends to be an interviewer so that you can practice answering those questions, and then they give you feedback on your responses. It can be helpful to videotape the mock interview so that you can look at it yourself later and think of ways to improve your answers, body language, or word choices.

Regardless of the questions asked, try to focus your answers on the following 3 objectives:

- Give examples of special achievements at school or work
- Explain your top strengths
- Customize your responses to the specific opportunity

Search "sample interview questions" online to find some great practice questions and write them in the space below.

PRACTICE QUESTIONS

Notes

What to Expect During an Interview

Every setting has its own set of norms and expectations. The interview setting is no different. It has its own norms, expectations, styles of dress, and communication that are different than other contexts. Remember the purpose of an interview is to build relationships and gather information through questions and responses. This section will help you prepare for navigating the unique interview setting as well as prepare for asking and answering questions.

> **TIP**
>
> *Are you nervous? Have awareness of how your body shows nerves by practicing in a mock interview. Through practice, you can find ways to calm your bodily reactions down and feel calm.*

Norms for an Interview Setting

Note: Read the "3" column of the Mock Interview Rubric to understand what a strong example of each norm looks/sounds like.

Enthusiasm. In whatever way you best share excitement, show the interviewer that you are excited and interested in the opportunity.

Communication. Your words are important! Ensure your questions, responses, and your body language are understood the way you intend them to be.

Handshake. When you first meet a new person in a professional setting, it is a norm that you shake hands. A firm handshake sends a message of confidence, especially when paired with eye contact. Practice before your interview.

Eye contact. Eye contact is an important skill for relationship building.

Body Awareness. Notice the way your body is positioned. We send non-verbal messages with the way our bodies are positioned. Search "body language meaning with pictures" to see examples.

Attentiveness. Taking notes can help keep your responses on track with the question asked. In addition, you can write down your questions for the interviewer ahead of time so you can easily reference them. You can also use your notebook to write down next steps, including names of anyone you want to write a thank you note to in the future.

Timeliness. Whether you are meeting in person or virtually for your interview, getting to the site or building can bring some unexpected challenges. Plan ahead for those by arriving early. The end of an interview is signaled by the interviewer standing or extending a hand for a handshake.

Visualizing an Interview

DIRECTIONS: Picture yourself in an interview. Draw a picture or describe in words what that will look like.

> **TIP**
> *Restate the question in your response. For example, if you're asked, "What's your greatest strength?" Start your reply with: "My greatest strength is…"*

Common Interview Questions

DIRECTIONS: Below are common questions employers will ask throughout the interview with tips on how to craft an outstanding answer. Practice responding to these questions using the exemplar answer guidelines.

What Makes an Exemplar Response to an Interview Question?

When answering a question, follow these general guidelines:

- Explain what you did / what the situation was.
- Explain what you learned from the situation.
- Explain how you plan to use what you learned in the future.

Note: *If you want to practice all of the questions, use the notes pages in the back of your book.*

Personality, Skills and Characteristics

Question	Description	Example Response
"What are three adjectives you would use to describe yourself? Explain why."	Think of your own personal "brand statement" that explains who you are. Identify which of your characteristics can benefit their organization. Your response should be 1-3 sentences.	
"What are you passionate about?"	This is your opportunity to share what is important to you. It doesn't need to be something related to the company, organization, or school you are interviewing at, but something you truly feel strongly about. Your response to this question is a great relationship builder. Even if it's not directly asked, you can work your passions into other responses.	
"What was the last book you read?"	Your interviewer is looking to see that you have a willingness to learn on your own. Also consider what your favorite book is.	
"In a group setting, what role do you typically play?"	Are you the leader? The organizer? The secretary? By answering this question, this gives the interviewer insight into what role you will naturally take at their organization.	
"What do you consider to be your strengths and weaknesses?"	As possible, provide strengths that relate to what you are applying for. When you provide a weakness, provide a true critique but be cautious not to paint yourself negatively.	

Practice Your Response!

DIRECTIONS: Select a question from those listed previously and practice scripting out your answer on the lines below.

Note: *Several of the questions about personality require a more open format than the template below allows.*

Explain the situation / what you did.

_____
_____
_____

Explain what you learned.

_____
_____
_____

Explain how you plan to use what you learned in the future.

_____
_____
_____

Unit 3: My Professionalism

www.educationopensdoors.org

Previous Experience

Question	Description	Example Response
"What accomplishment are you most proud of?"	Choose one accomplishment. To narrow your selection, think of what you are applying for and choose an accomplishment that aligns to the position.	
"To be your strongest self, what would you be doing at work everyday?"	Share a specific example of a time that shows what makes you your strongest self.	
"What extracurricular activities have you been, or would you like to be, involved in?"	This is your chance to share what you have been involved in outside of the classroom. If you have been involved in multiple clubs and sports, it is okay to reference your résumé, which includes all leadership roles and activities you have been involved in.	
"What are some of your past leadership roles?"	Begin by briefly explaining the club or organization you have held a leadership role in. Share what the organization's acronym stands for if applicable. Describe your responsibilities and specific examples of what you were able to accomplish in this role. You can also tell about a skill that you might have learned or improved on while in this role.	

Practice Your Response!

DIRECTIONS: Select a question from those listed previously and practice scripting out your answer on the lines below.

Explain the situation / what you did.

_____
_____
_____

Explain what you learned.

_____
_____
_____

Explain how you plan to use what you learned in the future.

_____
_____

	Challenges/Obstacles	
Question	Description	Example Response
"Describe an obstacle and how you overcame it."	Be prepared to share two obstacles/challenges you have worked to overcome. The point of this question is to give the interviewer an insight into how you work through problems. Include the lesson that overcoming this obstacle has taught you.	
"How would you resolve conflict in a group situation?"	Interviewers are looking for you to provide one specific example and then walk them through how you solved the conflict. Remember to end with a positive.	
"How do you handle stress?"	This interview question is often asked to gain insight on how you manage stress on the job and in your life. Provide a short example about a time you handled stress well to show you can work in stressful situations or environments if necessary.	

Practice Your Response!

DIRECTIONS: Select a question from those listed previously and practice scripting out your answer on the lines below.

Explain the situation / what you did.
_____
_____
_____
_____

Explain what you learned.
_____
_____
_____
_____

Explain how you plan to use what you learned in the future.
_____
_____
_____
_____

Unit 3: My Professionalism

Future, Goals, and the Closing		
Question	Description	Example Response
"What goals do you hope to accomplish in the next five years? Ten years?"	When answering this question, keep the role you are interviewing for in mind. If you are interviewing for a college, mention how admisson will help you reach your goal or plan for five (or ten) years down the road.	
"Why should we hire you rather than another candidate?"	When asked this question, compare your skills with the responsibilities of the position. Restate your interest in the organization and position, be positive and confident in your abilities.	
"What is something interesting about you that we wouldn't normally learn in an interview?"	Think outside the box. Think about what makes you unique and interesting.	
"Do you have any other questions?"	Now it is your turn to ask the questions. Have at least three prepared.	

Practice Your Response!

DIRECTIONS: Select a question from those listed previously and practice scripting out your answer on the lines below.

Explain the situation / what you did.
_____
_____
_____

Explain what you learned.
_____
_____
_____

Explain how you plan to use what you learned in the future.
_____
_____
_____

Notes

Preparing for a Mock Interview

BIG IDEA
During an interview, I should be enthusiastic, have strong communication, have good body awareness, be attentive and timely.

Practicing Interview Skills

What opportunity are you excited to interview for?

_____

_____

DIRECTIONS: In this mock interview activity, you will pretend you're interviewing for the opportunity you wrote above. You will need a partner. Your partner will ask you interview questions and score your overall interview on the following criteria:

- Body Awareness
- Enthusiasm
- Clear Communication
- Handshake
- Eye Contact
- Attentiveness

You will be the **interviewee** (the one being asked questions), and your partner will be the **interviewer** (the one asking questions). Then you will switch roles and repeat the same process.

Role as the Interviewer

- Ask interview questions.
- Take notes of responses in the interviewee's book.
- Answer follow up questions.
- Score the interviewee on the rubric by checking the appropriate box.
- Complete peer feedback protocol.

Role as the Interviewee

- Give the interviewer your book to take notes and score your mock interview
- Answer interview questions.
- Ask any follow up questions to interviewer.

150 © 2019 Education Opens Doors, Inc.

Mock Interview Template

Mock Interview Worksheet

> **BIG IDEA**
> *I can prepare for an interview by participating in a mock interview.*

DIRECTIONS: Utilize the following two pages during your mock interview. The interviewer will write notes about your responses in this template for you to review afterwards using the peer feedback protocol.

Interviewee Name: _____
Interviewer Name: _____

Personality, Skills, and Characteristics

What are 3 adjectives you would use to describe yourself? Explain why.
- _____
- _____
- _____

What are you passionate about?
_____
_____

What was the last book you read?
_____
_____

In a group setting, what role do you typically play?
_____
_____

What do you consider to be your strengths and weaknesses?
_____
_____

Previous Experience

What accomplishment are you most proud of?
_____
_____

To be your strongest self, what would you be doing at work everyday?
_____
_____

Unit 3: My Professionalism

What extracurricular activities have you been, or would you like to be, involved in?
_____
_____

What are some of your past leadership roles?
_____
_____

Challenges/Obstacles

Describe an obstacle and how you overcame it.
_____
_____

How would you resolve conflict in a group situation?
_____
_____

How do you handle stress?
_____
_____

The Future/Goals

What goals do you hope to accomplish in the next five years? Ten years?
_____
_____

In Closing

Why should we hire you rather than another candidate?
_____
_____

What is something interesting about you that we wouldn't normally learn in an interview?
_____
_____

Do you have any other questions?
_____
_____

Mock Interview Rubric

DIRECTIONS: Below is a rubric for a mock interview. Read the column labeled "3." This is the highest scoring column. Use this as a guide to help shape a great interview! To score an interviewee using this rubric, place a check mark in the box to indicate where they score.

EXAMPLE

	1 Interviewee…	2 Interviewee…	3 Interviewee…
Body Awareness	…appears **nervous** the whole time	…appears **relaxed some** of the time	…appears **relaxed** the whole time ✓

INTERVIEWEE

	1 Interviewee…	2 Interviewee…	3 Interviewee…
Enthusiasm	…**rarely** smiles and uses **no** positive body language (covering mouth with hand, arms crossed, frowning, etc.)	…smiles **occasionally** and uses **some** positive body language	…**smiles and uses positive body language** (facing interviewer, uses hands to make point, makes eye contact, etc.)
Clear Communication	…uses **numerous** slang words and "verbal ticks" (ex: like, um, yeah, este, so)	…uses **some** slang words and **some** "verbal ticks" (ex: like, um, yeah, este, so)	…uses **no** slang words and "verbal ticks" (ex: like, um, yeah, este, so)
Handshake	…**long, limp** handshake given when candidate introduces themself (> 3 seconds, like a dead fish)	…quick, **limp** handshake given when candidate introduces themself (1-2 seconds, like a dead fish)	…**quick, firm** handshake given when candidate introduces themself (1-2 seconds; almost hurts hand, but not quite)
Eye Contact	…looks **down and away** from interviewer, **rarely** making eye contact	…looks up towards the interviewer, **rarely** making eye contact	…looks up **confidently** at the interviewer, **often** making eye contact
Body Awareness	…appears **nervous** the whole time, **slouches** in chair, looks down as listening, fidgets hands or feet, and crosses arms	…appears **relaxed some** of the time, **sometimes** sits up straight, **occasionally** nods head as listening, **occasionally** fidgets hands or feet, or crosses arms	…appears **relaxed** the whole time, **sits up straight, nods head** in agreement or understanding as listening, does not fidget hands or feet, and keeps arms in open position
Attentiveness	…**does not have** notepad and/or pen, **does not ask** questions or next steps	…has notepad and pen, but takes **no** notes, writes down **no** questions and asks **no** follow up questions or next steps	…has notepad and pen, **actively takes notes** or **writes** down questions, **asks** follow up questions and next steps
Timeliness	…**not ready** to begin on time, leaves too early (**before** interviewer stands or extends handshake)	…**not ready** to begin on time but leaves **on time** (after interviewer stands or extends handshake)	…**ready to begin on time** and leaves **on time** (after interviewer stands or extends handshake)

Unit 3: My Professionalism

www.educationopensdoors.org

Peer Feedback Protocol

STEP 1 DIRECTIONS: Gain perspective from interviewee by asking the following questions and recording their responses.

How did you feel about the mock interview experience?
_____
_____

What parts were easy?	What parts were hard?

STEP 2 DIRECTIONS: Look at the rubric together and review each line. Tell the interviewee what their scores are and why you felt their score is what it is using the question prompts below. Remind them that a score of 3 is the highest and 1 is the lowest if necessary.

On items earning a 3, why did they earn the highest score?	What specifics can be praised?

On items earning less than a 3, why didn't they earn the highest score?	What can be improved for next time?

STEP 3 DIRECTIONS: Build empathy by asking follow up questions like the following. Record a paraphrase of their response.

How do you feel about this feedback?
_____
_____

STEP 4 DIRECTIONS: Share any additional recommendations for them the next time they are in an interview setting that you have not already shared. Ask them to repeat back to you the following 2 things and record their responses.

1. What needs to be fixed	2. How they're going to fix it

STEP 5 DIRECTIONS: Offer to do mock interviews together again to continue getting feedback.

Extending My Learning: Practicing for an Interview

DIRECTIONS: Review all of the interview preparation and practice tips in this section. Ask someone you trust to conduct another mock interview with you. Determine what skills you want to practice the most. Build a rubric in the space below and ask someone you trust to evaluate your mock interview based upon your own criteria.

Extending My Learning: Peer Feedback Protocol

STEP 1 DIRECTIONS: Gain perspective from interviewee by asking the following questions and recording their responses.

How did you feel about the mock interview experience?
_____
_____

What parts were easy?	What parts were hard?

STEP 2 DIRECTIONS: Look at the rubric together and review each line. Tell the interviewee what their scores are and why you felt their score is what it is using the question prompts below. Remind them that a score of 3 is the highest and 1 is the lowest if necessary.

On items earning a 3, why did they earn the highest score?	What specifics can be praised?

On items earning less than a 3, why didn't they earn the highest score?	What can be improved for next time?

STEP 3 DIRECTIONS: Build empathy by asking follow up questions like the following. Record a paraphrase of their response.

How do you feel about this feedback?
_____
_____

STEP 4 DIRECTIONS: Share any additional recommendations for them the next time they are in an interview setting that you have not already shared. Ask them to repeat back to you the following 2 things and record their responses.

1. What needs to be fixed	2. How they're going to fix it

STEP 5 DIRECTIONS: Offer to do mock interviews together again to continue getting feedback.

Notes

Unit 3 Summary: Professionalism: Showing Up As My Best Self

Success does not happen by accident! Remain focused and work hard to achieve your goals. Strive to be your best.

Checklist Check-In

1. Consider where you are in your educational journey. Check the corresponding box below.
    - ☐ 6th Grade
    - ☐ 7th Grade
    - ☐ 8th Grade
    - ☐ 9th Grade
    - ☐ 10th Grade
    - ☐ 11th Grade
    - ☐ 12th Grade
    - ☐ High School Graduate
    - ☐ GED Recipient

2. Turn to the "Grade Level Checklist" at the beginning of Unit 1. Locate your current grade level. **Review what you checked off at the beginning of the program and check off any other activities you have completed.**

Unit Review Opportunities

1. Go back to the "Extend Your Learning" pages in this unit. Research, ask questions, and locate resources to complete those activities.
2. Complete any remaining vocabulary tasks for this unit's vocabulary and use each word in a sentence this week.
3. Answer the questions on the unit cover page, and complete the directions in the white box.

Moving Forward…

Select one of the colors from the triangle to describe how you feel about new understandings gained from this unit. Justify your answer in at least 3 sentences.

_____
_____
_____
_____
_____
_____

UNIT 4
KNOWING MY OPTIONS AFTER HIGH SCHOOL

DIRECTIONS: Read the topics of this unit. Draw a picture of your emotions about this content.

- Unit 4 Vocabulary — page 160
- Options After High School — page 162
- Understanding My Why — page 171
- Exploring the Career for Me — page 175
- Soft Skills — page 177
- Understanding Career Pathways — page 179
- Degrees and Certification Programs — page 183
- Education Pays: Lifetime Earnings — page 190
- Choosing a Course of Study — page 193
- Playing a Sport While in College — page 203
- Unit 4 Summary — page 208

What are my options after high school?

What jobs are going to be relevant and well-paid when I graduate?

What is the difference between an Associate's and a Bachelor's degree?

How do I choose a career path?

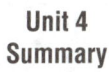

Unit 4 Vocabulary

DIRECTIONS:

1. DEFINE each word using the glossary in this book or a dictionary.
2. ANSWER the questions listed below for each word.

Vocabulary Word	Definition	Have you ever heard/seen this word before?	Explain how you have heard this word used before. If you've never heard or seen it, what other word (in any language) does it look like to you?
Postsecondary		Y N	
Certification		Y N	
Degree		Y N	
First Generation College Student		Y N	
Career		Y N	
Career Aptitude Test		Y N	
Soft Skills		Y N	
Credit Hours		Y N	
Associate's Degree		Y N	
Bachelor's Degree		Y N	
Undergraduate		Y N	

Vocabulary Word	Definition	Have you ever heard/seen this word before?	Explain how you have heard this word used before. If you've never heard or seen it, what other word (in any language) does it look like to you?
Master's Degree		Y N	
Doctoral Degree		Y N	
Dissertation		Y N	
Major		Y N	
Capped Major		Y N	
Minor		Y N	
NCAA		Y N	
College		Y N	
Credentials		Y N	
Graduate Degree		Y N	

Additional words to complete on notebook paper: _____
_____
_____

Unit 4: My Options

Options After High School

BIG IDEA
I have the power to choose my educational path after graduating high school.

Research Careers
Careers require various levels of education. Research your goal career to see what level of education you need to be successful in it.

TIP
Talk to your guidance counselor to gather more information.

First Generation College Student
A student whose parent(s) or legal guardian(s) have not completed an undergraduate degree program.

You have the power to choose your path after graduating from high school. There are so many excellent options to choose from! Explore your personal goals, skills, and passions to identify a choice that will bring you joy as an adult.

In year _____, you will graduate high school. What comes next is up to you!

Do others in your life have opinions about what you do after high school? If so, who?
_____
_____

Do their goals align with your personal goals? Why or why not?
_____
_____
_____
_____

What GOALS do you have for your future related to education level and career choice?

Education Level	Career Choice

If you're not sure what your goals are or you're not sure how to achieve them, who do you feel comfortable asking for help? If no one, who can you build a stronger relationship with to get to a level of being comfortable?
_____
_____
_____
_____

Public versus Private

Much like high school, there are two categories of colleges: public and private.

Public Colleges/Universities are schools that receive money from local and state governments through tax dollars, in addition to money from students (tuition) and alumni (donations). Typically, if you are a resident of that local or state community, you get discounted tuition. Without the discount, public schools outside of your state cost the same as many private schools.

Private Colleges/Universities do not get money from the government and rely on funding from students (tuition) and alumni (donations). As a result, they have more freedom in programming available as well as the mission of the school. Private schools often attract students from across the country rather than just the local or state communities and usually have a smaller total student body.

Within the two categories of colleges, there are countless types of schools, degree programs, and certificate offerings. In this section, we will learn about many school options, and determine what makes each of them unique.

Identify 3 questions you have about public or private schools.

- _____
  _____
  _____
  _____

- _____
  _____
  _____
  _____

- _____
  _____
  _____
  _____

Does one of the choices sound more interesting to you based upon what you know so far? Which type and why?

_____
_____
_____
_____

College
An institution of education where students study to earn a degree and/or certificate after high school.

In-State Tuition
A student who lives in the same state as a college may pay a lower tuition rate than students from other states.

For-Profit Colleges
For-profit schools are businesses rather than institutions and might not be accredited, which means credits cannot transfer to another school. Search "for-profit schools" in your area to see a list. These schools tend to have higher tuition costs and payment plans rather than financial aid, which means students tend to graduate with more debt.

Unit 4: My Options

Unique Types of Schools

Postsecondary
Any school after high school.

Each state has several public and private school options. Researching what is available in your state and across the US is important to determine what is the best fit for your goals. This section is not inclusive of every type of school. It does, however, focus on unique opportunities across both public and private schools.

TIP
Liberal Arts Colleges tend to be small and require students to take a variety of courses outside of their major to graduate.

Liberal Arts Colleges/Universities

Liberal arts schools tend to be small in size, providing an intimate learning environment where students have an opportunity to build strong relationships with professors. Liberal arts schools emphasize a "whole" education by offering a broad range of classes to all students, regardless of your degree plan. This allows students to take courses in a wide range of subjects to determine what career field they would like to pursue one day.

What makes a Liberal Arts School unique?

_____
_____
_____
_____

Community Colleges

Community colleges offer both technical/certificate programs and degree programs to prepare students for their futures. Often, campus locations are close to a student's home, making it convenient to live at home while in school. Community colleges also offer tuition rates lower than larger universities or colleges. For students who choose to continue their education or change degree programs, many community colleges have partnerships with other universities to make the credit transfer process easier.

What makes a Community College unique?

_____
_____
_____
_____

Minority Serving Institutions

MSIs are a category of schools whose student body is largely made up of a specific minority group. These schools are known for serving historically underrepresented students of color by offering an environment rich in tradition and pride, cultural immersion opportunities, and unique support for first generation college students. Within the category of MSI are: Hispanic Serving Institutions (HSIs), Tribal Colleges or Universities (TCUs), Asian American and Native Pacific Islander-Serving Institutions (AANAPISIs), Alaska Native-Serving Institutions, Native Hawaiian-Serving Institutions, Predominantly Black Institutions, Native American-Serving Nontribal Institutions, and Historically Black Colleges and Universities (HBCUs).

What makes an MSI unique?

_____

_____

U.S. Armed Forces

The United States Armed Forces has 5 branches, including the Army, Navy, Air Force, Coast Guard, and Marines. If you choose to join the military, you have options.

Options	Enlist after high school	Enter as an officer after college	Attend a military academy
Tuition Help	G.I. Bill	ROTC Scholarships	All expenses paid
Benefits	During active service or as a veteran, you have access to a G.I. Bill to get free college credits.	In joining the ROTC program (Registered Officer Training Program), the military will pay for some or all of your tuition in return for a 5 year commitment to active military service after graduation.	The US government funds 100% of the college experience for students at military academies, including: tuition, housing, food, medical and dental care, in addition to an annual salary to purchase uniforms, books, and supplies. In return, you will commit to 5 years of active service and 3 years of inactive duty with the Ready Reserves.
Resources	www.benefits.va.gov	Army: https://www.goarmy.com/rotc.html Air Force: https://www.afrotc.com Navy: http://www.nrotc.navy.mil Marines: http://www.nrotc.navy.mil/marine.html *The Coast Guard does not have an ROTC program.	https://www.usa.gov/military-colleges#item-34997

What makes the United States Armed Forces unique?

_____

_____

Unit 4: My Options

Online Classes for Degrees/Certificates

Sometimes online classes are cheaper than classes in person. Check with college admission counselors to ask if students can often complete online classes along with classes at a traditional university and count both types of classes towards their degree or certificate.

Online Schools

Many colleges and universities offer online degree and certificate programs. Taking classes online offers a lot of flexibility for where you choose to live as well as how you schedule your time.

What makes completing a degree or certificate program at an online school unique?

___
___
___
___

Historically Black Colleges and Universities (HBCUs)

HBCUs are colleges and universities that were initially established in the 1800s through the second Land Grant Act. As a result of this legislation, states were required to establish opportunities for black students to attend predominantly white institutions or allocate money to establish schools which would primarily serve black students. Today over 100 HBCUs exist in the US and are open to students of all races.

African American students who attend HBCUs report more positive experiences in a variety of ways (relationships with professors, higher grades, and professional success) than African American students who attend predominantly white institutions.

What makes an HBCU campus unique?

___
___
___
___

Ivy League Schools

The Ivy League is a network of 8 schools: Brown, Columbia, Cornell, Dartmouth, Harvard, Princeton, the University of Pennsylvania, and Yale University. These schools have a long history of successful job placement for graduates and are recognized worldwide as excellent schools.

What makes an Ivy League school unique?

___
___
___
___

Vocational, Trade, or Technical Schools

Vocational, trade, or technical school programs may result in an associate's degree, a certification, or a diploma, depending on the school and program. Instead of requiring classes in several different subjects, these programs typically include classes that focus directly on a specific career and offer a great deal of hands-on training, often from professionals already working in that career field. These schools are intended to lead to immediate employment upon graduation within a very specific role/skill set which students are trained for.

What makes a Vocational, Trade, or Technical School unique?

_____
_____
_____

> **Trade School Requirements**
>
> *Vocational and trade schools require a high school diploma or GED.*

> **Accreditation**
>
> *Always check that any school you are applying to is accredited by the U.S. Department of Education. Check* ope.ed.gov/accreditation.

Public Service Academy

Police officers, paramedics, emergency medical technicians, and firefighters are some examples of public service workers. The kind of education and training necessary to pursue a career in the public service field varies depending on which position you are interested in. Some of the careers require completion of a college degree, while others may require only a high school diploma followed by a specialized training academy. However, if this is a field that interests you, speak with your guidance counselor or contact public service agencies to ask about their application process and their requirements beyond high school graduation.

What makes a Public Service Academy unique?

_____
_____
_____

Transferring

*Students can start their college career at community colleges and then **transfer** to a traditional four-year school. This saves money on tuition. If you transfer, make sure your college credits transfer with you.*

BIG IDEA

I have many different options after high school, and I understand all possibilities.

In addition to these unique options, there are hundreds more! It's worth the research. Think of a special interest you have or specific population of people you might like to attend classes with and learn from. Search online for options fit for you. Some include: single-sex colleges, arts colleges or conservatories, religiously affiliated colleges, colleges for students who are hearing or visually impaired, amongst so many more!

What value, identity, idea, or interest is important to you?

_____
_____
_____
_____
_____

How important is it to find a college with like-minded people? Why?

_____
_____
_____
_____
_____
_____
_____
_____

What Appeals to You?

DIRECTIONS: In the ovals below, answer the question, "What makes this option appealing or not appealing to you?" Use the previous pages about postsecondary options to help make your selections. After filling in all of the outside ovals, answer the questions below.

Based on the information in the graphic organizer, what do you think is the best title to go in the center? Please write your answer in the central oval.

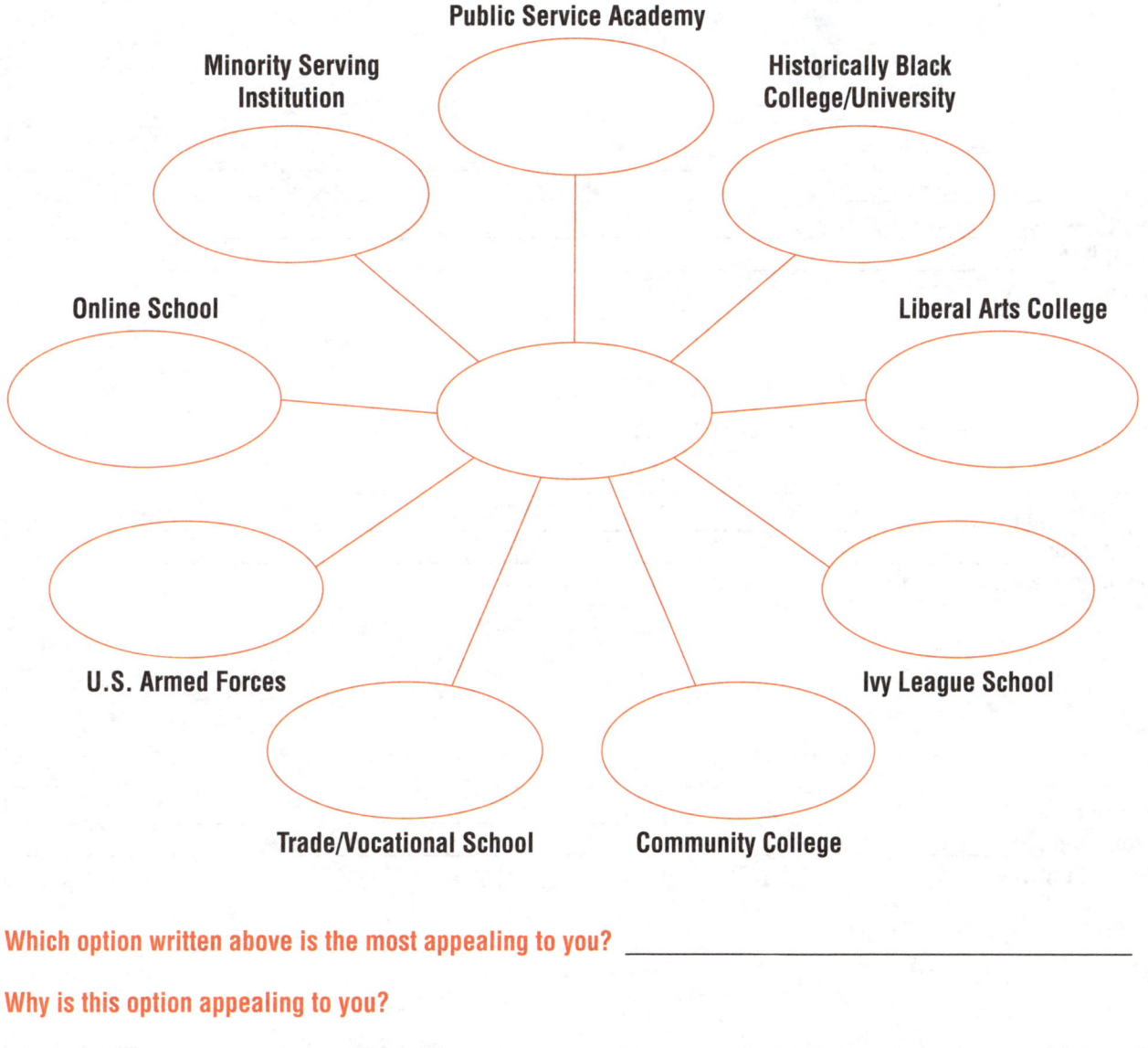

Which option written above is the most appealing to you? _____

Why is this option appealing to you?
_____
_____

Recall the goals you wrote earlier. Do you know what type of school will help you reach your career goal?
              Yes   No

How do you feel about enrolling in this option? (Circle all that apply)
Intimidated   Excited   Totally got this   Need more information

Unit 4: My Options

Extending My Learning: Exploring Options After High School

DIRECTIONS: Ask at least 5 adults about the pathway they took to arrive in their current job. Ask about the type of school(s) they attended, about credentials, degrees, and anything else that guided them to where they are today. Document your learnings in the space below.

Name of Person: _____
Current Role: _____
Steps in Pathway:

Name of Person: _____
Current Role: _____
Steps in Pathway:

Name of Person: _____
Current Role: _____
Steps in Pathway:

Name of Person: _____
Current Role: _____
Steps in Pathway:

Name of Person: _____
Current Role: _____
Steps in Pathway:

Understanding My Why

There are so many options to pursue after high school. Knowing the direction you are headed and why you're headed there are important steps in making your goal become true.

Setting Goals, Rooted in YOUR Why

PART 1

Did you know… Over 60% of jobs in the US require education beyond a high school diploma.

DIRECTIONS: There are 10 boxes below. Each box represents a job. This person has a high school diploma. As a result, they are eligible for less than 40% of jobs. Shade in 40% of the boxes below.

DIRECTIONS: There are 10 boxes below. Each box represents a job. This person has continued their education after high school. Depending upon the amount of education they complete they can be eligible for 100% of jobs. Shade in 100% of the boxes below.

High School Graduate

Continued Education After High School

If more than 60% of the jobs available in the future require continuing your education, how could that impact your life as an adult?

_____
_____
_____
_____
_____
_____

Unit 4: My Options

PART 2

DIRECTIONS: First, choose one of the boxes below and write in your name and response. Second, ask 3 people why they want to continue their education after high school. If you prefer to complete this activity individually, fill in the remaining squares with 3 additional reasons of your own.

My name is _____ **and I want to continue my education because** _____	**My name is** _____ **and I want to continue my education because** _____
My name is _____ **and I want to continue my education because** _____	**My name is** _____ **and I want to continue my education because** _____

PART 3

We asked a group of grown-ups the same question. Here's what they said:

I chose to continue my education after high school because…

I wanted to gain independence.	I wanted to develop a specific skill for a future career option.
I wanted to build relationships with others outside of my current community.	I wanted to gain perspective to pursue something I'm passionate about.

DIRECTIONS: First, circle one of the statements above that you can relate to the most. Second, create a goal statement for yourself by combining the statement you circled with the statement you wrote in the box above into one sentence.

_____

Extending My Learning: Understanding My Why

DIRECTIONS: Write a 1 page journal entry expanding on the goal you wrote on the previous page. Include details about what you anticipate influencing the path you choose after high school.

Today's Date: _____

Notes

Exploring the Career for Me

Career
A commitment to a field or job within a field for an extended time.

Career Reflection

Describe or draw what you would be doing to feel accomplished and excited about your work every day as an adult.

What resources can help me choose a career?

1. Evaluate career fields that are interesting.
2. Take a career aptitude test.
3. Research present and future employment statistics.
4. Explore how your soft skills relate to a career choice.

1. Evaluating Career Fields

Read the career fields in the space below. Circle ones that sound interesting to you.

Agriculture, Food, and Natural Resources	Hospitality and Tourism	Science, Technology, Engineering, and Mathematics	Architecture and Construction	Health Sciences
Government and Public Administration	Humanities	Transportation, Distribution, and Logistics	Arts, A/V Technology, and Communications	Information Technology
Education	Law, Public Safety, Corrections, and Security	Manufacturing	Marketing	Business Management and Finance Administration

List any additional career fields not already mentioned.

_____   _____   _____

Unit 4: My Options

> **Career Aptitude Tests**
>
> *Career aptitude tests can help focus your selection of a major or career. However, regardless of the results, you have all the power in choosing your path.*

2. Career Aptitude Tests

A **career aptitude test** has questions about your abilities, interests, and skills. Based upon your responses, it creates a list of career options. You can easily find them online by searching "career aptitude test" or "career inventory test."

Take 3 career aptitude tests and write your results in the space below.

- _____
  _____
- _____
  _____
- _____
  _____

3. Research Employment Statistics

Statistics are numbers that show a trend. What types of statistics could be interesting to collect about jobs?

[ ]

- Search "Employment Statistics Occupation Profiles" online.
- Look for a link from The Bureau of Labor and Statistics (bls), and look for a link on their page called "occupational profiles."
- From there you can see data for thousands of career choices. The BLS publishes data on salaries, availability of jobs based upon state, and in which state someone in that role will be paid the most.

Data from your city or county community is often available as well. Search the same things as above, but add the name of your city. Sometimes data is called "labor statistics."

Research the labor statistics on a career you are interested in and input 3 bits of information you find interesting below.

[ ]

4. Soft Skills

If someone said to you – "you have skills?" what first comes to mind?

_____

Perhaps also singing, running, typing, skateboarding, reading…these are all examples of hard skills. Jobs require several hard skills, and many you will learn on the job or receive specific training for. Soft skills are a different type of skill that are also developed over time.

Examples of **soft skills** are: communication, leadership, collaboration, and many more. When choosing a career, it's helpful to consider the soft skills you have or can develop and how they align with the requirements of the job.

Think of someone working as the front desk person at a school. What specific soft skills might that role require? Refer to the list below for ideas.

_____

What are My Soft Skills?

DIRECTIONS: Rate your soft skills by placing a check in the column that reflects your current development of each skill.

Soft Skill	Already Skilled	Developing	Not Sure
Problem-solving*			
Leadership*			
Adaptability*			
Collaboration*			
Creativity*			
Innovation*			
Work Ethic			
Dependability			
Self-Motivated			
Confidence			
Effective Communicator			
Honesty			
Emotion Management			

*Note: Research indicates that the highlighted words in the chart are the most important soft skills to employers.

What soft skill do you think is most important? Why?

_____

What soft skill(s) do you want to improve on? Why did you rate yourself still developing on these?

_____

Unit 4: My Options

Exploring the Career for Me

BIG IDEA
I can take a career aptitude test and research employment statistics to help determine my path after high school.

DIRECTIONS: Based on your current interests, select 2 or 3 careers that you are interested in. Complete the Career Cards below after researching online and/or speaking with someone with that particular career.

Challenge Yourself: Go a step further and locate a person in each career to interview.

Career Field: _____
Career: _____
Description: _____
_____
_____
_____

Helpful Soft Skills	Average Salary	Education Level Required
_____	_____	_____
_____	_____	_____
_____	_____	_____

Career Field: _____
Career: _____
Description: _____
_____
_____
_____

Helpful Soft Skills	Average Salary	Education Level Required
_____	_____	_____
_____	_____	_____
_____	_____	_____

Additional Notes

Understanding Career Pathways

Using a Process

DIRECTIONS: What is your favorite food? Answer the questions and describe the steps you take to make that food below.

What is your vision of the food once it's ready to eat?
_____
_____

Do you need to ask anyone for help to be successful?
_____

What resources do you need?
_____

What are the steps you take to make the food?
- Step 1: _____
- Step 2: _____
- Step 3: _____
- Step 4: _____
- Step 5: _____

If there are more steps, write them out in this space.
_____
_____
_____

It takes effort and work to make something really great. Why is it worth it?
_____
_____

When making food, we go through a process.

If we start with a vision of the end goal, plan out the steps, collect necessary resources, pay attention to the details of each step without losing sight of the end goal, and ask for help when we need it – we'll be successful!

The same process applies to choosing a career! Re-read the paragraph above, but replace "making food" with "choosing a career."

Unit 4: My Options

Process = Pathway to Success

Below are examples of the career pathways for two students, Jaime and Maria. Jaime wants to become a school principal. Maria wants to become a paramedic (emergency responder on an ambulance) for the fire department. Both want to gain experience before starting their ultimate careers. Both have access to the community's "Degree Promise Program," making them eligible for free community college attendance.

Credentials
Credentials represent the degrees or certificates a person has earned.

	Jaime	**Maria**
End Goal	School Principal	Paramedic for the Fire Department
Necessary Credentials	• Bachelor's Degree • Teaching Certificate • Teaching Experience • Master's Degree • Principal Certificate	• Associate's Degree • EMT-Basic Certificate • CPR Certification • Advanced EMT Training Certificate
Step 1	Graduate from a traditional High School with HS Diploma.	Graduate from an Early College High School with HS Diploma and Associate's Degree as a Certified Medical Assistant (CMA).
Step 2	Use Degree Promise to enroll in community college working towards a Bachelor's Degree in History.	Get a job in the emergency room at a hospital to gain experience and gain CPR certification.
Step 3	Transfer schools during junior year to a private university to finish Bachelor's degree in History with Education minor, including teaching certification.	Maintain job in emergency room and enroll in trade school to earn basic EMT certification.
Step 4	Begin working as a history teacher.	Begin working as a paramedic.
Step 5	Enroll in Masters of School Leadership program that includes principal certification.	While working, start Advanced EMT certificate program.
Step 6	Get a pay raise and promotion for continued education and start working as a school principal!	Get a promotion and pay raise for continued education as a paramedic for the fire department!

Multiple Pathways to the Same Place

What is one way Jaime could have changed the steps but still arrived at the same goal?
_____

What is one way Maria could have changed the steps but still arrived at the same goal?
_____

Becoming a Teacher

Think about teaching. There are two different pathways to become a fully certified teacher; neither is better than the other. Teachers with both types are able to get the same jobs. One certification is called the traditional route and one is called the alternative route. The steps for each are here:

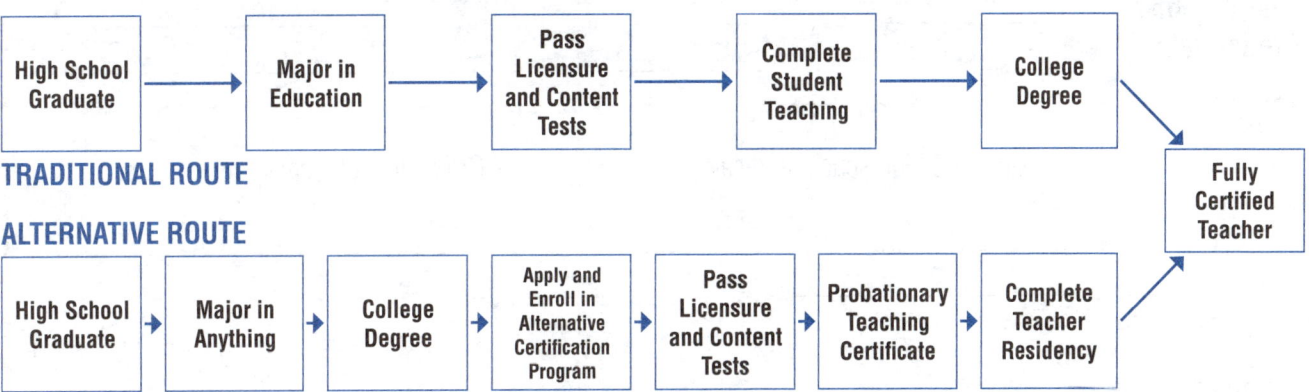

What is the biggest difference between these two certification types?
_____
_____

Talk to a Teacher

DIRECTIONS: Teachers are people passionate about making a positive impact on the next generation and often make a distinct choice to become a teacher. Take time to interview a teacher to ask about the pathway they took to arrive in their career. Take notes from your interview here.

_____
_____
_____
_____
_____

Extending My Learning: Visioning my Pathway

DIRECTIONS: Conduct interviews with people in your network and ask about their career and the education pathways they took to get there. Also research the "credentials for _____ career choice" to learn what degrees and certificates are required. Then, fill in the chart with 2 different pathways to your goal career choice.

	Option 1	Option 2
Ultimate Career Goal		
Education Requirements/ Credentials	• _____ • _____ • _____	• _____ • _____ • _____
Step 1	Graduate high school and earn a: _____	Graduate high school and earn a: _____
Step 2		
Step 3		
Step 4		
Step 5		
Step 6		

Degrees and Certification Programs

Planning with the end goal in mind is called backwards planning. If you think about the career you want to have one day, you can backwards plan to identify the type of degree and/or certifications you will need in order to be successful in that career.

Below are 3 key questions to consider when planning out which program is the right choice for you:

1. **How do you get the degree or certification?**
   i.e.: number of credit hours and length of time to complete

2. **Are there pre-requisites for the program or degree?**
   i.e.: classes or qualifications you need before enrolling

3. **What is unique about this option that I should know about before making my choice?**

Types of Degree Programs

Undergraduate Degrees

- Associate's Degree
- Bachelor's Degree

Graduate Degrees

- Master's Degree
- Doctoral Degree
- Professional Degree

Certificate Programs

BIG IDEA

An Associate's degree is usually 2 years, a Bachelor's degree is usually 4 years, and both are undergraduate degrees.

Degree

Degrees are what students get for completing a program of study at a college or university. There are three basic types of degrees: Associate's, Bachelor's, and Master's and Doctoral Degrees.

Certification

Certifications provide focused training in a particular skill or trade. Certifications are gained at all levels of education.

Credit Hour

The number of credits given for a course, which is then used to determine GPA.

Undergraduate Degree Programs

Undergraduate
A student who is pursuing an Associate's or Bachelor's degree.

Associate's Degree
Associate's Degrees are not typically offered at 4-year colleges or universities

Associate's Degree

An **associate's degree** is an undergraduate degree typically requiring 60 credit hours, or about 2 years of coursework for a full-time student. Students who have graduated high school or have an equivalent diploma (GED) can begin work towards an associate's degree at a college or university. In many cases, credits earned as a part of an associate's degree program can be transferred into credits towards a bachelor's degree program. This is not always the case though. Often, if the word "applied" is used in reference to the degree plan, the credits will not transfer.

Example Career Options at a School	• Teacher's Aid • Campus Police • Registrar

What are some other career examples with this level of education not listed here?

_____
_____
_____

Bachelor's Degree
You do not need to earn an associate's degree to obtain a bachelor's degree.

Bachelor's Degree

A **bachelor's degree** is an undergraduate degree usually requiring 120 credit hours, and takes about 4 years to complete coursework for a full-time student. In order to apply to a bachelor's degree program, you need to graduate from high school or have an equivalent (GED). Students do not have to complete all four years of coursework at the same school. There are 4 distinctions within a bachelor's degree; each will bring a different focus to your coursework. They are Bachelor of Arts (BA), Bachelor of Science (BS), Bachelor of Business Administration (BBA), and Bachelor of Fine Arts (BFA).

Example Career Options at a School	• Teacher • Librarian • School Nurse

What are some other career examples with this level of education not listed here?

_____
_____
_____

Graduate/Professional Degrees

Master's Degree

A **Master's degree** is a graduate degree usually taking 1-3 years after completing a bachelor's degree. Usually, students are required to complete a thesis as a final large project. In order to qualify for enrollment in a master's degree program, one must have a bachelor's degree or be enrolled in a "fast-tracked" master's program. Many master's programs are designed for full-time working professionals, so classes take place online, in the evenings, and on weekends.

Example Career Options at a School	• Instructional Coach • Principal • Assistant Principal

What are some other career examples with this level of education not listed here?

_____

_____

_____

Doctoral Degree

Doctoral degrees (PhD) are highly specialized degree programs where students become experts in their field of study. PhD's typically take 5-6 years to complete, and culminate with a project called a dissertation. A completed **dissertation** requires students to write a detailed report based upon original research and publish their conclusions. In order to enroll in a doctoral program, students must have a bachelor's degree and in some cases a master's degree. Many doctoral programs allow students to gain a master's while in pursuit of a PhD.

Example Career Options at a School	• Any individual at school who is addressed as "Doctor" • Professors in college setting

What are some other career examples with this level of education not listed here?

_____

_____

_____

BIG IDEA

A Master's degree is usually 1-2 years, Doctoral degrees are 3-5+ years, and professional degrees are 1-4+ years. They are all begun after completion of a bachelor's degree and are considered graduate degrees.

Graduate School/Student

Graduate programs are for students who want to study a subject area in further depth beyond their undergraduate studies.

Unit 4: My Options

> **Dissertation**
>
> *A dissertation is a requirement for a Doctoral Degree. The lengthy essay is based upon scholarly research, and it must be an original contribution to the field.*

Professional Degree

Professional degrees are programs where students become educated and trained for a career either through hands-on practice (practicum/residency/apprenticeship) or alternatively by passing a test. Professional degree programs range from 1 year to 7 years. Common professions requiring a professional degree are medical doctors, lawyers, social workers, veterinarians, pharmacists, and dentists.

Example Career Options at a School	• Licensed School Counselor

What are some other career examples with this level of education not listed here?

_____

_____

_____

Certification Programs

A student in a certificate program does not earn credit hours, but will earn a **certification** or license at the completion of the program. The length of time to complete the program and education level required all vary depending upon the program. People of all education levels obtain certifications. They provide focused training to help individuals specialize in a particular skill or trade.

> **BIG IDEA**
>
> *I am responsible for determining the steps I need to take in order to participate in educational opportunities after high school.*

Example Career Options at a School	• **Certificate with no college:** Cafeteria Cook, Maintenance Staff • **Certificate with associate's:** Campus Police • **Certificate with bachelor's:** Teacher, Nurse • **Certificate with master's:** Principal, School Counselor

Other Example Career Options by Education Level

Certificate with no college

Certified Electrician, Certified Beautician, Heavy Equipment Operator, Medical Technician, Commercial Pilot (non-airline), Certified Diesel Mechanic, Chef

Certificate with associate's degree

Dental Hygienist, Diagnostic Medical Sonographer, Licensed Practical or Vocational Nurse, Physical Therapist Assistant

Certificate with bachelor's degree

Film Production, Cardiovascular Technologist, Computer Network Administrator

What are some examples of certificate programs you might be interested in completing?

_____
_____
_____

What are some other career examples not listed here?

_____
_____
_____

Which Degree or Certification Program is for Me?

DIRECTIONS: In the space below, please write a complete sentence answering each question.

UNDERGRADUATE DEGREES

Associate's Degree
Bachelor's Degree

GRADUATE DEGREES

Master's Degree
Doctoral Degree
Professional Degree

CERTIFICATION PROGRAMS

What are the most significant differences between these options?

_____
_____
_____
_____
_____
_____

Is one of these options interesting to you? Why or why not?

_____
_____
_____
_____

How Long Will it Take Me to Accomplish My Goal?

DIRECTIONS: Look at the chart below. Take note of the year tracker across the bottom in **green**. Trace with your finger the path you would like to pursue for your future and then answer the questions.

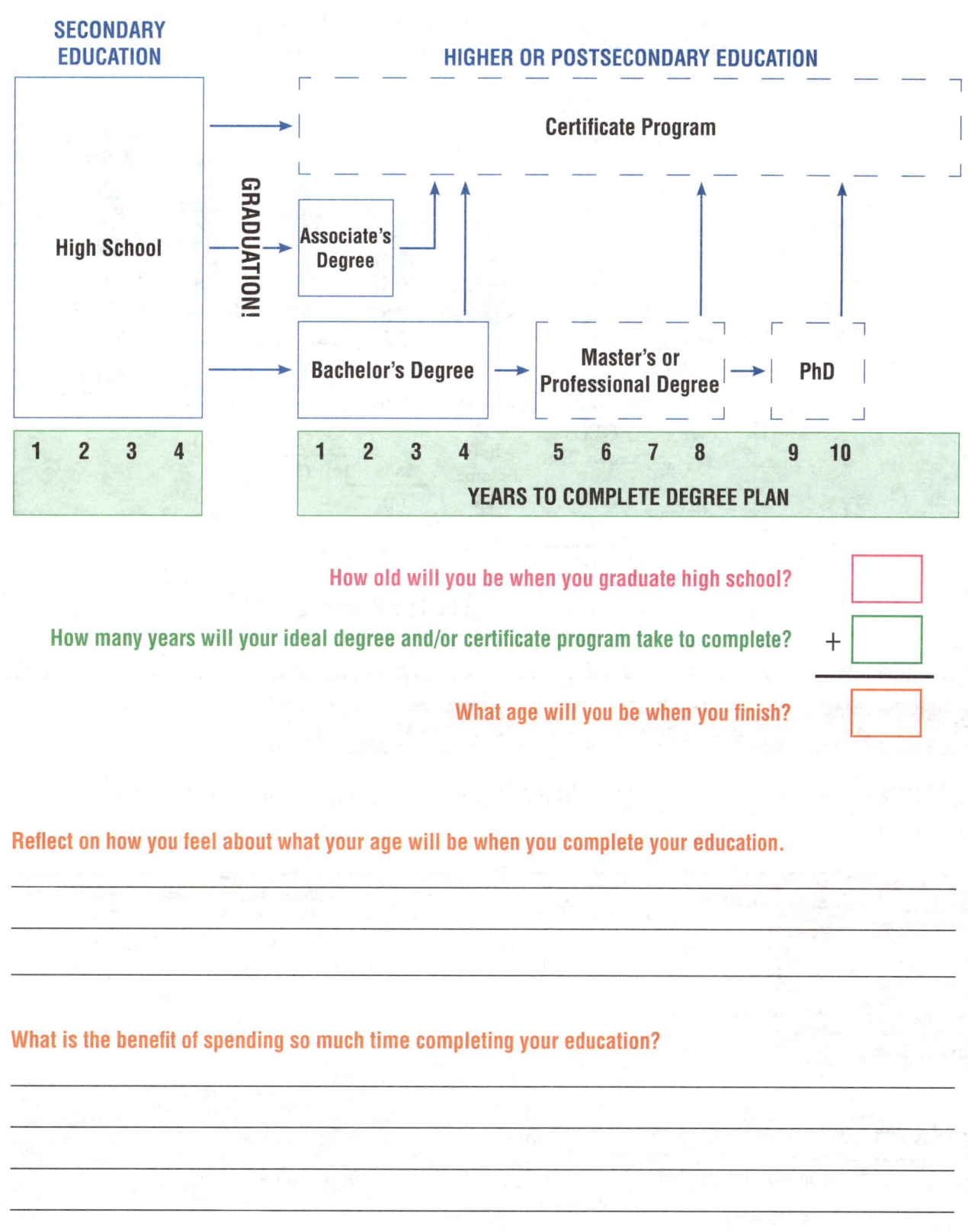

How old will you be when you graduate high school?

How many years will your ideal degree and/or certificate program take to complete? +

What age will you be when you finish?

Reflect on how you feel about what your age will be when you complete your education.
_____
_____
_____

What is the benefit of spending so much time completing your education?
_____
_____
_____
_____

Unit 4: My Options

Education Pays: Lifetime Earnings

The power of reaching higher levels of education, and making more money, actually increases over time. Take a look at the graph below.

According to this graphic, individuals who obtain a Bachelor's Degree make more than twice (2x) the amount of money that someone with only a high school diploma makes each year. Those workers with an Advanced Degree make roughly three times (3x) the money than workers with only a high school diploma.

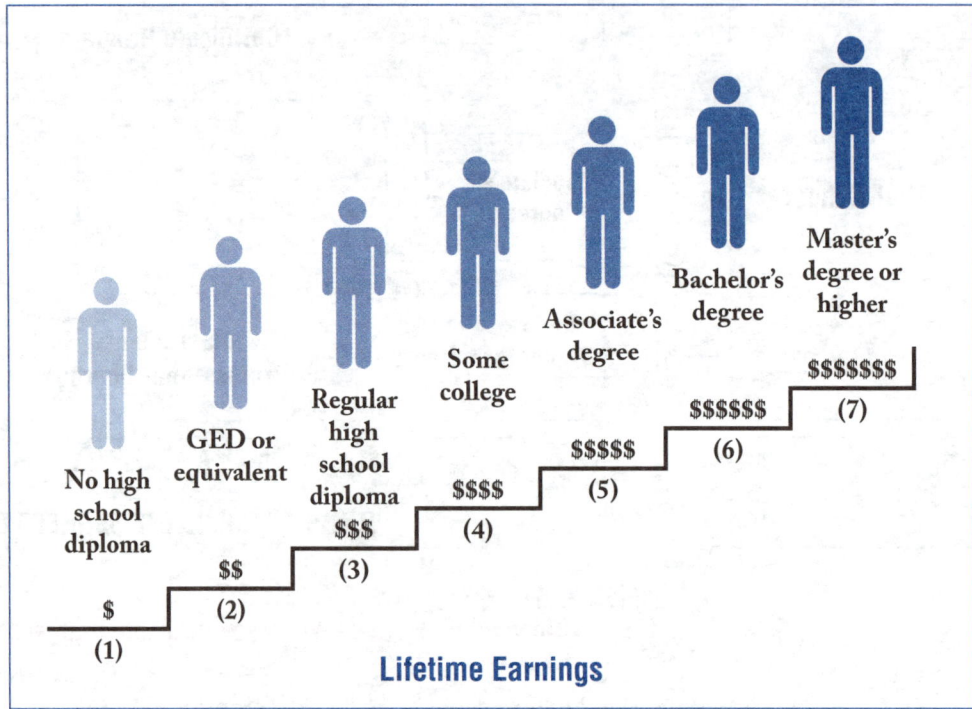

Lifetime Earnings

Education Pays

DIRECTIONS: Complete the table below by filling in $ and watch how lifetime earnings grow over four years!

Do the Math!	Lifetime Earnings After Year 1	Lifetime Earnings After Year 2	Lifetime Earnings After Year 3	Lifetime Earnings After Year 4
High School Diploma	$$$ (3)	$$$$$$ (6)	$$$$$$$$$ (9)	$$$$$$$$$$$$ (12)
Bachelor's Degree	$$$$$$ (6)			
Advanced Degree	$$$$$$$ (7)			

Fill in the blanks:

The _____ education I have, the _____ my lifetime earnings can be.
(more/less)   (higher/lower)

Extending My Learning: Credentials

Aa Bb Cc Dd Ee Ff Gg
Hh Ii Jj Kk Ll Mm Nn
Oo Pp Qq Rr Ss Tt Uu
Vv Ww Xx Yy Zz

example: Alicia Casey

DIRECTIONS: Select the cursive letters in your name from the chart above and practice signing your name.

Credentials are a representation of the degrees as well as certificates a person has. Many professionals place their credentials after their name when they use their signature.

Example: Alicia is a physician's assistant. She has a Bachelor's of Science, a professional degree as a physician's assistant, and has completed a certificate program for Phlebotomy.

This is how she signs her name with credentials:

Unit 4: My Options

Extending My Learning: Credentials

Create yours!

DIRECTIONS: Pretend you are a professional in your ideal career. You have completed degree and/or certification programs to become qualified. List them below:

Certificate(s): _____
Certificate(s): _____
Certificate(s): _____

Degree(s): _____
Degree(s): _____
Degree(s): _____

Create acronyms for each of the certificates and degrees. Do this by researching the real ones, or create some to use for now.

Write your signature with credentials!

_____

Choosing a Course of Study

To determine what course of study you will begin after high school, think about your end goal, your career choice (1). Then evaluate what type of degree and/or credentialing you will need to be successful in that job (2). Once you determine those, narrow your focus to determine what course of study you want to focus on (3). Once you know your major, it makes choosing a school much easier!

1
CAREER
What career do I want to have in the future?

2
TYPE OF DEGREE
What type of degree(s) and/or training do I need to be qualified for my career?

3
MAJOR
What course of study should I focus on after high school?

EXAMPLE:

CAREER
Chief Financial Officer (CFO) of a startup company

TYPE OF DEGREE
Bachelor's Degree

MAJOR
Business Finance
MINOR
Entrepreneurship

A **major** is a specialty in a specific subject area at a college or university that guides a student's course selection. Majors can also be called degree plans, degree programs, specialties, courses of study, or areas of focus.

A **minor** is a secondary specialty for a student and does not require as many credit hours as a major.

Choosing a major in an area that interests you can help to shape your career path. Schools offer different majors. Before making a final decision on your school choice, it is important to ensure the school offers the degree plan you hope to complete.

Even if you aren't sure what specific major you would like to focus on, you can narrow your focus based upon which career field interests you. The activity on the next page will help you determine which career field is interesting to you.

> **BIG IDEA**
> *A major is a student's area of study in college and is the degree a student earns upon graduation.*

> **TIP**
> *Not all colleges offer all majors.*

> **Can I Choose My Classes?**
> *While it is true that you have a lot of flexibility for your course selection in college, your major will determine most of your classes.*

Unit 4: My Options

Identifying a Career Field

BIG IDEA
The course of study I choose can relate to my personal, academic, and career interests.

Guidance Counselor
Talk to your guidance counselor to gather more information.

PART 1

DIRECTIONS: Fill in the big open spaces of the Venn Diagram below. Once all are complete, look for similarities in your answers. Write the common threads in the spaces connecting the circles. If there is something connecting all 3, perhaps that points to a career field you could look into! Refer to the example at the bottom of the page for help.

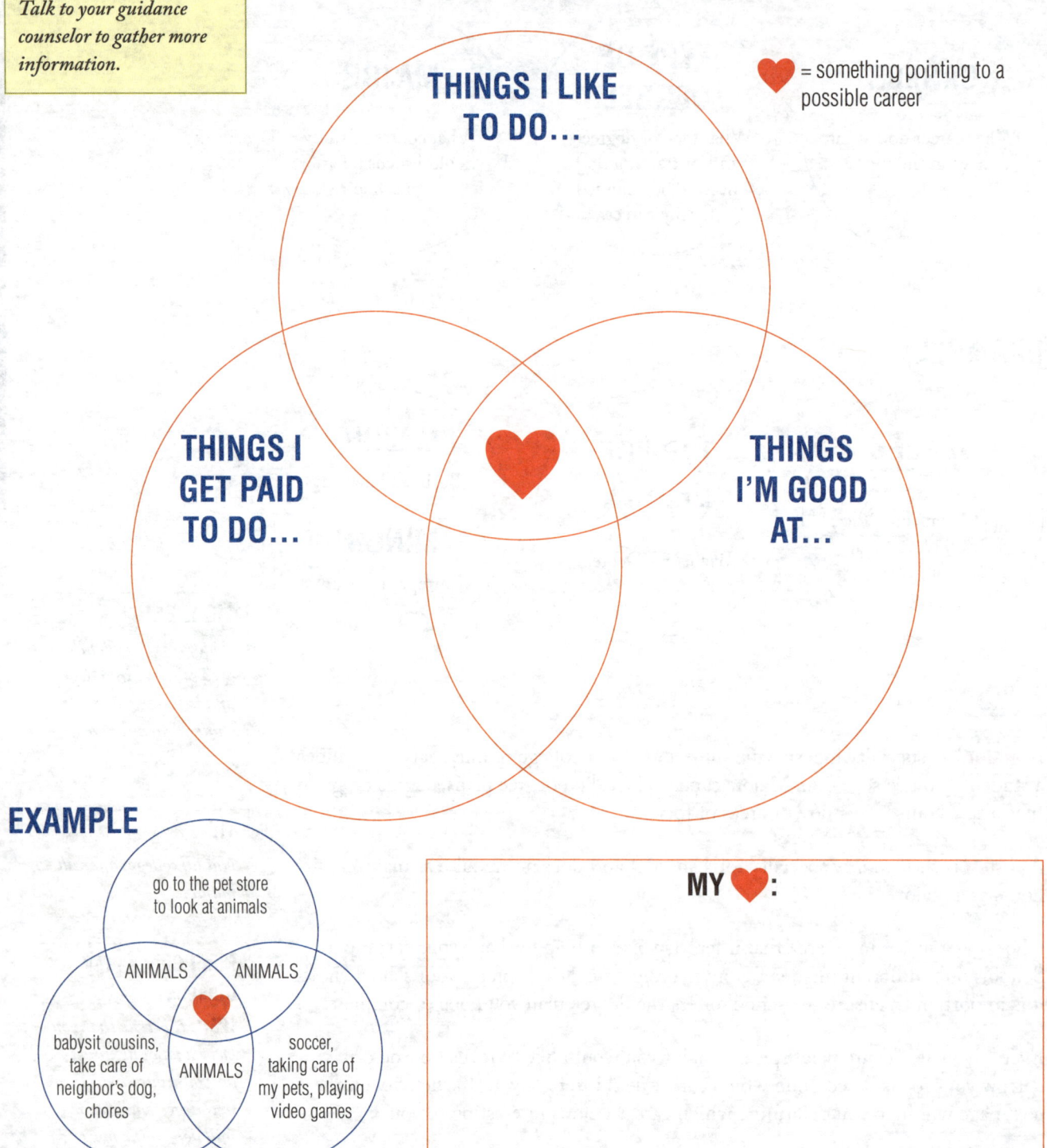

♥ = something pointing to a possible career

THINGS I LIKE TO DO...

THINGS I GET PAID TO DO...

THINGS I'M GOOD AT...

EXAMPLE

go to the pet store to look at animals

ANIMALS   ANIMALS

babysit cousins, take care of neighbor's dog, chores

ANIMALS

soccer, taking care of my pets, playing video games

MY ♥:

Identifying a Career Field (Continued)

PART 2

DIRECTIONS: Read the career fields in the space below. Circle ones that sound interesting to you. Place a ♥ next to any that are related to the interests you named in the previous activity.

Agriculture, Food, and Natural Resources	Hospitality and Tourism	Science, Technology, Engineering, and Mathematics	Architecture and Construction	Health Sciences
Government and Public Administration	Humanities	Transportation, Distribution, and Logistics	Arts, A/V Technology, and Communications	Infomation Technology
Education	Law, Public Safety, Corrections, and Security	Manufacturing	Marketing	Business Management and Finance Administration

PART 3

DIRECTIONS: The following pages contain HUNDREDS of possible majors related to the career fields named above, but there are even more than these listed here. Read through them and circle any that sound interesting to you! Search "majors in _____ career field" to locate more.

Capped Major

Some majors are "capped," meaning the school will only admit a certain number of students into the program each year because so many students desire that major.

Agriculture, Food, and Natural Resources

- Agricultural Business and Management
- Agricultural Economics
- Agricultural Journalism/ Communications
- Agricultural Mechanization
- Agricultural Technology Management
- Agriculture Science
- Agronomy and Crop Science
- Animal Systems
- Arboriculture
- Environmental Service Systems
- Floriculture
- Food Products and Processing Systems
- Forestry
- Geophysics
- Horticulture
- Livestock Management
- Natural Resource Conservation
- Plant and Soil Science
- Power, Structural, and Technical Systems
- Turf Management
- Wildlife and Fishery Science

Unit 4: My Options

www.educationopensdoors.org   **195**

Identifying a Career Field (Continued)

Architecture and Construction

Architecture
Building Inspection
Building Technician
Carpentry
Construction and Construction Management
Electrician
Industrial Design
Landscape Architecture
Maintenance and Operations
Plumbing
Surveying
Urban Planning
Welding

Arts, Audiovisual Technology, and Communications

Acoustics
Animation
Art
Art Education
Art History
A/V Technology and Film
Ceramics
Cinematography
Costume Design
Dance
Digital Communications and Multimedia
Graphic Design
Illustration
Jazz Studies
Journalism and Broadcasting
Lighting Specialist
Music
Music History
Music Management
Musical Theater
Painting
Performing Arts
Photography
Photojournalism
Piano
Playwriting and Screenwriting
Printing Technology
Radio, Television, and Film
Sculpture
Telecommunications
Theater
UX (User Experience) Design
Visual Arts

196 © 2019 Education Opens Doors, Inc.

Identifying a Career Field (Continued)

Business, Management, Administration, and Finance

Accounting
Actuarial Science
Administrative Support
Advertising
Banking Services
Business Administration
Business Finance
Business Information Management
Data Management Specialist
Entrepreneurship
Human Resource Management
Industrial Management
Insurance
International Business
Management Information Systems
Managerial Economics
Operations Management
Public Relations
Risk Management
Securities and Investments

Education

Administration and Administrative Support
Early Childhood Education
Elementary Education
Physical Education
Professional Support Services
Secondary Education
Special Education
Teacher Education

Government and Public Administration

Foreign Service
Governance
National Security
Political Science
Public Administration
Public Policy Analysis
Revenue and Taxation

Identifying a Career Field (Continued)

Health Sciences

Adult Development and Aging
Anatomy
Biomedical Science
Biometrics with Biostatistics
Biopsychology
Biotechnology Research and Development
Child Care and Development
Chiropractic
Dental Hygiene
Diagnostic Services
Dietitian
Educational Psychology
Genetics
Health Informatics
Industrial Psychology
Kinesiology
Massage Therapy
Medical Radiologic Technology
Medical Sonography
Medical Technician
Midwifery
Molecular Genetics
Neuroscience
Nursing
Nutrition
Occupational Therapy
Optometry
Pathology
Pharmacology
Pharmacy
Physical Therapy
Physiological Psychology
Pre-Dentistry
Pre-Medicine
Public Health
Radiation Therapist
Sport and Leisure Studies
Sports Management
Toxicology

Hospitality and Tourism

Culinary Arts
Event Planning
Food and Beverage Services
Hospitality
Hotel and Restaurant Management
Parks and Recreation Science
Travel and Tourism

Identifying a Career Field (Continued)

Humanities

- African Studies
- African-American Studies
- American History
- American Literature
- American Sign Language
- Ancient Studies
- Anthropology
- Art Therapy
- Asian-American Studies
- Biblical Studies
- Child Life Specialist
- Chinese
- Communications Studies
- Community Health and Preventive Medicine
- Comparative Literature
- Consumer Services
- Counseling and Mental Health
- Creative Writing
- Developmental Psychology
- East Asian Studies
- Economics
- English
- English Composition
- English Literature
- Ethnic Studies
- Family and Community Services
- French
- German
- Hebrew
- Hindi
- Hispanic-American Studies
- History
- Islamic Studies
- Italian
- Japanese
- Jewish Studies
- Korean
- Latin American Studies
- Linguistics
- Music Therapy
- Native American Studies
- Organizational Behavior Studies
- Pastoral Studies
- Personal Care Services
- Philosophy
- Portuguese
- Psychology
- Rehabilitation Counseling
- Religious Studies
- Romance Languages
- Rural Sociology
- Social Psychology
- Social Work
- Sociology
- Southeast Asian Studies
- Spanish
- Speech Pathology
- Technical Writing
- Theology
- Urban Studies

Information Technology

- Artificial Intelligence and Robotics
- Computer Programming
- Computer Repair Technician
- Content Management
- Digital Communications
- Gaming
- Health Administration
- Information Security Analysis
- Information Support and Services
- IT Management
- Network Design and Administration
- Online Design
- SEO Consulting
- Social Media Strategizing
- Software Development
- Systems Analysis

Unit 4: My Options

www.educationopensdoors.org

Identifying a Career Field (Continued)

Law, Public Safety, Corrections, and Security

Correction Services
Criminal Justice
Emergency and Fire Management Services
Land Use Planning and Management
Law Enforcement Services
Legal Services
Paralegal
Pre-Law
Security and Protective Services

Manufacturing

Health, Safety and Environmental Assurance
Logistics and Inventory Control
Maintenance, Installation, and Repair
Manufacturing Production Process Development
Production
Quality Assurance

Marketing

Apparel and Textile Marketing Management
Marketing Communications
Marketing Management
Marketing Research
Merchandising and Buying Operations
Professional Sales

Identifying a Career Field (Continued)

Science, Technology, Engineering, and Mathematics

Acoustical Engineering
Aerospace Engineering
Applied Mathematics
Applied Physics
Aquatic Biology
Architectural Engineering
Astronomy
Astrophysics
Automotive Engineering
Biochemistry
Bioethics
Biology
Biomedical Engineering
Botany/Plant Biology
Cell Biology
Chemical Engineering
Chemical Physics
Chemistry
Civil Engineering
Computer Engineering
Electrical Engineering
Engineering Design
Environmental Engineering
Environmental Science
Geography
Geological Engineering
Geology
Industrial Engineering
Marine Biology
Marine Science
Materials Science
Mathematics
Mechanical Engineering
Microbiology
Military Science
Mineral Engineering
Molecular Biology
Neurobiology
Nuclear Engineering
Oceanography
Paleontology
Petroleum Engineering
Planetary Science
Statistics

Transportation, Distribution, and Logistics

Automotive Mechanic
Commercial Pilot
Facility and Mobile Equipment Maintenance
Fleet Management
Health, Safety, and Environmental Management
Transportation Manager and Operations
Transportation Systems/Infrastructure
Logistician
Longshore Worker
Operations Technicians
Warehousing and Distribution

Unit 4: My Options

www.educationopensdoors.org **201**

Extending My Learning: Next Steps for College and Career Selection

Is This TOO Soon to Plan?
Don't worry about picking the "right" major at this point; you have plenty of time to choose!

BIG IDEA
Career aptitude tests and employment statistics can help determine what career path may be the best fit for you based on your skills and interests.

PART 1

DIRECTIONS: Answer the following questions after previewing the list of majors.

Do you feel ready to make a choice about your career?
_____
_____

What questions do you still have about choosing a course of study?
_____
_____
_____

What tools or resources can you use to help you choose a career or course of study?
_____
_____
_____

In addition to the resources you listed, a career aptitude test provides you with personal results aligned with your abilities and interests. It will generate career ideas you may not have considered. Using your results, you can then narrow down a college major that aligns with your personal career goals, strengths, and interests. Is it hard to narrow down to just one major? You can double major in 2 different content areas, or choose a minor to supplement your major. In either case, you will have specific coursework to complete each degree plan.

PART 2

DIRECTIONS: Make a list of majors you may be interested in pursuing. Next, research specific information about the majors you are interested in and complete the following questions.

TIP
Research which employment opportunities will have the most job opportunities based on market trends.

Potential Majors:

A. _____ B. _____ C. _____

How many months/semesters/years does it take to complete the major/program? _____

Does the major or program include on-the-job work experience (e.g. work study or internships)?
_____

Which type of qualification do you receive after completing the program (e.g. bachelor degree, associate degree, certificate)?
_____

Playing a Sport While in College

Colleges may recruit exceptionally committed and skilled athletes to play a sport at their school. Some schools offer athletic scholarships to student athletes. Talk to your coaches about opportunities for recruitment and scholarships. Students recruited as athletes must still go through the same admissions process as all other applicants to the college or university. Schools across the country with sports teams are members of athletic associations. Those associations determine many of the rules and regulations about which sports are included, how scholarship money can be dispersed, what uniforms must look like, etc. Below is a list of several athletic associations with a focus on the most widely known, the NCAA.

National Collegiate Athletic Association (NCAA) Sports

The **NCAA** is an organization that oversees athletic program participation, guidelines, and eligibility for competition at over 1,000 colleges and universities. More than 1,000 colleges are part of the NCAA with roughly 500,000 student athletes participating. The NCAA sanctions the following sports:

Baseball	Gymnastics	Swimming and Diving
Basketball	Ice Hockey	Tennis
Bowling	Lacrosse	Track and Field (indoor)
Cross Country	Rifle	Track and Field (outdoor)
Fencing	Rowing	Volleyball (indoor)
Field Hockey	Skiing	Volleyball (beach)
Football	Soccer	Water Polo
Golf	Softball	Wrestling

There are currently 3 emerging sports that have not been officially sanctioned by the NCAA yet. The three sports are: Rugby, Triathlon, and Equestrian. Schools can recruit athletes and even award scholarships for these 3 sports as they work towards becoming officially sanctioned sports.

> **BIG IDEA**
> *There are several different athletic associations, each with their own set of guidelines.*

> **Professional Athletes**
> *Depending on the sport, between 1% and 10% of college athletes make it to the professional league.*

Do Other Sports Exist?

DIRECTIONS: Write down any additional sports you know on the left side. Then write 1 you would like to appeal to the NCAA to include as a sanctioned sport so you or someone you know could play in the future.

Other sports you know of:	One sport you would like the NCAA to sanction:

Unit 4: My Options

NCAA Divisions

The NCAA is divided into 3 divisions. Each division offers different levels of competition and different scholarship levels.

> **Student Athlete**
> *In order to receive an athletic scholarship, athletes must also maintain a good GPA.*

Division 1 (D1)	Division 2 (D2)	Division 3 (D3)
1. Can offer FULL and partial scholarships to athletes	1. Can offer FULL and partial scholarships, but most are partial	1. Cannot offer athletic scholarships, but athletes can get academic scholarships
2. Most well known athletic programs are a part of this division	2. Fewer scholarships available each year than D-1	2. Division 3 athletes tend to have a more flexible practice and competition schedule than D-1
3. Highest level of competition	3. Less competitive than D-1	

Other Athletic Associations in the United States

Each of the associations below have their own guidelines, search the names of the conferences below to learn which schools and which sports are members. It's possible that the sport you would like the NCAA to sanction is already sanctioned by one of these associations!

- National Association of Intercollegiate Athletics (NAIA)
- United States Collegiate Athletic Association (USCAA)
- National Christian College Athletic Association (NCCAA)
- Association of Christian College Athletics (ACCA)
- National Junior College Athletic Association (NJCAA)
- California Community College Athletic Association (CCCAA)
- Northwest Athletic Conference (NWAC)
- Independent conferences

What College Coaches/Recruiters Look For

Once you have decided that you want to play a sport in college, start by doing research to find a program that's the right fit for you. High school coaches know your skill level, leadership qualities, and dedication better than others. They can help convey those skills to college recruiters.

Talent
Competing in college is a big step after high school. College coaches will look at video footage from your competitions and possibly come watch you in person.

Dedication
Recruiters and coaches will be interested in recommendations from your high school teachers and coaches to learn about your commitment to school, attendance at school and practice, and your work ethic.

Academics
Student athletes must maintain a minimum GPA in order to be eligible to play in college. The most widely known requirements are through the NCAA Clearinghouse, which ensures all Division 1 athletes have at least a 2.3 GPA in core classes as well as successfully complete the following classes in high school:

- 4 years of English
- 3 years of math (Algebra 1 or higher)
- 2 years of natural or physical sciences (including one year of lab science if offered by your high school)
- 1 extra year of English, math, or natural or physical science
- 2 years of social science
- 4 years of extra core courses (from any category above, foreign language, or philosophy)

*Note: Division 2 course requirements are different. Check collegeboard.com for more information.

Awareness and Goal Setting

BIG IDEA
Talent, dedication, and academic success can lead to personal and athletic achievement.

DIRECTIONS: Not everyone has hopes of being a student athlete, but the awareness and goal setting around your talents, dedication, and academics are all still relevant. Thoughtfully answer each of the following questions.

In which of those 3 areas do you feel you are the strongest right now?

    TALENT   DEDICATION   ACADEMICS

In which of these areas do you think you need the most work right now?

    TALENT   DEDICATION   ACADEMICS

What is one way you can strengthen that area?

_____

_____

Who is one person who can support you as you try to improve in that area?

_____

Extending My Learning: Student Athlete Time Tetris

DIRECTIONS: Imagine the schedule below being one you follow each week. Then, answer the questions about the schedule either in the space provided or on the schedule itself.

	Monday	Tuesday	Wednesday	Thursday	Friday	Saturday	Sunday
8:00	CLASS		CLASS		CLASS		
9:00	CLASS		CLASS		CLASS		
10:00	CLASS	CLASS	CLASS	CLASS	CLASS		
11:00		PRACTICE		PRACTICE	TUTORING	GAME PREP	
12:00		PRACTICE		PRACTICE		GAME PREP	
1:00	STRENGTH TRAINING	PRACTICE		PRACTICE		GAME PREP	
2:00	STRENGTH TRAINING					GAME PREP	
3:00						GAME PREP	
4:00			PRACTICE	PHYSICAL THERAPY		GAME PREP	
5:00	SCIENCE LAB		PRACTICE	PHYSICAL THERAPY		GAME	PRACTICE
6:00	SCIENCE LAB		PRACTICE		TEAM DINNER	GAME	PRACTICE
7:00			PRACTICE		TEAM DINNER	GAME	PRACTICE
8:00							

If this is your schedule, what additional activities would you like to have scheduled?
_____

How many hours of sleep do you think this athlete requires each night? _____

Based upon when they need to wake up in the morning, what time do they need to go to sleep to get at least 8 hours of sleep? _____

Locate 12 hours on this schedule for study time.

When do you think this athlete finds time to eat? _____

Notes

Unit 4 Summary: Knowing My Options After High School

There are many different paths for you to choose from after high school graduation. Research your options starting today. Some key things to consider are: the career you hope to pursue based on your interests and skills, the education required for that career, the selectivity of the educational programs you are interested in, how much money you would like to earn annually, and the likely employment rates for various levels of degrees and career. Typically those who attain advanced degrees or learn a specialty will earn considerably more money during their lifetime than those with only a high school diploma.

Start your research process now. This will help inform your decisions and bring you closer to the great things that await you in the future.

Checklist Check-In

1. Consider where you are in your educational journey. Check the corresponding box below.
   - ☐ 6th Grade
   - ☐ 7th Grade
   - ☐ 8th Grade
   - ☐ 9th Grade
   - ☐ 10th Grade
   - ☐ 11th Grade
   - ☐ 12th Grade
   - ☐ High School Graduate
   - ☐ GED Recipient

2. Turn to the "Grade Level Checklist" at the beginning of Unit 1. Locate your current grade level. **Review what you checked off at the beginning of the program and check off any other activities you have completed.**

Unit Review Opportunities

1. Go back to the "Extend Your Learning" pages in this unit. Research, ask questions, and locate resources to complete those activities.
2. Complete any remaining vocabulary tasks for this unit's vocabulary and use each word in a sentence this week.
3. Answer the questions on the unit cover page, and complete the directions in the white box.

Moving Forward…

Select one of the colors from the triangle to describe how you feel about new understandings gained from this unit. Justify your answer in at least 3 sentences.

_____
_____
_____
_____
_____
_____

UNIT 5
UNDERSTANDING MY FINANCES AFTER HIGH SCHOOL

What is financial aid and how do I apply for it?

| Financial Aid: The FAFSA page 234 | Comparing Financial Aid Packages page 240 | Financial Literacy page 245 | Establishing Financial Goals page 246 | How to Build a Budget page 248 | Making Your Money Work for You page 251 | Unit 5 Summary page 258 |

Understanding Financial Aid page 219

Calculating the Cost of Continuing My Education page 212

Unit 5 Vocabulary page 210

How does the FAFSA work?

When do I have to pay back student loans?

DIRECTIONS: Read the topics of this unit. Draw a picture of your emotions about this content.

How expensive is college?

Unit 5 Vocabulary

DIRECTIONS:

1. DEFINE each word using the glossary in this book or a dictionary.
2. ANSWER the questions listed below for each word.

Vocabulary Word	Definition	Have you ever heard/seen this word before?	Explain how you have heard this word used before. If you've never heard or seen it, what other word (in any language) does it look like to you?
Tuition		Y N	
Dormitory		Y N	
Room and Board		Y N	
Cost of Attendance		Y N	
Student Activity Fee		Y N	
Financial Aid		Y N	
Scholarship		Y N	
Grant		Y N	
Work Study		Y N	
FAFSA		Y N	
Loans		Y N	

Vocabulary Word	Definition	Have you ever heard/seen this word before?	Explain how you have heard this word used before. If you've never heard or seen it, what other word (in any language) does it look like to you?
Enrollment Status		Y N	
Subsidized Loan		Y N	
Unsubsidized Loan		Y N	
Federal Pell Grant		Y N	
Expected Family Contribution		Y N	
Verification		Y N	
Deposit		Y N	
Budget		Y N	
Compound Interest		Y N	
Interest		Y N	
Full-Time Student/ Part-Time Student		Y N	
Student Aid Report (SAR)		Y N	

Additional words to complete on notebook paper: **Satisfactory Academic Progress (SAP), College Scholarship Service (CSS) Profile, Stocks, Mutual Funds** _____
_____
_____

Unit 5: My Finances

Calculating the Cost of Continuing My Education

Anna's Story

Anna wants to buy a new laptop. How's she going to pay for it? She can…

1. Borrow money.
2. Wait, work, and save.
3. Participate in a community program that provides laptops to committed participants.

Weigh the Options

BIG IDEA
The costs for college are not limited to tuition.

DIRECTIONS: Consider each of Anna's options. In the chart below, fill in the pros (positives) and the cons (negatives) of each choice.

Option 1: Borrow Money		Option 2: Wait, Work, and Save		Option 3: Participate in Community Program	
Pros	Cons	Pros	Cons	Pros	Cons

Which option would you choose if you were Anna? _____

Why do you feel most comfortable with this option?
_____

Which item on your pro/con list influenced your decision the most?
_____

Laptops can be expensive! Have you considered these factors?

- Did Anna do enough research to make sure the laptop meets expectations?
- If Anna chooses to participate in the community program or work more, will there be enough time to maintain good grades?
- After getting the laptop, Anna might want or need some accessories (ex: headphones, case, apps, internet connection, etc.).

Do these factors change your decision on what you would do if you were Anna? Why or why not?
_____

What other factors would you consider if you were Anna?
_____

Connection to College

Anna wants to go to college, and college can be expensive. To pay for college, Anna can…

1. Borrow money.
2. Wait, work, and save.
3. Participate in a scholarship program.

Which option would you choose if you were Anna? _____

Is this different or the same as the option you would choose for purchasing a laptop?
_____
_____

Why do you feel most comfortable with this option?
_____
_____

What additional factors would you consider if you were Anna?

- _____
- _____
- _____

Breaking Down the Cost of College

Currently in the US, college is not free for everyone like secondary education is. Schools require tuition payments in addition to other fees. **Tuition** is the amount of money a student pays for classes they're enrolled in. Tuition usually does not include the cost of books or lab supplies.

Think about your school right now. If you had to pay to attend school there, what do you think you would need to pay for? Identify at least 3 factors that make up the cost of your education.

- _____
- _____
- _____

Expenses in college are more than just tuition, books, and class supplies. In college, students get to enjoy eating together, activities, sporting events, sometimes living on campus together, parking on campus, and much more. All of these things cost money.

TIP

Tuition costs per class are sometimes higher for part time students (less than 12 credit hours) than they are for full time students (more than 12 hours).

Room and Board

The cost for living on campus and participating in the campus dining plan.

Unit 5: My Finances

Below is an example of how much it might cost to attend a two-year public college. Living expenses are not included in this calculation.

Sample Two-Year College

Fee	Cost per Semester	Number of Semesters	Total
Tuition	$1,500	x 4	= $6,000
Textbooks/Supplies	$600	x 4	= $2,400
Student Activities	$750	x 4	= $3,000
Health Insurance	$450	x 4	= $1,800
On-campus Parking	$300	x 4	= $1,200
Personal	$450	x 4	= $1,800
		Total for 2 Years	**= $16,200**

Student Activity Fee

A fee that is separate from your tuition. These fees fund student organizations, activities, and other services provided on campus.

__Note:__ Expenses are a sample. School costs rise each year. Search "average tuition costs for _____ (insert current year)" to get an up-to-date number.

Calculating the Cost of 4-Year Colleges

DIRECTIONS: Using the numbers provided and referencing the sample above, calculate the cost of attending a Public Four-Year College.

Sample Public Four-Year College

Fee	Cost per Semester	Number of Semesters	Total
Tuition	$4,500	x 8	=
Room and Food - Year 1 (on-campus)	$5,000	x 2	=
Room and Food - Years 2-4 (off-campus)	$3,000	x 6	=
Textbooks/Supplies	$600	x 8	=
Student Activities	$750	x 8	=
Health Insurance	$450	x 8	=
On-campus Parking	$300	x 8	=
Personal	$450	x 8	=
		Total for 4 Years	**=**

__Note:__ Expenses are a sample. School costs rise each year. Search "average tuition costs for _____ (insert current year)" to get an up-to-date number.

Calculating the Cost of 4-Year Colleges

DIRECTIONS: Using the numbers provided and referencing the sample above, calculate the cost of attending a Private Four-Year College.

Sample Private Four-Year College

Fee	Cost per Semester	Number of Semesters	Total
Tuition	$11,000	x 8	=
Room and Food - Year 1 (on-campus)	$5,000	x 2	=
Room and Food - Years 2-4 (off-campus)	$3,000	x 6	=
Textbooks/Supplies	$600	x 8	=
Student Activities	$750	x 8	=
Health Insurance	$450	x 8	=
On-campus Parking	$300	x 8	=
Personal	$450	x 8	=
		Total for 4 Years	=

*****Note:** *Expenses are a sample. School costs rise each year. Search "average tuition costs for _____ (insert current year)" to get an up-to-date number.*

Now that you have calculated the cost of various types of schools, you may realize why choosing to continue your education is called an investment in your future!

Can you think of ways you can start planning for the costs of college today?

_____
_____
_____
_____

Do you believe that you have options to pay for your continued education after high school?

_____

What are some ways you could make your college experience less expensive?

_____
_____
_____
_____

> **BIG IDEA**
>
> *A number of factors affect the cost of college, and those factors vary by school.*

Unit 5: My Finances

Ways to Reduce the Cost of Continuing Your Education

BIG IDEA
There are several factors that affect the cost of college and they vary by school.

Dormitory
Dormitories, or residence halls, are buildings on college campuses where students live.

DIRECTIONS: Read the tips below and draw a box around the cost reducing tips you might actually use in your future.

Educational Cost Cutters

- **APPLY FOR SCHOLARSHIPS AND GRANTS** as soon as possible.
- **BUY USED TEXTBOOKS.**
- **TAKE PLACEMENT TESTS AND ADVANCED COURSES** to receive college credit without taking an actual class!
- **ATTEND AN IN-STATE SCHOOL.**

Lifestyle Cost Cutters

- **COOK WITH ROOMMATES** rather than eating out to share a grocery bill.
- **DON'T BRING A CAR.** Without your own car on campus, you will not need to pay for car insurance, parking passes, gasoline, or upkeep.
- When traveling home or to campus, find people to **CARPOOL** with.
- **LIVE WITH FAMILY**, if available as an option.

Why did you choose those particular tips?

_____
_____
_____
_____

Can you think of any additional cost cutters?

_____
_____
_____
_____

Notes

Extending My Learning: Cost Breakdown

COA (Cost of Attendance)

The estimated cost of completing one full year at a college or in a program. For college, it includes tuition, room and board (housing and food), student fees, books and supplies, and sometimes transportation costs.

TIP

Keep in mind that you can still attend college by only paying the tuition and student fees. If you live at home, you do not have to pay for room and board/rent or a meal plan on campus.

DIRECTIONS: Consider your ideal school option after high school. Search the school's website for a cost breakdown. Complete the chart below with real expenses for you to attend that school. Add any expenses not listed in the blanks at the bottom of the chart.

Note: *Determine the number of semesters you will need to be in attendance to complete the degree or certificate program.*

Fee	Cost per Semester	Number of Semesters	Total
Tuition	$_____	x ____	= $_____
Room and Food, Year 1 (on-campus)	$_____	x ____	= $_____
Room and Food, Years 2-4 (off-campus)	$_____	x ____	= $_____
Textbooks/Supplies	$_____	x ____	= $_____
Student Activities	$_____	x ____	= $_____
Health Insurance	$_____	x ____	= $_____
On-campus Parking	$_____	x ____	= $_____
Personal	$_____	x ____	= $_____
	$_____	x ____	= $_____
	$_____	x ____	= $_____
	$_____	x ____	= $_____
		Total for 4 Years	= $_____

NOTES

_____
_____
_____
_____
_____

Understanding Financial Aid

What questions or concerns do you have about paying for continuing your education?

_____

_____

> **BIG IDEA**
> *Financial aid is money that federal, state, college, and private sources offer students to help pay for college.*

For many students, paying for college is a concern. Fortunately, there are four types of financial aid, given based upon financial need, merit, or both. To determine if a school is a good financial fit for you and your family, contact their Financial Aid Office and ask how much financial aid current students receive.

Search "Federal Student Aid" online to find detailed information and resources. Specifically look for websites ending in **.gov** to ensure the information is coming from the federal government rather than a private company.

Needs-Based Financial Aid	Merit-Based Financial Aid	Needs and Merit Based Financial Aid
Eligibility is based only on funds available by the student's family. Academics/athletics/talents/interests are not considered.	Eligibility is based only on the academics/athletics/talents/interests of the student. Family finances are not considered.	Eligibility takes into consideration both the academics/athletics/talents/interests as well as funds available by the student's family.
Special Notes		
ALL Federal financial aid is needs-based, including the Pell Grant. They also require completion of the FAFSA.	University and private scholarships/grants can be merit-based.	University and private scholarships/grants can be needs based initially, and merit based for future semesters.

Four Types of Financial Aid

Grants

Grants are financial aid that do not need to be paid back! Federal grants are based upon your FAFSA. Grants can also be dispersed from the school or state, local, or federal government. They can be either merit based or needs based.

Work Study

Work study dollars do not need to be paid back, and are dispersed through the federal government after completing the FAFSA. **Work study** allows students to have a paying job on campus, and the payment received for the work can go directly towards school costs or be used to cover personal expenses.

> **Financial Aid**
> *Money students use to cover college expenses. Aid comes in the form of grants, scholarships, loans, and work-study.*

> **Work Study**
> *Work study is a paid campus job you can be awarded by filling out a federal form called the FAFSA.*

> **FAFSA**
> *The FAFSA is an application for financial aid, including loans, grants, college work study, and other federal and state funding. It is often required before a student can be considered for scholarships.*

Unit 5: My Finances

www.educationopensdoors.org

BIG IDEA
Scholarships and grants do not need to be paid back, while loans DO need to be paid back (typically with interest).

Use Free Searches
You should never have to pay to find scholarships that you can easily find yourself!

Scholarships

Scholarships are financial aid that does not need to be paid back! Scholarships can be given from the school or from a private company/organization. They can be either merit based or needs based. A benefit of private scholarships is that you can use them at the school of your choice. Thousands of private scholarships are available and range in the amount of money they disperse. Ask local companies, religious institutions, and community organizations about scholarship opportunities.

Loans

Loans are financial aid that does need to be paid back after you graduate. Loans come from the government (based on FAFSA), or from a private company like a bank. All student loans have an interest rate associated with them; some are very high (above 10%) and some are very low (0%). Be aware of the interest rate on the loan as well as the terms of repayment. The higher the interest rate, the larger the sum of money you will repay in total. Terms of repayment include: length of time after graduation before payments start, whether or not interest is collecting while you're still in school, and if there is a grace period available if you choose to join the Peace Corps or another service organization.

Compare Types of Financial Aid

DIRECTIONS: Fill out the chart below. At the bottom, be sure to list pros and cons about each type of financial aid.

	Loan	Grant	Scholarship	Work Study
Where does the money come from?				
Does the money have to be paid back?				
Does interest for fees accumulate on the money you receive? (Meaning you have to pay back more than you received)				
Does a student need to fill out the FAFSA to get this award?				
PROS (+)				
CONS (-)				

Paying for College Activity

DIRECTIONS: Complete the worksheet to determine Michael's left over need and read about ways it can be covered.

Michael's Sample Financial Statement

Tuition Cost	$9,000
Room and Board Cost	$10,000
Books Cost	$1,200
Other Fees	$3,900
Total Cost of Attendance	$_____

Financial Aid	$15,000
Michael's Contribution	$1,800
Parent Contribution	$1,800
Total Aid and Family Contribution	$_____

[ ] − [ ] = [ ]

Total cost of attendance (including room and board) − Total aid and family contributions = Left over need

Ways to cover left over need:

- Locate a summer job and start saving!
- Apply for scholarships not offered by the University (YMCA, private donors, large stores, etc.). Ask your guidance counselor at school about options.
- Talk to family members about starting a family savings plan for your college. There are savings accounts that will accumulate interest as your money sits in the bank account. Talk to a local bank or credit union about your options.
- Consider student loans for the amount of unmet need.

Can you think of other ways to cover left over need?

_____
_____
_____
_____

It's also possible to reduce your costs in college. Look back at the "Cost Cutters" lists for some tips on ways to do so.

Apply Early
College funding and financial aid are usually distributed on a first come, first serve basis.

Be Cautious
Be cautious when accepting loans and ONLY accept what you absolutely need.

Unit 5: My Finances

Extending My Learning: Exploring Personal Contributions

DIRECTIONS: Search the website or call the financial aid office at your top choice school to locate a cost breakdown for current students, including average financial aid. After inputting those numbers, complete the rest of the worksheet with your parents, guardians, or anyone who may be making financial contributions to continuing your education.

Note: *Some websites share information for the total to complete a degree/certificate and some share on a 1 year or semester basis. Make sure your numbers throughout the whole worksheet are representative of the same amount of time.*

School Name: _____

Tuition Cost	
Room and Board Cost	
Books Cost	
Other Fees	
Total Cost of Attendance	$_____

College financial aid forms include a number called "Expected Family Contributions" which is a dollar amount that the school feels your family will be able to pay towards your school. This number is determined based upon your family's income and expenses through taxes and other forms.

Questions to discuss with your family:

- Is there a plan in place already for covering costs of college in the future?
- If we pretend I am planning to attend college next year, what is an estimation of how much our family could contribute?
- If there is not a plan in place, would you all like to partner with me to learn more about college savings accounts and other options?

Average financial aid given	
My estimated contributions	
Estimated parent's/guardian's contributions	
Total Aid and Family Contribution	$_____

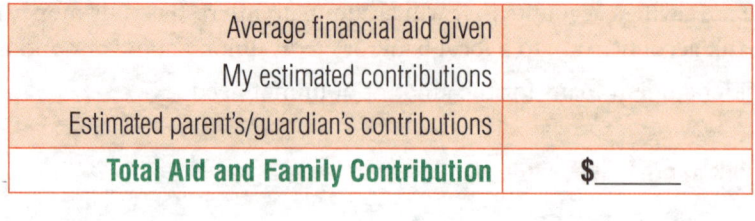

Total cost of attendance (including room and board) − Total aid and family contributions = Left over need*

*__Note:__ *The financial aid used in this calculation is an average. It is not a representation of all students. Contact the financial aid office at your top school to ask what financial aid averages are for students with a similar financial history to your family.*

Grants

Grants are a form of financial aid that does not need to be paid back, similar to a scholarship.

University Grants

Universities, especially private schools, have funding sources for financial aid for students. Often alumni of universities will contribute towards grants and scholarships for current students. These grants can be needs or merit based. They often are named after a person or position at the university or the school itself. For example, The University Chancellor's Grant.

Government Grants

Federal and state grants are usually awarded based upon financial need. Financial need is based upon each student's FAFSA. If you are eligible for a grant, it will appear as a part of your financial aid package from schools after you apply. Search online for grants awarded by your state or local government.

Popular grants

- **Federal Pell Grant**
  This grant awards up to $6,095* per year to college students. Priority is given to students from low income families.
- **Federal Supplemental Educational Opportunity Grant (SEOG)**
  This grant awards up to $4,000* per year to college students. Priority is given to students from low income families.

Community Specific Grants

Communities have focused initiatives, and many of them provide funding for students to continue their education. Ask questions about college funding available through organizations or institutions who are aligned with your career goals and/or your current skill sets, or are local to where you currently live.

Examples of Community Specific Grants:

- Living to Serve Grant is awarded to students in the Future Farmers of America (FFA) organization who are demonstrating impactful community involvement.
- Broadcast Education Association Grant is awarded to high performing students who have a desire to pursue a career in broadcast journalism or media arts.
- Wyoming Space Grant is awarded to any student pursuing space science in Wyoming.

*__Note:__ *This number is reflective of 2019 values.*

Student Grant Basics

DIRECTIONS: Answer the question below. Then, after doing some research, fill in examples and special notes in the chart.

Can you think of a place in your community you could go to ask about local, city, or state grants?

_____
_____
_____
_____

	How to Find Them	Examples	Special Notes
Community Specific Grant	Local government offices, online searches		
Federal Grant	Financial aid office at college	Pell Grant, SEO Grant	You must complete the FAFSA to be eligible.
University Grant	Financial Aid office at college		Some schools will require you to complete the FAFSA to be eligible, but not all.

Work Study

Work Study Positions

Based upon your FAFSA, you may be granted work study to cover additional tuition costs. **Work study** allows students to have a paying job on campus, sometimes related to one's major. College work study wages cannot be less than minimum wage, and students typically work 20 hours per week or less.

Most college campuses in the United States have work study programs. To determine your eligibility to participate in work study, the college looks at a student's **Expected Family Contribution** (or EFC). Some work study positions are available to students who do not qualify based upon their financial aid packages. Be sure to check with opportunities at your top choice school.

Working While in School (not as a part of work study)

Students may have a job off campus to pay towards tuition, pay rent and grocery expenses, or to have some extra spending money. While in school, having a part-time job can be a great way to earn income, practice time management skills, and gain critical job skills.

Part-Time Versus Full-Time Student

It is important to note that there are two statuses you can have as a student! A **full-time student**, meaning you have to take at least 12 credit hours per semester, or a **part-time student**, which is any commitment under 12 credit hours per semester. Keep in mind that being a part-time student can affect your financial aid status.

Enrollment Status

A full-time student is enrolled in 12 or more credit hours in a semester. A part-time student is enrolled in less than 12 credit hours in a semester.

Scholarships

BIG IDEA
The four main types of scholarships students can apply for are identity based, popular, local, and university scholarships.

Scholarships are financial aid dollars that do not need to be paid back. They come from a wide variety of sources. The company, individual, school, or organization providing the scholarship has the opportunity to state the eligibility and application requirements. Since they're not all the same, read the application requirements carefully before you submit them.

Identity/Experience Based Scholarships

In some cases, individuals, companies, or organizations make scholarship money available to students of a specific identity group or experience. Identity/experience groups can be based on, but not limited to, race, ethnicity, nationality, gender identity, sexual orientation, income level, religion, family circumstances, and many more.

How to Find Them	Example Scholarship Sources
Look for organizations and programs who serve people within specific identity groups.	• Black Excel: The College Help Network • United Negro College Fund • Congressional Hispanic Caucus Institute Regional Scholarships • The Hispanic Scholarship Fund • Latino College Dollars • American Indian College Fund • Native American Rights Fund • Catching the Dream • Asian and Pacific Islander American Scholarship Fund • Educators for Fair Consideration (E4FC) New American Scholars Program • The Dream US Scholarship (for **DACA** eligible youth) • Point Foundation: College Scholarships for LGBT Students • Girl Inc. Lucile Miller Wright Scholars Program • The Islamic Society of North America (ISNA) • The Islamic Scholarship Fund • First in Family Scholarship • Girls Scouts Gold Award Scholarship • Hispanic Scholarship Fund • Gates Millennium Scholars

Special Notes

There are hundreds more scholarships and organizations providing scholarships based upon identity; this list is just a starting point. Ask your guidance counselor and other individuals in your community about more options.

Can you think of an organization or community resource that provides services to people within an identity group that you are a part of?

_____

_____

_____

Popular Scholarships

Popular scholarships are often easy to locate through a quick scholarship search online.

> **BIG IDEA**
> *You can begin applying for college scholarships as early as 9th grade.*

How to Find Them	Example Scholarship Sources
• The College Board Scholarship Search • FastWeb • CSS/Financial Aid Profile from the College Board **These resources can be used to locate all types of scholarships, not just popular ones.*	• Many large companies and organizations offer scholarships: Target, Google, Apple, Pepsi, Ford, McDonalds, Kohl's, etc. • Coca-Cola Scholars Program • National Merit Scholarships • Ron Brown Scholar Program

Special Notes

Application requirements can be minimal, allowing thousands of students to locate and apply for these scholarships each year.

Have you ever heard of someone receiving a scholarship from a large company? Which one?

_____

Local/Regional Scholarships

Local or regional scholarships are less well known, and can be more difficult to locate. They are usually only available to residents of a particular community (city, neighborhood, county, school district, etc.)

How to Find Them	Example Scholarship Sources
The best way to find local and regional scholarships is to search "scholarships in _____" and see what you can find, then contact the institution or organization offering it and ask how to apply.	• Dallas County Promise • Dr. Anson L Clark Scholarship Fund • Grady Graves Scholarship Fund • Elizabeth Anne Ala Scholarship

Special Notes

In addition to an online search, utilize relationships you have with guidance counselors, coaches, community leaders, or others where you live and go to school. Ask questions about available scholarships from alumni of your high school as well.

Have you ever heard of someone receiving a local or regional scholarship? Which one?

_____

> **BIG IDEA**
>
> *Scholarships can be offered through organizations I am a part of, businesses I frequent, non-profit organizations, and professional organizations, amongst many more.*

University Scholarships

Universities set aside money each year to provide students with scholarships. Scholarships are merit based (grades, athletics, fine arts, etc.) or needs based (how much money is available to pay for school).

How to Find Them	Example Scholarship Sources
Contact the Financial Aid Office at the university you plan to attend and ask about scholarship eligibility and how to apply.	They often are named after a person or position at the university or the school itself and as a result names vary. An example is The University Chancellor's Scholarship.

Special Notes

These scholarships can be needs or merit based.

Do you know someone who has received a scholarship from a school?
_____

Was the scholarship merit based or needs based?
_____

Scholarship Eligibility

DIRECTIONS: Go back through the scholarship pages. Underline or highlight at least five websites, resources, or locations where you can find scholarships that you are eligible for.

| IDENTITY/EXPERIENCE BASED SCHOLARSHIPS | POPULAR SCHOLARSHIPS | LOCAL/REGIONAL SCHOLARSHIPS | UNIVERSITY SCHOLARSHIPS |

NOTES

_____
_____
_____
_____
_____
_____

Community Scholarship Hunt

DIRECTIONS: Read the ideas of places to ask for scholarships. Think of one more place and write it in the bubble. Then develop a list with specific places in your community you can look for scholarships.

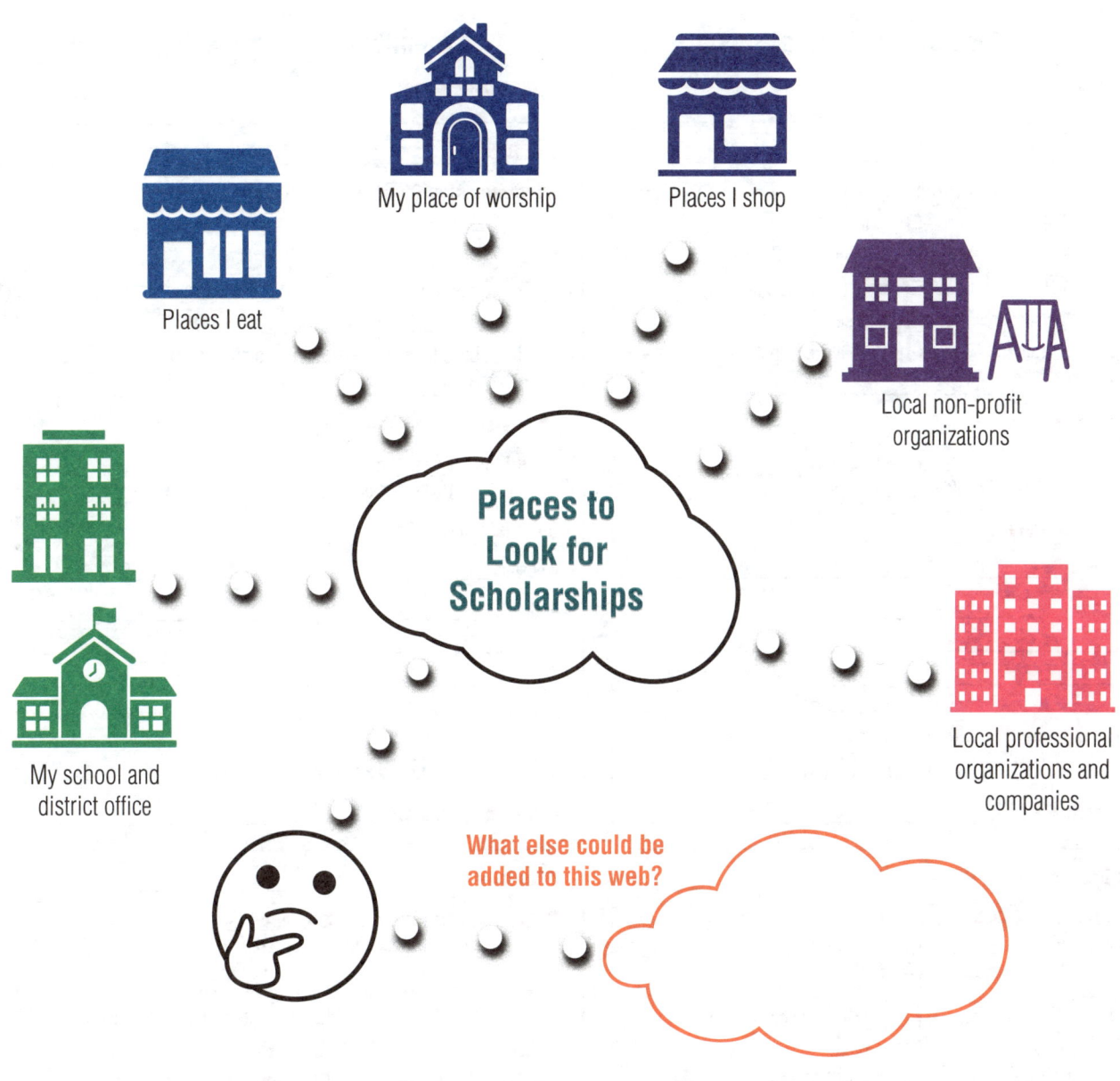

My school and district office	Places I eat	My place of worship	Places I shop	Local non-profit organizations	Local professional organizations or large companies	Other ideas I have

Extending My Learning: Scholarship Organizer

DIRECTIONS: Fill out this template for scholarships you are considering in each category. This will allow you to better understand the eligibility requirements, keep yourself organized, and prioritize the scholarship due dates.

Popular Scholarship

Scholarship Name: _____

Due Date: _____

Requirements: (Check all that apply)
- ☐ GPA
- ☐ SAT
- ☐ ACT
- ☐ Transcripts
- ☐ US Citizen
- ☐ Major Specific
- ☐ Community Service
- ☐ Letter of Recommendation
- ☐ Essay
- ☐ Ability to reapply
- ☐ Other _____

Scholarship Amount: _____

Time Line: Due to High School Counselors: _____
Due to Scholarship Committee: _____

Submission Details:
Website: _____
Address: _____

Identity Based Scholarship

Scholarship Name: _____

Due Date: _____

Requirements: (Check all that apply)
- ☐ GPA
- ☐ SAT
- ☐ ACT
- ☐ Transcripts
- ☐ US Citizen
- ☐ Major Specific
- ☐ Community Service
- ☐ Letter of Recommendation
- ☐ Essay
- ☐ Ability to reapply
- ☐ Other _____

Scholarship Amount: _____

Time Line: Due to High School Counselors: _____
Due to Scholarship Committee: _____

Submission Details:
Website: _____
Address: _____

Local/Regional Scholarship

Scholarship Name: _____

Due Date: _____

Requirements: (Check all that apply)
- ☐ GPA
- ☐ SAT
- ☐ ACT
- ☐ Transcripts
- ☐ US Citizen
- ☐ Major Specific
- ☐ Community Service
- ☐ Letter of Recommendation
- ☐ Essay
- ☐ Ability to reapply
- ☐ Other _____

Scholarship Amount: _____

Time Line: Due to High School Counselors: _____
Due to Scholarship Committee: _____

Submission Details:
Website: _____
Address: _____

University Scholarship

Scholarship Name: _____

Due Date: _____

Requirements: (Check all that apply)
- ☐ GPA
- ☐ SAT
- ☐ ACT
- ☐ Transcripts
- ☐ US Citizen
- ☐ Major Specific
- ☐ Community Service
- ☐ Letter of Recommendation
- ☐ Essay
- ☐ Ability to reapply
- ☐ Other _____

Scholarship Amount: _____

Time Line: Due to High School Counselors: _____
Due to Scholarship Committee: _____

Submission Details:
Website: _____
Address: _____

Types of Federal Loans

Loans are a type of financial aid that you will eventually pay back. Before you accept or decline loans you are offered in your financial aid package, understand the pros and cons of each type.

State Specific Loan Programs

In addition to federal loans, states also have loan programs. Programs will vary from state to state. Research your state's Department of Education by visiting their website for details about state-specific loans available at the school you plan to attend. Many states have financial aid programs available for students who are not eligible to apply for FAFSA.

How do interest rates affect my loan?

Pretend Michael chooses to take out a loan of $5,000 to cover the majority of their unmet need. Their $5,000 loan has an interest rate of 5%.

> Year 1 after graduation: $5,000 x .05 = $250
>
> Total amount Michael will repay = $5,250

Michael will only need to make a minimum payment on the loan at first. Each loan type has different standards for how repayment works. Some are 3 years and some are 10+ years.

The interest does continue to add on to the total every year though, so the sooner they can be paid off, the better.

Loan Amounts
Any loan amounts referenced are subject to change annually. Search the name of the loan online to find the most up-to-date information.

TIP
Some loans begin accruing interest from the day you receive the loan rather than after graduation.

Perkins Loan

The Perkins Loan is a federal low-interest loan. Students can receive a Perkins loan from any accredited college institution in the United States. The college, not the federal government, determines the loan amount based upon FAFSA information. Perkins loans are given to students demonstrating the greatest financial need.

Benefits of a Perkins Loan

- The interest rate is low.
- There is a 9-month grace period after graduation until you have to start paying it back.
- There are ways you can become eligible for loan cancellation (meaning you would no longer have to pay your loans back). Some include teaching, military work, working for the Peace Corps, AmeriCorps, or working in law enforcement.

www.educationopensdoors.org

Subsidized Loans

Subsidized loans do not build interest for at least the first half of one's college education.

Unsubsidized Loans

Unsubsidized loans are federally funded and not based on financial need, therefore interest begins to build on the loan as soon as the student borrower starts college.

Is Your Loan Enough?

If not, you can find additional loans through banks if your financial aid package does not cover all of your unmet need. Stay aware of interest rates.

Stafford Loan

The Stafford Loan is a federal loan. Stafford loans may be offered as either subsidized or unsubsidized loans.

Subsidized vs. Unsubsidized

A subsidized loan is the best choice for a student because of its low interest rate. These loans are based on financial need and do not build interest while you are in school for at least half of the time (which means less money you will have to pay back!). They are called **subsidized loans** because the government "subsidizes" (or pays) any interest that builds for at least the first half of your college education.

An **unsubsidized loan** is federally granted and is based on merit rather than financial need. Interest builds as soon as you begin school and the government does not pay any of it for you.

Benefits of a Stafford Loan

- **Subsidized Loan**
  - Interest rates could be as low as 5%*
  - No payments required while in school
  - No interest accrued (or built) for at least the first half of education

- **Unsubsidized Loan**
  - Can borrow larger sums of money if needed
  - Fixed interest rate of 6.6% ("fixed interest rate" – will remain constant until changed by law)
  - No payments required while in school

PLUS Loan

A PLUS loan is one borrowed by a parent on behalf of a student to help pay for tuition and other expenses. For a parent to take out a PLUS loan, the student must be enrolled in at least part time education, and the parent or guardian must go through a credit check. PLUS loans are not need-based and have a fixed interest rate.

PLUS Loan Benefits

- Fixed interest rate of 7.6%*
- Can fund up to the total cost of a student's education minus other aid received
- Have up to 10 years to repay loan

*****Note:** *Rate based upon 2019 values*

Student Loan Basics

DIRECTIONS: Complete this chart to help guide conversations about loans with your parents as well as help you understand types of loans. Research any information not included on the book pages.

	Perkins	Stafford Subsidized	Stafford Unsubsidized	State Loan Program	PLUS Loan
Interest Rate (Include fixed or variable)					
How do you qualify?					
When do you start paying the loan back?					
When do interest payments start?					
Other special information					

Financial Aid: The FAFSA

> **BIG IDEA**
> *In order to be eligible for federal financial aid, I must fill out the FAFSA; the earlier I apply, the more money I am likely to receive.*

What is the FAFSA?

To be eligible for federal financial aid, you must fill out the **Free Application for Federal Student Aid (FAFSA)** when you're applying to college AND every year you are in college. The FAFSA gives a view into your family's finances and helps determine how much financial aid a student receives. Filling out the FAFSA will automatically enable you to be eligible for many scholarships, grants, and loans.

Who gets federal financial aid?

Any student who meets eligibility requirements can receive student aid. Find out more details at **studentaid.gov/eligibility**. Below are some basic requirements:

- Family demonstrates financial need
- Student is a U.S. citizen or an eligible noncitizen (search "eligible noncitizen FAFSA")
- Student has a valid social security number
- Male students register with the selective service if you are between ages 18-25
- Student maintains satisfactory academic progress in college or career school
- Student completes admission requirements for a college or career school
    - Have a HS diploma, GED, or state-recognized equivalent, OR
    - Complete a high school education in a setting approved under state law, OR
    - Enroll in an eligible career pathways program

If you do not meet these eligibility requirements, refer to section "Resources for students not eligible for FAFSA."

What are the steps to complete FAFSA?

STEP 1

During your junior year, create your FSAID **AND** have your parents create an FSAID.

- Create your username and password at **studentaid.gov/fsaid**

Special notes for FSAID:

- Students and parents will need their own e-mail addresses that will continue to be used after high school graduation.
- If your parents are not documented citizens, they will not be eligible to get an FSAID, but instead must print and sign a form. Ask your guidance counselor for help if this pertains to you.

STEP 2

During your junior year, prepare documents and practice completing FAFSA with your parents.

Necessary Documents:

- Social security number
- Driver's license or state ID number
- Your W-2 form if you've had a job over the past year
- Your parent's tax return documents

> **Note:* Check **FAFSA.gov** *for the most up to date information on necessary documents.*

Practice the FAFSA
- Preview the form and get an idea of how much aid you're likely to receive by searching "FAFSA 4Caster" online and complete the form.

STEP 3

Decide what schools you want your FAFSA to be sent to as a part of your application *(up to 10)*.

STEP 4

On October 1st, complete and submit your FAFSA.
- With all necessary documents, go to **www.fafsa.gov** or call 1-800-4-FED-AID.
- For help, search "five-minute FAFSA" for a video with instructions on how to submit online.

STEP 5

Receive student aid report!
- After you get your student aid report, use your FSAID to log in and send your report to any additional schools needed (keep in mind you can only send it to 10 total).
- If you have had significant financial changes since your FAFSA was submitted or if you notice something is wrong, contact the financial aid office at ALL of the colleges you applied to, share the information with them, and ask for advice.

Step 6

Every year you're in school, gather updated tax documents and on October 1st use your FSAID and the IRS Data Retrieval Tool to complete your FAFSA again.

FAFSA Basics

DIRECTIONS: The FAFSA, filling it out, and keeping track of all of the information is a lot. Answer the questions below about FAFSA basics.

In your own words, what is the FAFSA?
_____
_____

Where do you access the FAFSA?
_____

Who can you ask to help you fill out the FAFSA?
_____

When should you submit FAFSA? _____

How often do you have to submit the FAFSA? _____

Verification

Verification occurs when a student's FAFSA is selected either by random selection or due to an issue with their application. It means additional information in required for acquiring financial aid.

TIP

Schools often have resources to help students complete the FAFSA. Ask your guidance counselor for help or refer to websites ending in ".gov" for additional assistance and help to complete your FAFSA.

Common FAFSA Issues

Some students' FAFSAs are flagged for verification either by random selection or due to an issue with their application.

Common issues are:

- FAFSA is incomplete
- FAFSA information is inconsistent with tax documents
  - Date of birth
  - Social security number
  - Parent's marital status on the FAFSA form does not match how they submit taxes
  - Parent who claims student on taxes is not the one who FAFSA was filed with
  - Student does not enroll as a full-time college student

If this occurs, it does not mean you cannot receive financial aid. There are steps to take to ensure you have the right information and documents. These steps will vary by individual students. The best source of information will be the financial aid office at your college or university; explain the circumstances and ask for advice.

Plan Ahead

DIRECTIONS: Based upon the common errors listed above, write a plan for how you might be able to prevent your FAFSA from being verified.

1. _____
2. _____
3. _____
4. _____
5. _____
6. _____
7. _____
8. _____
9. _____
10. _____

Unique FAFSA Situations

If any of these situations pertain to you, contact your guidance counselor at your high school to help you determine the best plan of action before you submit your FAFSA. You can also contact the financial aid office at the schools you plan to attend for guidance.

- My parents do not file their taxes as "married", they file separately.
- My parents file separately and do not live together, and I am not sure which one claims me as a dependent.
- I live with a guardian or outside of my parents' home, but my parents claim me as a dependent on their taxes.
- I live alone or with a guardian, and no one claims me as a dependent on their taxes.
- My parents live outside of the US and do not file US taxes.
- My parents have assets outside of the US and do not claim them on US taxes.
- I am unable to get my parents' tax information, and/or I do not know if I am claimed as a dependent.

> **BIG IDEA**
> *I can ask my guidance counselor, look for community resources, or refer to online resources for additional assistance in completing my financial aid applications.*

Students who do not meet federal aid eligibility requirements

Unable to Demonstrate Financial Need
- Locate scholarships that are merit based rather than needs based

Non-US Citizen/Non-Eligible Citizen
- Complete applications for state-based aid
- Apply for private scholarships and grants
- Contact the financial aid office at the school you plan to attend and ask for guidance

Selective Service Registration
- Currently in the US, males between the ages of 18 and 25 must complete the selective service registration
- Search "selective service registration" to locate the form and complete it

Enrolled in school
- In order to be eligible for aid, you must maintain a certain GPA. The requirement varies based upon the aid received.

Do not have high school diploma or GED
- In order to apply for student financial aid, you must be college-bound and in order to apply for college, students must have a high school diploma or GED.

Frequently Asked Questions about FAFSA

How Much Aid Can You Expect?
Your FAFSA is based on the tax information of the person who claims you as a dependent; this is usually your parent. Work with your family to fill it out.

Cost of Attendance (COA)
The estimated cost of a full-time student completing one full year of college.

How does the government determine my financial aid?

The government uses a basic equation to determine student need. This equation is:

Cost of Attendance – Expected Family Contribution = Financial Need

Any aid that does not cover your financial need is called "unmet need."

What does Expected Family Contribution (EFC) on the FAFSA mean?

This is an extremely important part of the FAFSA. It is the government's way of determining your financial need based on the amount of money that your family could contribute to your college education. Basically, the less your EFC, the more aid you can expect to receive. Many factors go into calculating your EFC – family size, current earnings, number of family members in college, and family savings.

I'm a U.S. citizen but I don't have a social security number. What do I do?

Go to a social security administration office in your city, and visit **http://www.ssa.gov.** Use this as a resource for detailed application steps as well as a list of required documents.

If my parents are divorced or don't live together, whose information do I report?

Think about the last 12 months. Which parent have you lived with more? Which parent claims you as a dependent on their taxes? That is the parent that you should provide information for. If you split the time pretty equally, list the one who provided you with more financial support in the last year.

What if I have a major life change after filing my FAFSA (parent lost job, passed away, etc.)?

You need to contact the Federal Student Aid Office and update your FAFSA through filing an appeal. If you've already received your financial aid reward packages, you should contact the financial aid offices at the colleges in which you were accepted.

Do I have to fill out the FAFSA online?

You may complete the application online or you may print it out and mail it.

What happens after I fill out the FAFSA?

The Student Aid Report (SAR)

After you have filed your FAFSA, the government will send a **Student Aid Report (SAR)** to you and the colleges you filed on your application. After you have been accepted to a few colleges, they will send a financial aid package based on your EFC from the SAR. You should apply to multiple schools in order to determine the best financial aid package for you. Wait until you receive all of your financial aid packages before accepting any, yet make sure that you accept your offers before their deadlines pass. Remember, finding money for college can be difficult – but it's not impossible!

> **Student Aid Report (SAR)**
> *If you would like to send your SAR to a school that wasn't listed on your FAFSA, do so immediately so that you don't miss opportunities or deadlines!*

Can I lose my financial aid package?

Yes, you can lose your financial aid package, but you would know about it in advance and have an opportunity to fix the issue(s). Some reasons you can lose your financial aid package are: changing from a full-time to a part-time student, leaving or being expelled from your campus, deciding not to attend the school, or your GPA falling below an acceptable standard (deemed by the provider). A federal aid accountability system called **Satisfactory Academic Progress (SAP)** states that students receiving financial aid under federally supported programs must follow certain standards to continue receiving aid. These standards include holding a certain GPA and completing a minimum number of credit hours per semester.

> **Full-Time Enrollment/ Part-Time Enrollment**
> *A full-time student is enrolled in 12 or more credit hours in a semester. A part-time student is enrolled in less than 12 credit hours in a semester.*

Will my financial aid package always cover all of my tuition and expenses?

Some financial aid packages will not cover all of your financial needs. If this is the case, you will have to pay for any "unmet need" on your own (in addition to your family contribution).

Are there other options than the FAFSA to get financial aid?

Yes, search for aid from your state, the university you are applying to, your county, and your school district in high school.

What is the College Scholarship Service (CSS) Profile?

The **College Scholarship Service (CSS) Profile** is another application students may fill out to receive nonfederal student aid. Over 500 colleges, universities and scholarship programs in the United States use the information on the CSS Profile to determine student aid packages. Once you register for the CSS Profile online, you will be sent a personalized application based on your needs and financial situation. Fill out this application as soon as you know where you will attend college.

Unlike the FAFSA, the CSS is not a free application – it costs $25 for the application and initial school report and $16 for every scholarship or college program you wish to attend. Fee waivers are available! So why use the profile? Some colleges require the FAFSA and the CSS. On the other hand, in many cases, the CSS is not necessary to fill out. Therefore, you need to research colleges you are thinking about applying to and see whether they need one, or both.

> **CSSP**
> *The College Scholarship Service Profile is another application students may fill out to receive nonfederal student aid.*

Comparing Financial Aid Packages

BIG IDEA
Financial aid packages include grants, scholarships, loans, and work-study; all of which I can accept or decline.

Financial aid factors to remember:

- You do not have to take all of the financial aid offered.
- Scholarships and Grants are FREE money.
- There are options to pay for unmet need:
  - Seek more scholarships from local/regional sources as well as identity-based groups and popular national scholarships
  - Although loans need to be repaid, some have very low interest rates and are worth the investment in your education.
  - Wait, work, and save.

Selecting Financial Aid

DIRECTIONS: This section has 3 sample financial aid letters. Read items available in this student's financial aid package. Look back at the financial aid content in this unit to locate specifics about each type of financial aid. Choose whether you accept or decline each offer by circling your choice (Accept | Decline). Then write in how much you plan to accept of each type of aid.

Achievement Community College

Total Cost of Attendance for Year 1 = *$3,000
*Includes tuition and student fees, no housing or food costs are included

Financial Aid Award Package

Achievement County **Scholarship**	$1,500	Accept	Decline	Total accepted: $_____
Federal Subsidized Stafford **Loan**	$1,500	Accept	Decline	Total accepted: $_____

Total Aid Accepted: $_____

$3,000 Total Cost of Attendance for Year 1
− $_____ Total Aid Accepted for Year 1
_____
$_____ Unmet Need

If you chose not to accept the loan, what other options can you pursue to avoid collecting student debt?

_____

240 © 2019 Education Opens Doors, Inc.

Roadmap Private University
Total Cost of Attendance for Year 1 = *$45,000
*Includes tuition, housing, meal plan, and student fees
Financial Aid Award Package

Roadmap University **Scholarship**	$24,000	Accept | Decline	Total accepted: $_____
College of Health Science **Grant**	$2,000	Accept | Decline	Total accepted: $_____
Federal Pell **Grant**	$8,500	Accept | Decline	Total accepted: $_____
Federal SEO **Grant**	$2,000	Accept | Decline	Total accepted: $_____
Federal Perkins **Loan**	$5,500	Accept | Decline	Total accepted: $_____
Federal Subsidized Stafford **Loan**	$5,000	Accept | Decline	Total accepted: $_____
Parent PLUS **Loan**	$20,000	Accept | Decline	Total accepted: $_____
Federal **Work Study**	up to $2,000	Accept | Decline	Total accepted: $_____

Total Aid Accepted: $ _____

$45,000   Total Cost of Attendance for Year 1

− $ _____   Total Aid Accepted for Year 1

$ _____   Unmet Need

Why is the total award package higher than the total cost of attendance? What factors could the university be considering as additional costs for attendance?

_____
_____
_____

Work study is something students earn by having a job on campus. If you make $15 per hour in your work study position, how many hours would you have to work in order to earn $2,000?

_____
_____
_____

Unit 5: My Finances

Success Public University

Total Cost of Attendance for Year 1 = *$20,000
*Includes tuition, housing, meal plan, and student fees

Financial Aid Award Package

Success University **Scholarship**	$3,000	Accept | Decline	Total accepted: $_____
Federal SEO **Grant**	$1,000	Accept | Decline	Total accepted: $_____
Federal Pell **Grant**	$5,000	Accept | Decline	Total accepted: $_____
State **Grant**	$2,000	Accept | Decline	Total accepted: $_____
Federal Subsidized Stafford **Loan**	$5,000	Accept | Decline	Total accepted: $_____
Federal **Work Study**	up to $2,000	Accept | Decline	Total accepted: $_____

Total Aid Accepted: $_____

$20,000 Total Cost of Attendance for Year 1

− $_____ Total Aid Accepted for Year 1

$_____ Unmet Need

What are ways you could cover the unmet need?
_____
_____

All of your meals and housing are included in this cost; does that factor into your decision? Do you think it would it cost more or less for you to live and eat somewhere off campus?
_____
_____

Life in college has financial needs not listed like clothing, enjoying a dinner off campus with friends, social activities, transportation to and from home to visit family, etc. What could it look like for you and your family to cover those costs in addition to the unmet need?
_____
_____
_____

Weigh My Decision

DIRECTIONS: Now that you've had a chance to look at each financial aid offer in depth, it's time to weigh the pros (positives) and the cons (negatives) of each of the three options offered. Remember, there is no one right choice for everyone. Where you will be happiest and find the most success in college is truly up to you! Use the questions below to help you weigh your decision. Keep in mind, these financial aid packages only cover 1 of 4 years in college.

Achievement Community College		Roadmap Private University		Success Public University	
Cost of Attendance		Cost of Attendance		Cost of Attendance	
Amount of Aid in Loans		Amount of Aid in Loans		Amount of Aid in Loans	
Unmet Need		Unmet Need		Unmet Need	
Pros	Cons	Pros	Cons	Pros	Cons

Questions to Consider as You Make Your Choice

Which financial aid package offers the most grants/scholarships? Is it enough to completely cover your cost of attendance?

_____

Which financial aid package offers more loans? If you need to accept loans, which loans have the best interest rates and repayment terms?

_____

_____

Consider the type of college connected to the financial award. Does it align with your goals to choose that type of school? Why/Why not?

_____

_____

My Choice Is: _____!

Unit 5: My Finances

Extending My Learning: Financial Aid

DIRECTIONS:

STEP 1: Read and complete activities on Grants and Loans to learn more about federal financial aid.

STEP 2: Search "Practice FAFSA" and locate the FAFSA-4-Caster link.

STEP 3: Complete the FAFSA practice form with your family. Write questions you or your family has below.

STEP 4: Ask your guidance counselor or someone you trust who knows a lot about financial aid to help you and your family answer those questions.

Question	Answer

Financial Literacy

BIG IDEA
It is never too early to begin saving money and establish strong financial habits.

If someone has literacy on a topic, that means they have knowledge and understanding on the topic. Do you feel you have literacy on finances? In other words, do you have knowledge and understanding of how to manage money?

What is 1 question you have about managing money?
_____
_____

This section of the book will cover budgeting, saving and spending habits, bank/credit union accounts, credit cards/debit cards, and investing. Knowing how each of these works can give you confidence in the decisions you make about your money as you continue into adulthood. Gathering information about money management is a practice that continues throughout life as income, expenses, and opportunities change.

Is It Affordable?
How can you tell if you can afford something? If the purchase requires you to spend more money than you have in your account, it may not be affordable at the present time.

Saving and Spending Habits: Self Evaluation

DIRECTIONS: You won $60 in an art contest! Answer the following questions to get a general idea of your saving and spending habits.

How do you feel most comfortable using your $60 prize? Circle your choice.

1. Spend all ($60).
2. Save half ($30) and spend half ($30).
3. Save one quarter ($15) and spend three quarters ($45).
4. Save all ($60).

Pretend you chose either option 2 or 3. What would you do with the money? Circle your choice.

1. Keep it in your wallet or piggy bank.
2. Keep it in a bank account or credit union account.
3. Let your 5-year-old sibling hold it for you.

List 1 advantage you can think of for each option.

1. _____
   _____

2. _____
   _____

3. _____
   _____

Unit 5: My Finances

www.educationopensdoors.org

Establishing Financial Goals

What is something you look forward to purchasing in your life?
_____

What is the estimated cost of that thing? _____

How long do you think it would take to save enough money to purchase that thing?
_____

> **TIP**
> *In the long run, small differences in spending and saving make a BIG impact!*

A Little Bit Goes a Long Way

DIRECTIONS: Calculate the possible outcomes of the following scenario. You work a part-time job after school and make $400 each month. You hold this job all through high school and college – a total of 8 years (96 months). At the end of those 8 years,…

How much money would you have if you SAVED ALL of it?	At the end of 8 years, what could you purchase with this amount of money?
$400 (each month) **x 96 months =** $_____	

How much money would you have if you SPENT HALF AND SAVED HALF?	At the end of 8 years, what could you purchase with this amount of money?
$_____ (each month) **x 96 months =** $_____	

How much money would you have if you SAVED $100 each month?	At the end of 8 years, what could you purchase with this amount of money?
$_____ (each month) **x 96 months =** $_____	

Assuming you had a job paying $400 per month, would one of these three options enable you to be able to purchase the thing you wrote above?
_____

Establishing a Budget Based Upon Financial Goals

Making a **budget** means you determine how much of your income you want/need to allocate for specific things. Because income changes over time, developing a budget based upon percentages is helpful.

For example, if you are saving for a big purchase, you can increase your percentage of savings and decrease your "wants" allocation. That would mean you spend less on small purchases, but are able to make a big purchase later instead.

Evaluating Spending Habits

DIRECTIONS: Read the scenario below and answer the following questions.

To make $400 per month ($100 per week), pretend you earn $10 an hour working 10 hours per week. You and your friends like to go see a movie every Friday, and you always like to purchase a snack. The movie costs $12 and your snack costs $4.

How much does that cost you per week? _____

Does this fit within your weekly budget for "wants?" _____

Based upon your financial goals, which of the following would help you achieve your goals?
1. Go to the movies every Friday, but don't purchase a snack.
2. Go to the movies one Friday a month and get a snack.
3. Locate a cheaper option to have fun with your friends.

Saving Within Your Budget

Here is a list of some helpful tips to get you started!

1. Set Goals
If you really want something, set a goal to buy it and save a little bit each month until you can afford it. Don't buy something you cannot afford!

2. Separate Your Savings
Wherever you keep your money (we recommend a bank or credit union), divide your money into two separate accounts labeled "Spending" and "Saving." Many banks and credit unions will already do this for you if you ask for a second account.

3. Save First
Whenever you get money, first put some of it into your savings account, according to your goals.

How to Build a Budget

BIG IDEA
An FDIC bank or credit union is the safest location to keep money because it is always secure and available to me anytime.

Deposit
A deposit is money placed in a bank account, usually to gain interest.

STEP 1: Calculate how much money you make each month (income).

STEP 2: Calculate your expenses for each month.

STEP 3: Based upon your financial goals, determine what percentage of your money is available to allocate to costs outside of "necessities".

STEP 4: Calculate your budget allocations based on percentages of your income.

A common budget breakdown is as follows:

Percentage	Allocations	$ based on $400 per month
50%	**Necessities** (place to live, food to eat, utilities)	$50/week
20% - 25%	**Wants** (food outside of necessities, travel, fun activities, extra purchases)	$20-$25/week
20%	**Saving**	$20/week
5% - 10%	**Giving to others**	$5-$10/week

Based on your financial goals and desired lifestyle, what percentage budget allocations do you want to create?

Percentage	Allocations	$ based on $400 per month
_____%	Necessities	$_____/week
_____%	Wants	$_____/week
_____%	Saving	$_____/week
_____%	Giving to others	$_____/week

Spending within Your Budget

What do you usually spend money on? List expenses.

_____
_____
_____

What do you choose to save money for? List expenses.

_____
_____
_____

Tools for Money Management

Bank and Credit Union Accounts

Banks and credit unions are safe places to keep your savings and spending accounts. FDIC member banks have security systems and your money is insured by the U.S. government. You can access your money easily from an ATM or by using the cash back feature when making a purchase with a debit card.

Some banks require a minimum deposit to open your first savings account. Search "checking accounts for teens" for details about multiple account types.

Credit unions are an excellent alternative to a traditional bank. As an independent (owned by the members) non-for profit cooperative, their fees tend to be lower, customer base is smaller, and have better customer service. However, due to their size, they may not carry the same conveniences as a bank. Be sure to check the National Credit Union Administration website for local and reliable options.

> **Banking Fees**
> *Sometimes banks will try to charge you a fee for setting up an account. Check multiple options before paying any fees.*

Credit Cards

Credit cards are not linked to the amount of money in your bank account, so it is possible to spend more money than you have available. When you apply for a credit card (you must be 18 years old), you are given a credit limit. That means you can use your credit card to buy anything you like until you reach the credit limit. At the end of the month, you must pay the credit card company for all purchases you made. If you do not pay the entire bill, you are charged interest on top of what you already paid for the item.

For example, pretend you bought a new backpack and it cost $40. You paid for it with your credit card. When the credit card bill came, you could only pay $10. If your card had an interest rate of 20%, you will now owe an additional $36 rather than $30. Interest is charged every month until you pay it all.

Debit Cards

Debit cards work like cash. They are linked to your bank account and you can never spend more money than is available in your account. You can get cash from an ATM with them as well as get cash back when making other purchases.

Reflection

DIRECTIONS: Write a reflection on each of the following questions.

What are some steps you can take today to begin saving for your education after high school?

_____

What is 1 spending habit you would change as a result of the information you learned in this lesson?

_____

Unit 5: My Finances

Extending My Learning: Stay on Track with a Transactions Log

DIRECTIONS: Log your monthly income and expenses using the charts below.

*****Note:** Search "monthly budget tracker" online to locate an interactive version that you can update regularly and with some you can enter your financial goals and it will calculate the percentages for you.*

INCOME

CATEGORIES: paycheck, bonus, gift, other

Date	Category	Amount	Description of Income

EXPENSES

CATEGORIES: home, food, gifts, health, transportation, personal, pets, utilities, travel, other

Date	Category	Amount	Description of Expense

Making Your Money Work for You

Which would you rather receive? Circle one of the following:

| Get $1,000.00 a day for 30 days. | or | Get one penny and double your total every day for 30 days. |

BIG IDEA

Compounding interest from a bank adds money to your savings account to increase its value over time.

Justify your answer.

_____
_____

In this scenario, if you chose to receive $1,000 a day for 30 days, in the end you would have a total of $30,000. If you chose to start with 1 penny and double your total each day, you would end up with $5,368,709.12 at the end of 30 days.

How is this possible? Compounding interest.

Compounding Interest

In that example, the account is gaining 100% interest every day. Although the idea of compounding interest is real, an account growing at that rate is not realistic. In real life, investments usually earn interest ranging from less than 1% (savings accounts) to over 20% in unique and sometimes risky investments.

The Power of Compounding Interest

Another great reason to save your money in a bank is because in a savings or investment account, they pay you for every single dollar you keep with them. Seems crazy, right? But it's true.

Banks pay YOU money – called **interest** – on your savings account. The money you put in your savings account is called a **deposit**. For example, if you deposited $100 in the bank at a 1% interest rate and your money stayed in the bank for the entire year untouched, you would have $101. That's right, that $1 is free money!

Even better, banks today pay interest on the total amount in your account, including any interest you've already earned! This is called **compound interest**. This means next year, your bank will be calculating the 1% based on the $101 that is already in there.

Compounding interest works over time. Just as a penny did not seem like much at the beginning, neither does this one extra dollar.

Bonds and CDs

If you want to start long term (can't access money right away) savings to get a higher interest rate, a common option is investing in a Savings Bond or Certificate of Deposit (CD). Search online and check with your bank for more information.

Great Resource!

There are many great resources online to help you learn more about ways to put your money to work for you. Search "investing for minors" to learn what's possible before turning 18.

Unit 5: My Finances

Regular vs. Compound Interest

DIRECTIONS: The table below helps to explain the banking tips on the previous pages. It shows the difference in the growth of your money over time depending on whether you have a bank account with a regular interest rate or a compound interest rate. To help express this point, take some time to review this first example and answer the questions below.

*****Note:** *Interest rates of 5% would likely be investment accounts, not savings accounts.*

Interest Rate of 5%	Amount Deposited	Years in the Bank				
		1	2	5	15	25
Regular Interest	$100.00	$105.00	$110.00	$125.00	$175.00	$225.00
Compound Interest	$100.00	$105.00	$110.25	$127.63	$207.89	$338.64

Compound Interest (Banking Setting)

Earned interest on the total amount of money in the account, including past interest earned.

Interest (Banking Setting)

A deposit into your account from the bank based upon the amount of money you have deposited into the account.

Based on the table, what type of interest rate should you choose for your bank account? Circle your answer.

> Regular Interest   or   Compound Interest

After 25 years, how much more money would the bank account with compound interest make compared to the bank account with regular interest?

_____

_____

In two sentences, describe what happens to your money the longer it stays in the bank regardless of whether you have a regular interest or compound interest account?

_____

_____

_____

Are you ready to start saving?

> Yes   or   No

Saving $100 with Compound Interest

DIRECTIONS: It's clear that compound interest is even more powerful at growing your money than regular interest, but how much does the amount of money you invest matter? The table below shows the difference in the growth of two bank accounts at the same compound interest rate of 5 percent. The difference this time is that one smart saver has chosen to deposit money each year, instead of just one time. Review the table and then answer questions 1 and 2 below.

Compound Interest of 5% for Both	Amount Deposited	Years in the Bank				
		1	2	5	15	25
$100 Once	$100.00	$105.00	$110.25	$127.63	$207.89	$338.64
$100 Each Year	$100.00	$105.00	$215.25	$580.19	$2,265.75	$5,011.35

Does saving a little bit each year make a difference? Circle your answer.

Yes or No

After 25 years, how much more money would you make if you deposited $100 into your account each year vs. $100 just once?

_____

_____

savings account with no compound interest

savings account with compound interest

Investing with Compound Interest

What do you already know about investments?	What do you WANT to know about investments?

Do you know anyone who invests their money?
_____

Do you know of some ways people invest?
_____
_____

In order for compounding interesting to work, investments must stay untouched in the account for a long time. If you cannot access the money for a long time, why would you choose to invest?
_____
_____

What Is Investing?

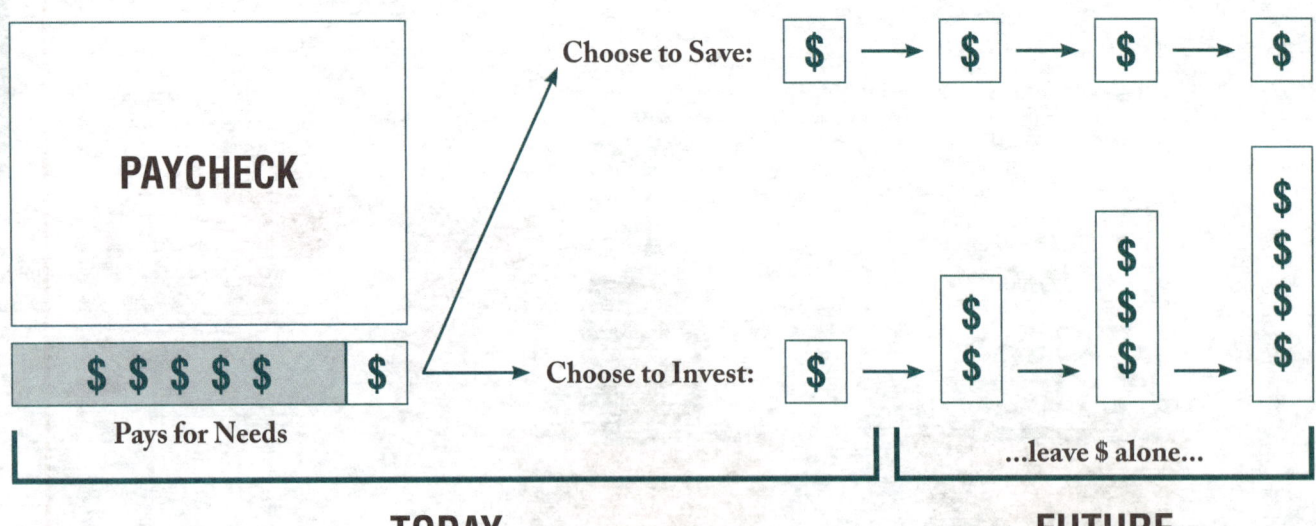

When in life does it benefit you the most to start investing?
_____
_____

Understanding How to Invest

If you are considering investing your money, the first step is to find someone you trust to help you understand how it works. Ask financial professionals at a bank and ask grown-ups if they know much about investments and if they would be willing to help you understand. Also search "understanding investments" online for several books, videos, and tutorials on how investments work. Keep in mind, investments can be risky. The risk in investing is knowing that just as easily as money is gained, it can be lost.

What are the most common types of investments?

Although there are many more investments, two common ones are stocks (like the stock market) and mutual funds.

Stocks are money raised by a business through sharing partial ownership of the company with the stock purchaser. When a company is publicly traded like this, when the company does well, everyone with purchased stock will earn money. When the company does not do well, everyone who purchased stock in the company will lose money.

Mutual Funds are similar to stocks but raise money to invest in many different kinds of businesses rather than just one. By investing in a mutual fund, you are purchasing stock of several different companies at once. Your money is diversified. Meaning, if one company does well, everyone gets a very small percentage gain, but if all of the companies do well then everyone gets a larger gain. The gains can also cover the potential losses. However, there is still risk involved because gains may not always cover losses.

What did you learn about investments in this lesson?

_____
_____
_____
_____
_____
_____
_____
_____

> **BIG IDEA**
> *I have options for saving and investing my money.*

> **TIP**
> *In addition to stocks and mutual funds, additional investment types are: Bonds, CDs, Hedge Funds, Index Funds, Private Equity, Real Estate, Retirement Accounts, and Savings Accounts. Search these key words online to learn more information.*

Extending My Learning: Double a Penny for 30 Days

DIRECTIONS: Calculate how much money you would earn each day if you doubled the value each day starting with a penny.

Day	Double Your Money	Total at the End of the Day
Day 1	$0.01	$0.01
Day 2	$0.01 x 2	$0.02
Day 3	$0.02 x 2	$0.04
Day 4		
Day 5		
Day 6		
Day 7		
Day 8		
Day 9		
Day 10		
Day 11		
Day 12		
Day 13		
Day 14		
Day 15		
Day 16		
Day 17		
Day 18		
Day 19		
Day 20		
Day 21		
Day 22		
Day 23		
Day 24		
Day 25		
Day 26		
Day 27		
Day 28		
Day 29		
Day 30		

Notes

Unit 5 Summary: Understanding My Finances After High School

Continuing your education after high school can be very expensive, but there are many different options available to help finance your education. Scholarships and grants are money which you do not have to pay back, so apply for them as you are able to. Start a savings account as early as possible.

Checklist Check-In

1. Consider where you are in your educational journey. Check the corresponding box below.
   - ☐ 6th Grade
   - ☐ 7th Grade
   - ☐ 8th Grade
   - ☐ 9th Grade
   - ☐ 10th Grade
   - ☐ 11th Grade
   - ☐ 12th Grade
   - ☐ High School Graduate
   - ☐ GED Recipient

2. Turn to the "Grade Level Checklist" at the beginning of Unit 1. Locate your current grade level. **Review what you checked off at the beginning of the program and check off any other activities you have completed.**

Unit Review Opportunities

1. Go back to the "Extend Your Learning" pages in this unit. Research, ask questions, and locate resources to complete those activities.
2. Complete any remaining vocabulary tasks for this unit's vocabulary and use each word in a sentence this week.
3. Answer the questions on the unit cover page, and complete the directions in the white box.

Moving Forward…

Select one of the colors from the triangle to describe how you feel about new understandings gained from this unit. Justify your answer in at least 3 sentences.

_____
_____
_____
_____
_____
_____

UNIT 6
COMPLETING MY APPLICATIONS

What are the steps for applying to college?

DIRECTIONS: Read the topics of this unit. Draw a picture of your emotions about this content.

- Unit 6 Vocabulary — page 260
- College Rankings and Selectivity — page 261
- Types of College Admission — page 264
- Choosing A School — page 267
- My Top College Research — page 272
- The College Application Process — page 273
- About the SAT and the ACT — page 276
- Application Essay — page 281
- Application Tracker — page 290
- Practice College Application — page 291
- Unit 6 Summary — page 296

Whose help do I need in the application process?

Do I need to take the SAT and ACT?

Unit 6 Vocabulary

DIRECTIONS:

1. DEFINE each word using the glossary in this book or a dictionary.
2. ANSWER the questions listed below for each word.

Vocabulary Word	Definition	Have you ever heard/seen this word before?	Explain how you have heard this word used before. If you've never heard or seen it, what other word (in any language) does it look like to you?
Early Admission		Y N	
Early Decision		Y N	
Binding Application		Y N	
Early Action		Y N	
Regular Admission		Y N	
Rolling Admission		Y N	
Candidates Reply Date Agreement		Y N	
Transcript		Y N	
SAT/ACT		Y N	
Admission Committee		Y N	
		Y N	

College Rankings and Selectivity

College Rankings

In the same way that seniors graduating from high school are given a class rank, colleges and universities are ranked on factors ranging from cost to academic quality. Rankings can play a role in your decision about where to go to college; future employers sometimes would rather hire graduates of a top ranked college than a graduate of a low ranked college. One of the most commonly used list of rankings is U.S. News & World Report.

Sometimes even if a university may not be ranked highly, a particular program or college at that university can be very highly ranked in the field. E.g. University of Wisconsin, Madison: overall rank #44; teaching program ranked #3.

> **BIG IDEA**
> *Schools range in their selectivity: highly selective, selective, moderately selective, and open enrollment.*

> **TIP**
> *When choosing your college, compare academic ranking!*
> *http://colleges.usnews.rankingsandreviews.com/best-colleges*

College Selectivity

Before choosing which schools to apply to, consider their selectivity to estimate your chances of acceptance. Here, we use acceptance rates to determine the selectivity. Acceptance rates are determined by comparing the number of students who applied to the number of students who were accepted in a given year. Schools fluctuate in their selectivity year to year. For the most up to date information search "acceptance rate of _____ university". The four categories used here are: highly selective, selective, moderately selective, and open.

School Type	Highly Selective	Selective	Moderately Selective	Open
Representative Enrollment Community	<17%	<50%	50-75%	75%
Private School Examples	• Harvard • Yale • Princeton • Brown • Dartmouth • Columbia • University of Pennsylvania • Cornell • Juilliard • Stanford • Duke • Vanderbilt • Northwestern	• Wake Forest • University of Southern Califormia • Boston University • TCU • Tulane	• Samford • Clemson University • Baylor University	
Public School Examples	• University of California - Berkeley	• University of Virginia • University of North Carolina - Chapel Hill • University of Texas - Austin	• Oklahoma University • University of Arkansas • Michigan State University	• Community Colleges • Online Schools • Grossmont College (CA) • El Centro College (TX) • Bunker Hill Community College (MA)

Unit 6: My Applications

BIG IDEA
There are no schools that accept every applicant; all schools consider many factors when determining admission.

Are You a Match?
The perfect school is the one that is the right fit for you! Spend time to compare GPA, class rank, test scores, programs available, and the values of the school to find the best school for you.

Visit School Websites
Generally, colleges post their expectations for prospective students on their school website. Take advantage of this information.

Highly Selective

The acceptance rate of highly selective schools is less than 17%. These schools are often very highly ranked and are the most difficult to gain acceptance to. Accepted applicants tend to have high grades and test scores, are in the top 10% of their class, have leadership and unique experiences, strong recommendation letters as well as application essays, and are highly involved in their community.

Selective

The acceptance rate of selective schools is less than 50%. These schools are well ranked as well. Each school varies in who it accepts. Check their websites for a list of admission requirements. Accepted applicants tend to be highly involved in their community, have a GPA above 3.2 with good test scores, have strong recommendation letters, and leadership and unique experiences.

Moderately Selective

The acceptance rate of moderately selective schools is between 50% and 75%. The majority of colleges in the US fall into this category. These schools tend to have a lot of applicants every year. Accepted applicants generally have a GPA above 3.0, good test scores, some community involvement, leadership or unique experiences, and strong recommendation letters.

Open

The acceptance rate of open enrollment schools is above 75%. These schools are often actively seeking students to apply. This model is becoming more popular because as online coursework continues to become more accessible, schools can grant admission to a larger number of students. Accepted applicants have met high school graduation requirements, have strong recommendation letters, and are involved in their community.

College Selectivity Debrief

DIRECTIONS: Fill out the chart below with facts that you have learned about colleges and their relative levels of selectiveness. Once finished, use the information from the table to answer the questions below.

> **Applying Early Helps!**
> *Applying early does significantly increase your chances of getting accepted to the university of your choice.*

College Selectiveness	
Highly Selective Fact 1: Fact 2: Example School:	**Selective** Fact 1: Fact 2: Example School:
Moderately Selective Fact 1: Fact 2: Example School:	**Open Admission** Fact 1: Fact 2: Example School:

What type of college is the most difficult to get into?

- A. Selective
- B. Open Admission
- C. Highly Selective
- D. Moderately Selective

Put an X on the factors that a college would NOT consider.

- ○ Grades
- ○ Hometown
- ○ Clubs/Organizations
- ○ Friends
- ○ Test Scores
- ○ Age

What is one reason that a student would attend a college that is highly ranked in academics?

_____
_____
_____

Unit 6: My Applications

Types of College Admission

BIG IDEA
Applying early can increase my chances of admission.

Binding Application
A binding application binds the student to that particular college or university that they are applying to. This means that if they are accepted to that college or university that they applied to, they must attend the following semester.

Priority Deadline
Regardless of the admission you choose, do not miss the Priority Deadline. The priority deadline is the date by which your application (for admission, student housing or financial aid) must be received.

There are three types of **admission** you can apply for as a student: early, regular and rolling. In many cases colleges offer more than one. For example, a college may offer early admission if you apply by a certain date, but still offer regular admission past that date. However, the different types of admission influence your chances of getting admitted, so you should investigate which types of admission the colleges you would like to apply to offer. Once you know this, pick the one that is going to maximize your chance of getting in. Most importantly, familiarize yourself with the deadlines for application and financial aid requests at each of your potential colleges or universities.

Early Admission

Some schools offer **early admission**. Students apply earlier in the year. Applicants choose to do this because generally you have a better chance of being admitted since the university knows you are sincerely interested in attending. There are two types of Early Admission.

Early Decision (ED) programs are commonly binding. **Binding** means that the applicant must attend the school if their application is accepted. Early decision applicants are expected to submit only one early decision application to one school.
Note: *You may not receive your Financial Aid Package until after the application deadline.*

Early Action (EA) programs are non-binding. Students get an early response to their application but do not have to make a decision immediately. This allows students the opportunity to consider other colleges and compare financial aid packages.

Although a school can decide to move your file from the early admission consideration to a later deadline consideration, you can only apply once.

Regular Admission

Regular admission is the type of admission that is most advertised. There is a set deadline by which an applicant has to submit their application. After this, all of the college's admission decisions are sent out around the same time. You can apply for regular admission to as many schools as you want and, once you receive your offers of admission, you can pick whichever school you would like to go to.

Rolling Admission

Rolling admission means that a college will assign a large window (up to six months) during which applicants can submit an application at any time until the college has filled all of its freshman class.

What's the Difference?

Plan Ahead
Don't miss the priority deadline for the college of your choice!

DIRECTIONS: Go back through the text one more time and pull out what makes these admission processes unique. Record 1 or 2 ideas in each box of the chart below.

Early Decision	Early Action

Regular Admission	Rolling Admission

College Admission Debrief

Ask Yourself
Is there a school you feel strongly enough about that you would apply using one of the types of Early Admission?

DIRECTIONS: Fill in the blank with the phrase you think makes sense.

If you want the highest chance of getting accepted to a highly selective university, you should choose _____ (**early** or **regular**) **admission.**

I should apply early to _____ (**all** or **only my top choices**)**.**

I should apply to _____ (**one** or **several**) **schools.**

I should _____ (**wait** or **start early**) **on college applications.**

Unit 6: My Applications

www.educationopensdoors.org

Extending My Learning: Organizing Schools by Selectivity

DIRECTIONS: Write down your Top 10 List of schools. Research their "acceptance rate" and place them into the column representing their selectivity

My Top 10 List of Schools	Public or Private?

School Type	Highly Selective	Selective	Moderately Selective	Open
Representative Enrollment Community	<17%	<50%	50-75%	75%
Private Schools				
Public Schools				

Choosing a School

My Top 10

DIRECTIONS: Flip back to the "Options After High School" section of the book in Unit 4 to review the various types of schools. Based upon schools you have heard about before or have researched since then, create a list of your top 10 schools to learn more about as we progress through this unit. You can change your Top 10 in the future! This is a starting point.

If you cannot think of 10 schools now, there is a list of several schools shown by selectivity in the previous section.

My Top 10 List of Schools	Public or Private?

TIP

It is important to consider personal fit when choosing a college, including majors offered, selectivity, location, size, and cost.

College Selection

You can only apply to a limited number of schools. There are thousands of options inside the United States and even more available with international options. Finding a good match is important. The best way to find your match is through self-evaluation of what you want and to research schools that cater to your desired outcomes. Every school is different and every student is different – it's your responsibility to find your path!

One helpful tool to learn about various schools is The College Board. Search "the college board, college search" to find statistics colleges have posted about their most recent class of applicants. Schools post average test scores, GPAs, costs of attendance, average financial assistance given, and much more.

Prioritizing College Characteristics

TIP
Remember to talk to your guidance counselor to gather more information.

DIRECTIONS: Based on your own feelings about each characteristic, place a checkmark under "Not Very Important," "Somewhat Important," or "Very Important." When you are done, look at the characteristics you marked as "Very Important." These will help you narrow down the most important factors to you in choosing a college or university.

College Characteristic	Importance Rating		
	Not Very Important	Somewhat Important	Very Important
1. Variety of majors offered			
2. Selectivity			
3. Distance from home			
4. Size of the student body			
5. Cost of attending			
6. Guidance and personal attention to students, especially first generation college students			
7. Extracurricular activities			
8. Sports programs			
9. Diverse student body			
10. Job and graduate school placement			
11. Values of the school align with mine			
12. Campus housing and food options			

School Categories

College applications take time, money, and hard work. Since it's not feasible to apply everywhere, breaking down your Top 10 into categories based upon their selectivity will help you focus on which ones to apply to first.

The three categories are: Foundation Schools, Target Schools, and Reach Schools.

- **Foundation schools** are ones that you have a very good chance of being admitted to.
- **Target schools** are ones that you have a good chance of being admitted to, but aren't sure.
- **Reach schools** are ones that you will have a difficult time being admitted to, but are excited to pursue the opportunity and try!

> **BIG IDEA**
>
> *Categorizing my Top 10 List as foundation schools, target schools, and reach schools will help me determine my top choice and best fit for me.*

Organizing Schools by Category

DIRECTIONS: Using your Top 10 List, what you have learned about selectivity, and your current GPA, complete the chart below.

Selectivity Codes:

HS = HIGHLY SELECTIVE (less than 17% acceptance)
S = SELECTIVE (less than 50% acceptance)
MS = MODERATELY SELECTIVE (between 50% and 75% acceptance)
O = OPEN (more than 75% acceptance)

My Top 10 List of Schools	Selectivity	Foundation | Target | Reach

At Education Opens Doors, we recommend you apply to at least 8 schools. Of those 8 schools, 4 should be target schools, 2 should be foundation schools, and 2 should be reach schools.

Unit 6: My Applications

> **Family Visit**
>
> *Involve your family in the college visit process by making a trip out of it or visiting colleges in cities you live in/near or travel to.*

Visiting Schools

Visiting schools is the best way to get an overall feeling about the school alongside the rankings, majors and extracurricular activities available. Call the admissions office to arrange a tour with a student guide to further help you make an informed decision.

Questions for Your Student Guide(s):

- Do people have an easy time transitioning from high school to this school?
- What do the professors expect of students?
- What tutoring resources are available to me as a freshman? Do a lot of freshmen need tutoring support?
- What is life like for students socially?
- What types of clubs/groups/activities are available to freshmen?

Questions to Ask Yourself:

- How do my GPA, class rank, and SAT/ACT scores compare to the average on this campus?
- What do I really like and dislike about the campus?
- Do I feel comfortable here? Why or why not?
- Do I want to attend here after high school?

What other questions do YOU think would be important to ask on a college visit?

- _____
  _____

- _____
  _____

- _____
  _____

- _____
  _____

- _____
  _____

Virtual School Tours

Virtual tours of college campuses are a great option if you cannot travel to a campus. Check the school's website or search "_____ virtual tour."
                                        campus name

Take a Campus Tour

DIRECTIONS: Locate a campus virtual tour to each of your Top 10 schools. Take notes here, as well as on your Top 10 College Research Pages.

_____
_____
_____
_____
_____
_____
_____
_____
_____
_____
_____
_____
_____
_____
_____
_____
_____
_____
_____
_____
_____
_____
_____
_____
_____
_____
_____

Unit 6: My Applications

Extending My Learning: My Top College Research

DIRECTIONS: Research your Top 10 universities and colleges, using these questions below as a template.

*****Note:** *Make copies of this page for future use.*

Investigate!
The list of questions to the left is a starting point. Ask as many questions as you feel are necessary in order to find the school of your dreams!

Name of University or College

Basic Information

Type of College? Circle all that apply.   Two-Year   Four Year   Public   Private

Location: _____

Founded in the year: _____   Number of students: _____

School mascot/ Team name: _____

Programs (sports, activities, and support available): _____

Student Diversity: _____   School Ranking: _____

Does it offer the major you're looking for? _____

Core values of the school: _____

How can you apply? Do they accept the Common Application?
_____

Graduate job/grad school placement: _____

How much is tuition (cost of classes) for a year? _____

What are the housing and meal plan options and costs for freshmen? _____

How much financial aid did the average freshmen receive in recent years? _____

What is the average range of scores on the SAT /ACT for students there? _____

Traditions: _____

Unique fact about the college: _____

Your question: _____
_____

Your question: _____
_____

The College Application Process

BIG IDEA
Use our timeline and seek help from your guidance counselor to complete the college application process.

Applying to college has a lot of steps. Based upon what you already know, completing a timeline will help simplify the process. Refer to the next page for an explanation of each step.

Application Timeline Exploration

DIRECTIONS: Complete the timeline by filling in the empty boxes with the words in the word bank below.

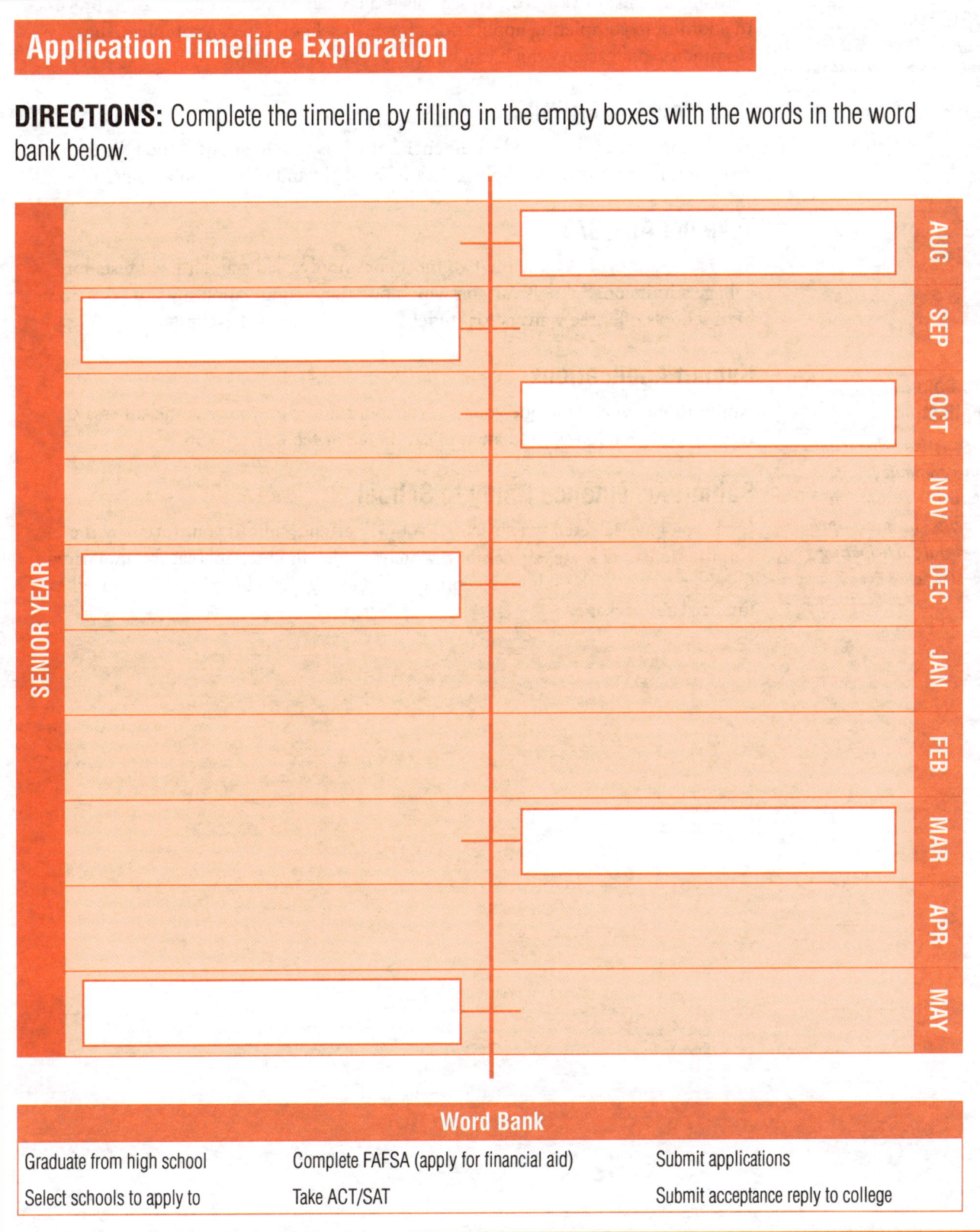

Word Bank

Graduate from high school	Complete FAFSA (apply for financial aid)	Submit applications
Select schools to apply to	Take ACT/SAT	Submit acceptance reply to college

College Application Process Defined

Graduate from High School

In order to graduate, you must complete all graduation requirements. Talk to your guidance counselor about requirements and graduation plans at your school.

Select Schools to Apply to

Developing a list of your Top 10 schools is a crucial part of the application process. In addition to completing applications for each school, you can complete The Common Application, which can be sent to several schools.

Complete the FAFSA

This is how you apply for federal financial aid; it is free to apply. If the FAFSA isn't an option for you, you can apply for state based aid and other scholarships.

Take the ACT/SAT

The ACT and the SAT are the two most commonly used standardized tests for college admission. Schools vary on which one they require applicants to take. Some high schools offer fee waivers for students to take each of these tests.

Submit Applications

Applications usually include your high school transcript, your résumé, an essay, recommendation letters, and an application fee or fee waiver form.

Submit Acceptance Reply to School

Once you have selected which school you will attend, submit your forms by the **Candidate Reply Date Agreement**, which is a deadline schools set for applicants to return forms to the school accepting or declining the admission offer as well as financial aid package.

Transcript

A transcript is a record of your classes and grades earned as well as honors and awards earned while in school. A school registrar provides both official and unofficial transcripts for students upon request.

The Common Application

The Common App is an undergraduate college admission application that students may use to apply to several participating schools at once.

Detailed Timeline for Senior Year

DIRECTIONS: Read each of the steps on the timeline. Fill in the correct months in the big bubbles. The timeline begins in August and ends in May.

Note: Refer to the appendix for a timeline after high school graduation.

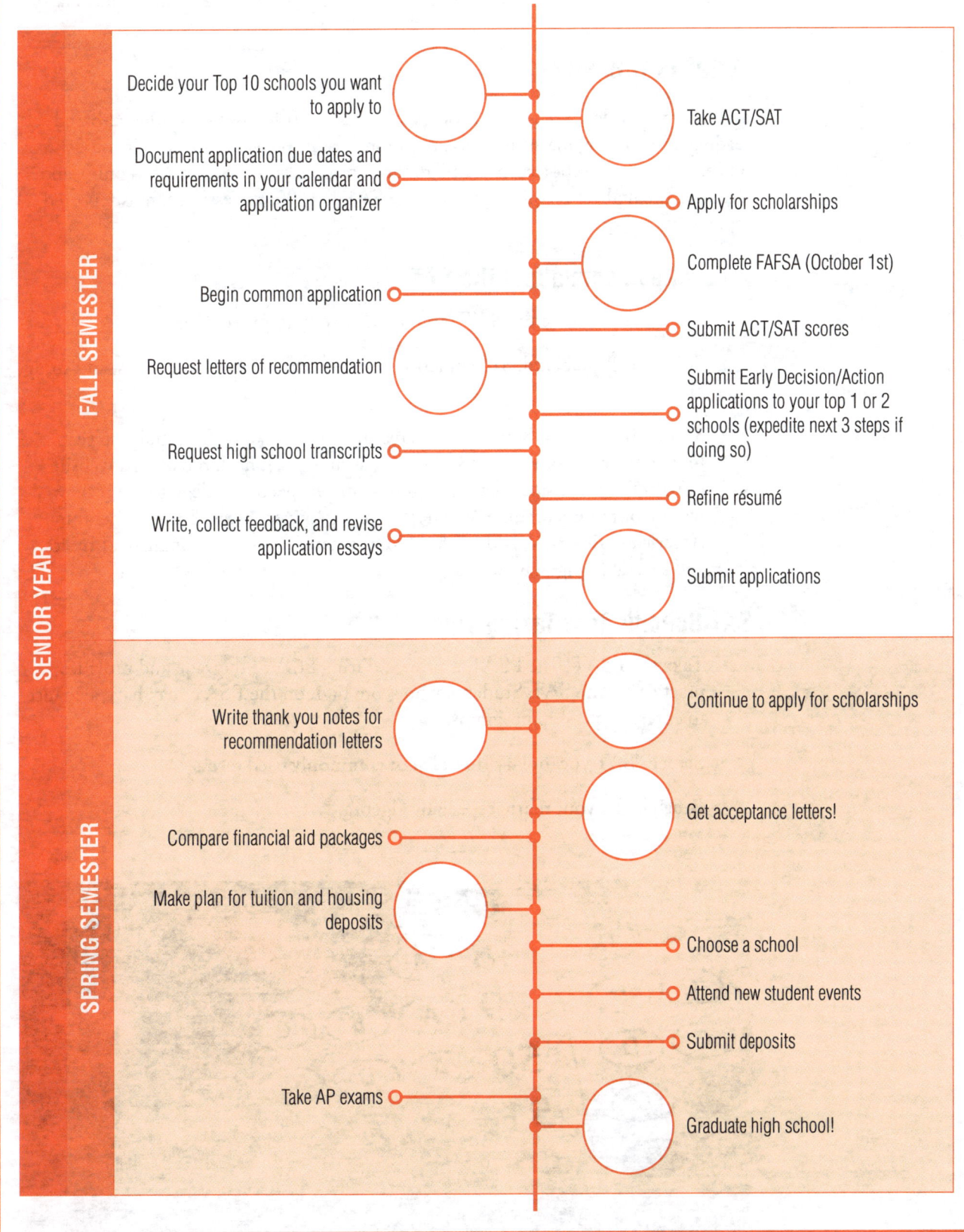

About the SAT and the ACT

Why Are the ACT and SAT Important?

Colleges use test scores to help determine admission and scholarships. They may also use your test results for course placement and course credit. This means if you have already mastered college-level content, you may test out of some foundational classes.

What is the SAT?

The SAT is a widely used test in college admissions. It focuses on evidence-based reading and writing, math, and has an optional essay. It includes three kinds of questions: multiple-choice, student-produced responses (in mathematics only), and an essay. The highest possible score for the SAT is 1600; the essay score is reported separately.

A Few Key Facts about the SAT

- Most students take the SAT more than once to improve their score.

- Search "college board, SAT practice" for free practice questions, tests, and study guides.

- SAT Subject Tests: Some colleges require you to take an SAT Subject Test to demonstrate competence in individual subjects. Check the official website or with the admissions department of your prospective college to see if they require or prefer certain SAT Subject Tests. Subject areas include Literature, American History, World History, Mathematics, Biology, Chemistry, Physics, and several foreign languages.

SAT Specific Test Taking Tips

- **Take the PSAT!** The PSAT is offered during 8th or 9th grade and provides practice for the SAT. Students who score high on the PSAT may have a chance to enter scholarship programs.

- Search "SAT vocabulary" for a list of commonly used terms.

- Brush up on your math, especially algebra.

What is the ACT?

The ACT, or "American College Test," is a standardized test used in the college admission process. The ACT is a curriculum based achievement test that is meant to measure information you have learned during high school.

A Few Key Facts About the ACT

- You can take it up to 12 times, so do not be afraid to retake it.

- By answering questions about your interests and courses, ACT develops a profile for you including your work in high school and your career choices. It also shows your strengths and weaknesses in the subject areas tested. This information is informative both for you and for colleges.

- Registration is usually required about a month prior to the date you take the test.

- Search "ACT.org" for free study guides and practice questions.

ACT Specific Test Taking Tips

- **Answer the questions you find easiest first.** Come back to the others last.

- **Don't waste time.** You shouldn't spend more than a minute or two on any question.

- **Answer every question.** There is no penalty for guessing and the easy questions are worth just as much as the hard one, when answered correctly.

Unit 6: My Applications

BIG IDEA
The SAT and ACT can impact my college admission and scholarship dollars available.

TIP
Although you must pay a fee to register for the SAT and ACT, there are fee waivers available for students who are eligible.

Comparing the SAT and ACT

SAT		ACT
3 hours + 50-minute essay (optional)	Testing time	2 hours, 55 minutes + 40-minute essay (optional)
7 times a year, August to June	Administrations	7 times a year
Evidence-Based Reading and Writing, Math + optional essay	Components	English, Math, Reading, Science + optional essay
No	Is there a penalty for wrong answers?	No
154	Number of questions	215
1 minute, 10 seconds	Time per question	49 seconds
400–1600 (SAT Essay: reported in 3 dimensions, each 2–8)	Score range	1–36 (writing domain scores: 2–12)
Yes. All of your scores are sent to the colleges you choose	Are ALL scores automatically sent?	No. Students can choose which scores schools will receive if the test is taken more than once.
Reading Test 65 minutes 52 questions	Text length and timing	**Reading Test** 35 minutes 40 questions
Writing and Language Test 35 minutes 44 questions		**English Test** 45 minutes 75 questions
Math Test 80 minutes 58 questions		**Math Test** 60 minutes 60 questions
		Science Test 35 minutes 40 questions
Sending scores - You can send your scores to 4 colleges for free.	Fees	Sending scores - You can send your scores to 4 colleges for free.
Registration - Check the SAT website for costs. There are fee waivers available to eligible students.		Registration - Check the ACT website for costs. There are fee waivers available to eligible students.
Late Fee Waivers - The SAT has late fee waivers available for eligible students.		Late Fee Waivers - The ACT does not have late fee waivers available at this time.

Where can you find the most up to date information on college admission tests?

_____

_____

Explain three ways in which the SAT or ACT are different than a typical classroom test or final.

_____

_____

Set up for Test Taking Success

General Test Taking Tips

- **Dress comfortably,** as there is no dress code and you're going to be testing for several hours.

- **Get plenty of sleep** the night before. You won't perform nearly as well if you're tired.

- **Eat a big breakfast** with a good amount of protein before the test. Studies have shown this leads to a significant increase in performance on tests.

- **Wear a reliable watch** so that you can keep track of time as you work on each section of the test.

- **Remember to bring photo identification** with you to the testing center on test day. You will need it to register.

- **Write neatly** so that others can read your handwriting with no confusion.

- **On multiple-choice questions, consider all answer choices before you choose one.** Use the process of elimination to narrow your choices. You will not be penalized for wrong answers that you give, so it's still worth your while to guess.

- **Make your essay structured:** a clear introduction, supporting paragraphs and a conclusion. Graders will take only 60 to 90 seconds to grade each essay, and they'll look for clear, evidence-based arguments more than stylish, graceful writing.

Envision My Test Success

DIRECTIONS: Draw a picture of yourself showing up on test day. Be sure to include all of the tips on the list above.

Unit 6: My Applications

Extending My Learning: College Application Organizer

DIRECTIONS: Complete this organizer for each of your top schools.

Note: Make copies of this page for future use.

School Name: _____
School Address: _____
Regular Application Deadline: _____
Applying Early? Yes | No
Early Decision Application Deadline: _____
Application Fee: _____
Type: Foundation | Target | Reach

Required Documents:

- ☐ ACT Score   ☐ Essay
- ☐ SAT Score   ☐ Résumé
- ☐ Official Transcript   ☐ Application Form
- ☐ Recommendation Letter(s), how many _____
    - From whom: _____

Notes: _____
_____
_____

School Name: _____
School Address: _____
Regular Application Deadline: _____
Applying Early? Yes | No
Early Decision Application Deadline: _____
Application Fee: _____
Type: Foundation | Target | Reach

Required Documents:

- ☐ ACT Score
- ☐ SAT Score
- ☐ Official Transcript
- ☐ Recommendation Letter(s), how many _____
    - From whom: _____

Notes: _____
_____
_____

School Name: _____
School Address: _____
Regular Application Deadline: _____
Applying Early? Yes | No
Early Decision Application Deadline: _____
Application Fee: _____
Type: Foundation | Target | Reach

Required Documents:

- ☐ ACT Score
- ☐ SAT Score
- ☐ Official Transcript
- ☐ Recommendation Letter(s), how many _____
    - From whom: _____

Notes: _____
_____
_____

School Name: _____
School Address: _____
Regular Application Deadline: _____
Applying Early? Yes | No
Early Decision Application Deadline: _____
Application Fee: _____
Type: Foundation | Target | Reach

Required Documents:

- ☐ ACT Score
- ☐ SAT Score
- ☐ Official Transcript
- ☐ Recommendation Letter(s), how many _____
    - From whom: _____

Notes: _____
_____
_____

Application Essay

What Is an Application Essay?

Essays could be a part of applications for several different opportunities - college applications, scholarship applications, internship applications, job applications, etc.

An application essay is written in response to a set of essay questions chosen by a selection committee or employer. This is the part of the application that gives the selection committee a glimpse into who you are outside of school. Your essay can also help them identify what makes you the right fit for their school, internship, job, or scholarship.

> **BIG IDEA**
> *Application essays provide an opportunity for you to tell colleges about who you are, what makes you ready for college, and why you would be a great fit for the opportunity.*

Who Reads My Application Essay?

A selection committee reads applications and essays. Who sits on the committee will vary by opportunity. Regardless of who is on the committee, they are looking for applicants who tell their story in a compelling and authentic way.

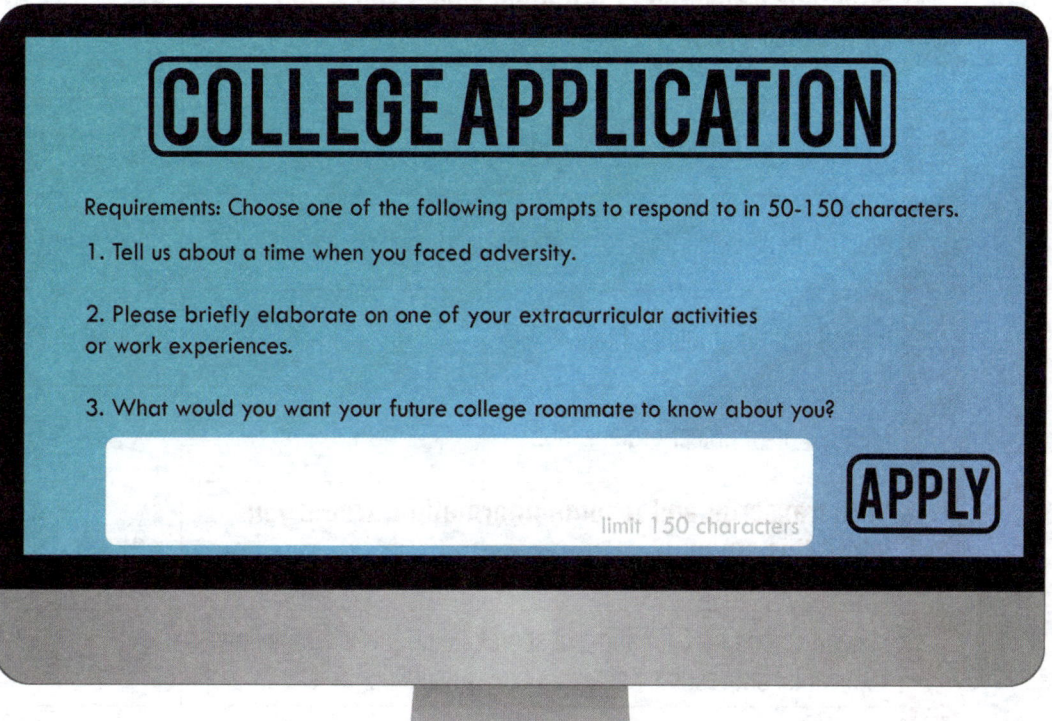

Why Does My Essay Matter?

Without an essay, the selection committee only knows the basic facts about you presented on your résumé and transcript. The essay serves as your voice in the application process. It's a very important element of the application process!

www.educationopensdoors.org

Admission Committee Decisions

Admission Committee
An admission committee is a group of people who select application essay topics, review submitted college applications, and make decisions on acceptance.

DIRECTIONS: Pretend you are on the admission committee for a selective private school (less than 50% of applicants are admitted). Read the application elements for applicant #2765 below and circle "thumbs up" or "thumbs down" for each element of their application.

Applicant Transcript Highlights		👍	👎
	Best SAT: 1260, Best ACT: 27	👍	👎
	GPA: 3.3	👍	👎
	Class Rank: Top 33% (247 / 750)	👍	👎
	Class Load: 2 AP classes, 3 years of science, 4 years of math, 2 years of Spanish	👍	👎
	With only transcript information would you admit applicant #2765?	👍	👎

Applicant Résumé Highlights			
	Worked as a lifeguard, coach, and swim instructor	👍	👎
	Held multiple leadership roles at work and school	👍	👎
	Record setting student athlete	👍	👎
	Member of volunteer organization	👍	👎
	With transcript and résumé information, would you admit this student?	👍	👎

Applicant Essay Highlights			
	Stated reasons for GPA and test scores being lower than fellow applicants, but résumé and experiences make up for it	👍	👎
	Made a compelling argument for why they would make an excellent addition to the school community	👍	👎
	Explained that they had to work 30+ hours a week to help cover expenses at home	👍	👎
	Shared an interesting story + an explanation of its impact on their life	👍	👎
	With transcript, résumé, and essay content would you admit this student?	👍	👎

IN REAL LIFE, APPLICANT #2765 WAS ACCEPTED!!

Admission committees are not only looking for applicants with excellent grades and test scores. They want students who will make positive impacts on their campus and the world as they become alumni.

Courtney is a real person, a graduate of TCU, and one of the authors of this guidebook. How did TCU's admission committee know Courtney would be a great asset to the community? Because they made a case for themselves in their essay!

Attending TCU was Courtney's dream. It was their "reach school" so they applied early decision to increase their odds of getting accepted and it worked!

Reflection

DIRECTIONS: Did you agree with the admission committee at TCU? Why or why not? Every student has a "reach school." What is the best reason(s) you have to compel the admission committee to admit you? Write your response below.

_____
_____
_____
_____
_____
_____
_____
_____
_____
_____

Sample College Application Essay

By Christian Duarte
Dallas, Texas

An Impactful Trade-Off

I arrived home, exhausted from working after my 6-hour shift. Walking through the door to my home, I was greeted by a wave of intense heat. Baffled, I asked my mother who was sitting on the couch drenched with sweat, "Why is it so hot in here?" She replied that the air conditioner had broken again. "Then call someone to fix it," I said, as I began to strip off my grease-stained work uniform. "I would, but we don't have the money to pay for it," she responded. I knew exactly where this was heading. I smacked my lips, gave out a huge sigh, and asked her how much she needed. Before she could answer, I had already started to head to my room to get the $400 that I had been setting aside for new parts for our car. Responsibility is a heavy weight, one that I choose to bear everyday for the sake of my family and pursuit of my dreams.

My family asks for help on a regular basis. Since my mother's divorce, we have struggled financially. She works two full-time jobs as a shift leader at two different restaurants for 70-80 hours a week. I have an older brother who just finished high school this past year and a younger sister who lives with my grandmother because we cannot support her financially. Since I turned 15, my responsibilities at home grew significantly. I became a full-time employee, brother, son, and high school student. Starting the summer before my junior year, I joined my mother at work to help pay some of the bills that were accumulating at home. Every week I work 40 hours. Although I'm exhausted and can barely keep my eyes open, I always push for more hours because I know that my hard work helps alleviate my family's financial struggles.

Almost every day I leave school for my job at 4p.m. and come home after 11p.m. to start my homework. I know that my responsibilities do not end when I come home from work. I know that if I don't continue to push myself to complete my homework assignments to the best of my ability, I will never move past this job or my grease-stained uniform. I continue to perform as a top student, always taking the most rigorous classes available at my school. No matter what, I refuse to let my academics suffer because of my financial responsibilities at home.

This summer I received a unique opportunity to be one of three students in my senior class selected to intern at The Millennium Foundation. Through the foundation I helped support my school's college access program. For the first time I worked in an environment where I was able to apply what I learn at school to projects that truly challenged me, and my perspective. I worked for the Director of College Admissions for my school district and saw how my summer research projects directly impacted the training of the college counselors at my high school. I saw the path of my long-term goals become clear by rooting myself in the importance of my continued education.

I know for me, that my high school job is temporarily patching the financial problems in my family. My goal is to gain a higher education that will push me toward a different career path. I know that college is the only solution for me. I will break barriers by going to college as the first person in my family to take this leap. I will show my younger sister, older brother, and mother how education will pay off as I am able to support them better when I return. I am proud of my mother and brother for working hard every day to support the family, but I know that my time there is coming to an end. I look forward to the next stage of my life and am ready to trade my grease-stained uniform for a degree, facing the challenges ahead and pushing limits to turn my dreams into a reality.

How Do I Start Writing?

DIRECTIONS: Read the step on the left and its explanation on the right. Then complete the questions and activities related to each step.

STEP 1	
Find a place to write	Find a place where you can focus on your essay for at least 1 to 2 hours and get all of your necessary tools in one place.

Describe or draw an environment where you feel you can focus well.

STEP 2	
Establish what the essay is about	Many essays have similar prompts. If you have already written an essay for a different application and it is a strong essay, then you can rewrite the essay with similar ideas and concepts. Some applications only give one essay prompt; others provide several to choose from. Choose a topic that addresses information you have not shared about in other parts of your application.

Do you have an electronic portfolio that you save all of your work to? _____

If not, it could be helpful so you can re-use parts of essays you've previously written.

Unit 6: My Applications

How Do I Start Writing? (continued)

STEP 3	
Brainstorm about yourself	Use the questions below to process your strengths, goals, and other elements that make you unique.

Use the prompting questions below to brainstorm for your essay. Write or draw your ideas in the box below.

- What are you especially good at?
- What are the things you struggle with?
- What are the things you are interested in?
- What are your character strengths?
- When have you demonstrated leadership abilities?
- What extracurricular activities have you participated in?
- Describe your work experience.
- What are your goals and dreams?

STEP 4	
Create your personal brand statement	A personal brand statement defines you as a unique applicant. It often goes at the end of the opening paragraph.

Draft one statement that defines you as a unique applicant.

_____

_____

_____

How Do I Start Writing? (continued)

STEP 5

Outline your essay
- Choose a hook that will grab your audience's attention by using a quote, action, or describing a scene.
- Organize your thoughts in a logical way in order to outline important points.
- As you are writing, make sure you are following the directions that were laid out for you by the prompt.

What could be a good hook for your essay? Write your idea.

Organize your brainstormed thoughts into categories. Add more categories as needed.

STEP 6

Begin writing essay
- Turn your outline into a flowing narrative (not a list)
- Keep the details simple
- Focus on grammar, syntax, and paragraph structures
- Search "sample personal statements" online to see how others have formatted their essays

Syntax
The way words and phrases are arranged to create well-formed sentences.

STEP 7

Gather feedback, edits, and revise
After writing a draft of your essay, ask others to read your work and recommend edits.

Extending My Learning: Writing an Application Essay

DIRECTIONS: Choose one of the following essay prompts. Use the space provided or a computer to write out a draft of your essay.

Topic A: Write an essay to discuss the impact of one person in your life.

Topic B: Choose an issue that is important to you. Explain the immediate significance of that issue on your life.

Topic C: What single adjective do you think would be most frequently used to describe you by those who know you best?

Topic D: Tell us about a conversation you've had that changed your perspective or was otherwise meaningful to you.

Topic E: Evaluate a significant experience or achievement that has special meaning to you.

Topic F: Name one book you have read in the past year. Describe your reason for considering the book significant and what you gained from reading it.

Topic G: Write an essay describing information you want considered as part of your admissions application. This information should demonstrate how you will contribute to the institution's diverse learning environment.

For example:

- academic credentials
- personal responsibilities
- exceptional achievements
- talents
- obstacles
- educational goals

Unit 6: My Applications

Application Tracker

Track My Submitted Applications

DIRECTIONS: Use this college application tracker, or create a soft copy version to save on your computer, to organize each of your applications and stay on top of all the necessary deadlines and details.

Application Number	Name of School	My Application ID Number	Date App Submitted	Test Scores Sent?	FAFSA Sent?	Transcript Sent?	App Fee/ Waiver Sent
1				☐	☐	☐	☐
2				☐	☐	☐	☐
3				☐	☐	☐	☐
4				☐	☐	☐	☐
5				☐	☐	☐	☐
6				☐	☐	☐	☐
7				☐	☐	☐	☐
8				☐	☐	☐	☐
9				☐	☐	☐	☐
10				☐	☐	☐	☐

Practice College Application

Below you will find a practice college application. While this is not an exact copy of the application you will be asked to complete, the questions and information below are modeled after real applications as closely as possible.

> **The Common Application**
>
> *While many schools do accept the Common App, some schools require their own application and many request supplemental (additional) documents as well. Search "The Common App" to find more information.*

SCHOOL

FIRST CHOICE	School	
	Major	
SECOND CHOICE	School	
	Major	

BIOGRAPHICAL INFORMATION

Date of Birth	____ / ____ / ____ (mm/dd/year)	
Full, legal name	Last/Family Name	
	First Name	
	Middle	
	Suffix	*(Example: Jr., III, etc.)*
Other names or aliases	*If you attended school using a different name or took a standardized test (ACT/SAT) using a different name, please list them below.*	
	Last/Family Name	
	First Name	
	Middle	
	Suffix	*(Example: Jr., III, etc.)*
Place of Birth	City	
	State/Possession	
	Country	
Status as a current U.S. military service member, veteran, or dependent	*A U.S. military service member is a person who is serving in any branch of the U.S. Armed Forces, including the National Guard or Reserves. Please select any of the following that apply to you. I am a:*	
	☐ Veteran (former U.S. military service member)	
	☐ Current U.S. military service member	
	☐ Spouse or dependent of a veteran or a current U.S. military service member	
	☐ Spouse or dependent of, or a veteran or current U.S. military service member with an injury or illness resulting from military service (service-connected injury/illness)	
	☐ Spouse or dependent of a deceased U.S. service member	
Your Permanent Address	City	
	State/Possession	
	Country	
Your Phone Number	Phone Number	
	Type	☐ Cell ☐ Work ☐ Home
Your Personal Email Address		

www.educationopensdoors.org

BIOGRAPHICAL INFORMATION

Emergency Contact

Name	
Relationship to You	
Phone Number	
Address	
Email	

Family's Educational Background

Please indicate the highest level of your parents' or legal guardians' educational background.

Father	☐ No High School ☐ Some High School ☐ High School Diploma or GED ☐ Some College ☐ Associate's Degree ☐ Bachelor's Degree ☐ Graduate/Professional Degree ☐ Unknown
Mother	☐ No High School ☐ Some High School ☐ High School Diploma or GED ☐ Some College ☐ Associate's Degree ☐ Bachelor's Degree ☐ Graduate/Professional Degree ☐ Unknown

Language

What language(s) are you fluent in?

	Speaking	Reading	Writing
Language:	_____	_____	_____
Language:	_____	_____	_____

Household Size

How many people, including yourself, live in your household? _____

Family Commitments

Do you have any family obligations that prevent you from participating in extracurricular activities?	YES	NO
If yes, do you...		
Have to work to supplement family income?	YES	NO
If yes, describe:		
Provide primary care for a family member?	YES	NO
If yes, describe:		
Have other family obligations that prevent you from participating?	YES	NO
If yes, describe:		

© 2019 Education Opens Doors, Inc.

EDUCATION INFORMATION

High School

School Name	
City or County	
State	
Expected Gradution Date: ____ / ____ (month/year)	
Number of college credits at high school graduation?	
Are you home schooled?	YES NO
Do you plan to graduate with an IB (International Baccalaureate) diploma?	YES NO
If you did not graduate from high school, do you have a GED?	YES NO

College

List all colleges you have attended, including dual credit courses in high school.

Name of Institution	
Location *(city, state)*	
Dates of Attendance	____ / ____ (month/year) to ____ / ____ (month/year)
Major	
Degree Date	____ / ____ / ____ (mm/dd/year)
Type of Degree	*(Associate's, Bachelor's, etc.)*

Coursework

List all of the courses you will complete your senior year. Place an X in each box that is applicable after writing each course name.

Course Name	(Example: Physics)	☒ AP/IB Credit ☐ Dual Credit
Course Name		☐ AP/IB Credit ☐ Dual Credit
Course Name		☐ AP/IB Credit ☐ Dual Credit
Course Name		☐ AP/IB Credit ☐ Dual Credit
Course Name		☐ AP/IB Credit ☐ Dual Credit
Course Name		☐ AP/IB Credit ☐ Dual Credit
Course Name		☐ AP/IB Credit ☐ Dual Credit

Standardized Tests

Indicate tests that you have taken or plan to take. Please have official test scores sent directly from the testing agency to your top choice schools to which you apply.

ACT	Date taken or plan to take: ____ / ____ (month/year)
SAT	Date taken or plan to take: ____ / ____ (month/year)

WORK EXPERIENCE AND COMMUNITY INVOLVEMENT

Experience/Involvement

Organization/Activity Name	
Participation	

Activity Level	☐ Local ☐ Regional	☐ City ☐ National	☐ District ☐ International	☐ State
Years *(circle all that apply)*	Positions Held	Elected?	Hours per Week	Hours per Year
Freshman		YES NO		
Sophomore		YES NO		
Junior		YES NO		
Senior		YES NO		

Experience/Involvement

Organization/Activity Name	
Participation	

Activity Level	☐ Local ☐ Regional	☐ City ☐ National	☐ District ☐ International	☐ State
Years *(circle all that apply)*	Positions Held	Elected?	Hours per Week	Hours per Year
Freshman		YES NO		
Sophomore		YES NO		
Junior		YES NO		
Senior		YES NO		

Experience/Involvement

Organization/Activity Name	
Participation	

Activity Level	☐ Local ☐ Regional	☐ City ☐ National	☐ District ☐ International	☐ State
Years *(circle all that apply)*	Positions Held	Elected?	Hours per Week	Hours per Year
Freshman		YES NO		
Sophomore		YES NO		
Junior		YES NO		
Senior		YES NO		

Experience/Involvement

Organization/Activity Name	
Participation	

Activity Level	☐ Local ☐ Regional	☐ City ☐ National	☐ District ☐ International	☐ State
Years *(circle all that apply)*	Positions Held	Elected?	Hours per Week	Hours per Year
Freshman		YES NO		
Sophomore		YES NO		
Junior		YES NO		
Senior		YES NO		

*Note: A paper résumé is not an alternative to filling out the information below. You must also complete the information below and the FAFSA to be considered for scholarships.

AWARDS AND HONORS

Award/Honor/Distinction
- Name of Award/Honor/Distinction:
- Date(s) of Award: ____ / ____ / ____ (mm/dd/year)
- Describe the award, honor, or distinction (description, basis, sponsor, etc.).

Award/Honor/Distinction
- Name of Award/Honor/Distinction:
- Date(s) of Award: ____ / ____ / ____ (mm/dd/year)
- Describe the award, honor, or distinction (description, basis, sponsor, etc.).

Award/Honor/Distinction
- Name of Award/Honor/Distinction:
- Date(s) of Award: ____ / ____ / ____ (mm/dd/year)
- Describe the award, honor, or distinction (description, basis, sponsor, etc.).

Award/Honor/Distinction
- Name of Award/Honor/Distinction:
- Date(s) of Award: ____ / ____ / ____ (mm/dd/year)
- Describe the award, honor, or distinction (description, basis, sponsor, etc.).

Award/Honor/Distinction
- Name of Award/Honor/Distinction:
- Date(s) of Award: ____ / ____ / ____ (mm/dd/year)
- Describe the award, honor, or distinction (description, basis, sponsor, etc.).

> **Keep Track!**
> *Document the role and dates of employment for as many jobs, internships, activities, and experiences you have while you're in high school. It will make your application so much easier to complete later on!*

CAREER PATH

College Plans

- Semester and year you expect to enter: ____ / ____ (month/year)
- Intended Major:

If you plan to pursue a pre-professional program, please indicate which one.

- ☐ Pre-Law
- ☐ Nursing
- ☐ Medicine
- ☐ Veterinary
- ☐ Physical Therapy
- ☐ Other: _____

What certifications do you intend to attain?

Unit 6: My Applications

Unit 6 Summary: Completing My Applications

Consider the steps we recommended in order to apply to college: maintaining a strong GPA, building an awesome résumé, performing well on national assessments, requesting recommendations, preparing an essay, and submitting application materials on time. With your diligence, hard work, and early preparation, you can attain college acceptance.

Checklist Check-In

1. Consider where you are in your educational journey. Check the corresponding box below.
   - ☐ 6th Grade
   - ☐ 7th Grade
   - ☐ 8th Grade
   - ☐ 9th Grade
   - ☐ 10th Grade
   - ☐ 11th Grade
   - ☐ 12th Grade
   - ☐ High School Graduate
   - ☐ GED Recipient

2. Turn to the "Grade Level Checklist" at the beginning of Unit 1. Locate your current grade level. **Review what you checked off at the beginning of the program and check off any other activities you have completed.**

Unit Review Opportunities

1. Go back to the "Extend Your Learning" pages in this unit. Research, ask questions, and locate resources to complete those activities.
2. Complete any remaining vocabulary tasks for this unit's vocabulary and use each word in a sentence this week.
3. Answer the questions on the unit cover page, and complete the directions in the white box.

Moving Forward…

Select one of the colors from the triangle to describe how you feel about new understandings gained from this unit. Justify your answer in at least 3 sentences.

_____
_____
_____
_____
_____
_____

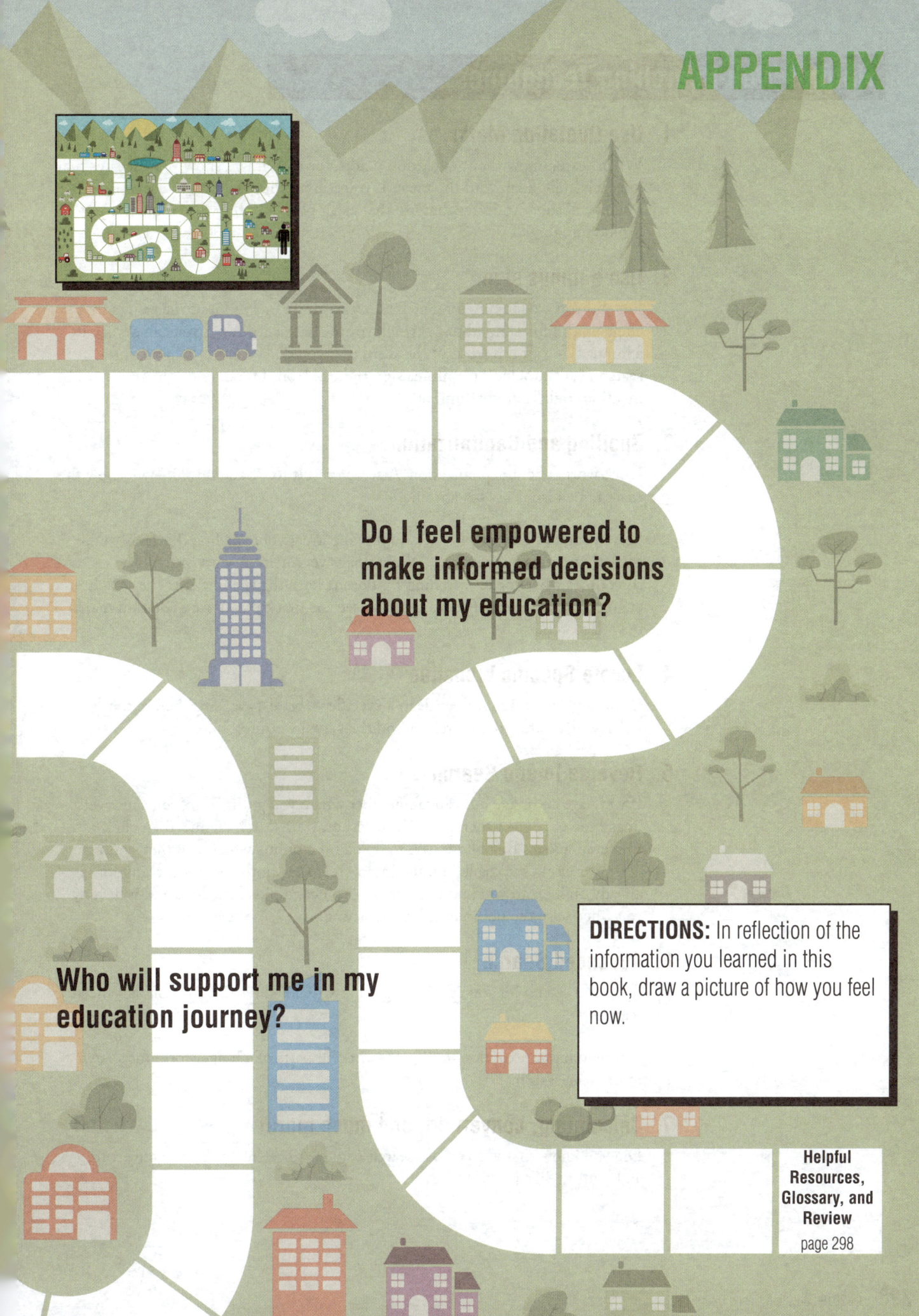

Helpful Web Searching Techniques

1. Use Quotation Marks " "
When searching without quotation marks, the search will show you the sites that use each individual word the most. If you search using quotation marks, then the results will show you sites that use that exact phrase in the word sequence you are looking for.

2. Use a minus sign
Pretend you are looking for a recipe that has milk in it; a lot of the results that come up call for almond milk, which you're allergic to. What you can do is put a minus sign right in front of the word that you don't want to pop up in the search results. Including a minus sign right in front of "almond," the results will mention "milk" but not "almond."

3. Spelling and Capitalization
Don't worry about capitalization. A search result for "San Antonio" will show the exact same results as "san antonio."

Search engines have spell check, so it will correct your spelling if it feels you've spelled something incorrectly. While this is very helpful most of the time, sometimes what you're searching for doesn't have the spelling that the search engine thinks it does. If that's the case, see the first tip and use quotation marks in your search.

4. Locate Specific Websites
If you want to search for words in a specific website, type "site:" before the website URL and your search to find the actual website.

5. Reverse Image Search
If you have an image but can't remember where you got it from, you can reverse image search. To get there, click "Images" on your search engine, then click the camera icon. That allows you to upload the photo, which will then show wherever else it's uploaded on the internet. If the photo you're searching for is already online and you know where it is, you can upload the link, and it'll show you where else the photo is uploaded as well.

6. Advanced Search
After you search for something, to get more detailed results, click on "advanced search."

You then have the option to fill out any or all parts of a longer form for a new, more clear, search.

7. Calculating, converting, and much more!
Did you know that you can use search engines to calculate things, convert things, and more? Give it a try!

Students in Foster Care and Students Who Are Homeless

If you do not have housing that is fixed, regular, and adequate, and are not in the physical custody of an adult, you may benefit from this sheet. If you do not live with your biological parents or live with someone unrelated to you (this can include group homes, residential care facilities, etc), you may also benefit from this sheet.

FAQ

At what age do I age out of foster care?
This depends on the state you live in. Some people age out of foster care as early as 18 years old, and some as late as 23 years old. It's important to know your state's "age out" policy as this can affect your access to financial aid, health insurance, and other supports.

What is an Educational Training Voucher [ETV]?
An ETV is an annual federal grant that is given to states so they can give youth who have aged out of the foster care system funds to pursue education after high school. Funds can be used for tuition, books, housing, and student loan payments.

I can't afford the fee to take the ACT and SAT. Can I get a waiver for those?
Yes! You may use up to 2 waivers for the ACT exam. You may also use up to 2 waivers for the SAT, and 2 for the SAT subject tests as well. Look up the "fee waiver eligibility requirements" for the current year to determine if you qualify.

Do I need a stable address to apply for FAFSA?
No, you only need a mailing address as a backup. (This can be a friend or extended family member's address.) With permission, you can use the address of the college[s] to which you're applying as well!

How do I know if I'm financially independent?
If at any time since you turned 13 years old both of your parents were deceased, you were in foster care, or you were a dependent or ward of the court, you may be considered financially independent for FAFSA.

What is a UHY?
UHY stands for Unaccompanied Homeless Youth. Being designated UHY means that you will not need a parent signature on your FAFSA as you will be considered an independent student.

What can I do if I don't have a place to live during college breaks?
Some colleges offer year-round and emergency housing for homeless and at risk [homeless] students. Some colleges offer school-sponsored service trips, and study-abroad grants as well. These are options for winter and summer breaks.

What about healthcare?
Many colleges offer college health plans, which allow you to access basic healthcare while on/near campus. Some hospitals have programs that reduce the costs for homeless and other people with a low income as well.

Do I have extra options for tuition help?
Many universities and colleges that offer automatic free tuition once you meet certain marks that include but are not limited to your: GPA, income level, and SAT/ACT score[s]. There are some scholarships and financial aid options available specifically to students who are homeless or in foster care. Depending on which school and state, foster students may qualify for certain partial and full tuition waivers and scholarships. In later years,

becoming an RA (resident assistant) may be an option. In many colleges, it comes with the perk of having free room and board. Look into those opportunities at the college[s] of your choice!

What is an academic retention center? [Also known as "academic advising" and "retention" centers.]

These are places dedicated to supporting students to continue pursing higher education.

What's "Job Corps?"

Job Corps is a free program that offers education and vocational training to people ages 16 through 25. They also help people get GEDs or high school diplomas if they don't already have one.

Do I need any copies of identity documentation to continue my education?

Before you graduate high school, get a copy of your birth certificate, social security card and a state ID card if you don't already have them. They should all be in the exact same name. If you are in foster care, your caseworker can help you with this. Be sure to keep your social security card in a safe place- DON'T carry it around with you, and don't share its number unless absolutely necessary (to apply for FAFSA, public health insurance, etc).

What if I need extra academic support?

Some colleges offer free live online tutoring. The great thing about these partnerships is that they often offer 24/7 availability and are one-on-one, meaning that you can get tutoring according to your schedule and work on exactly what you want to work on. Other colleges often have free workshops with student tutors.

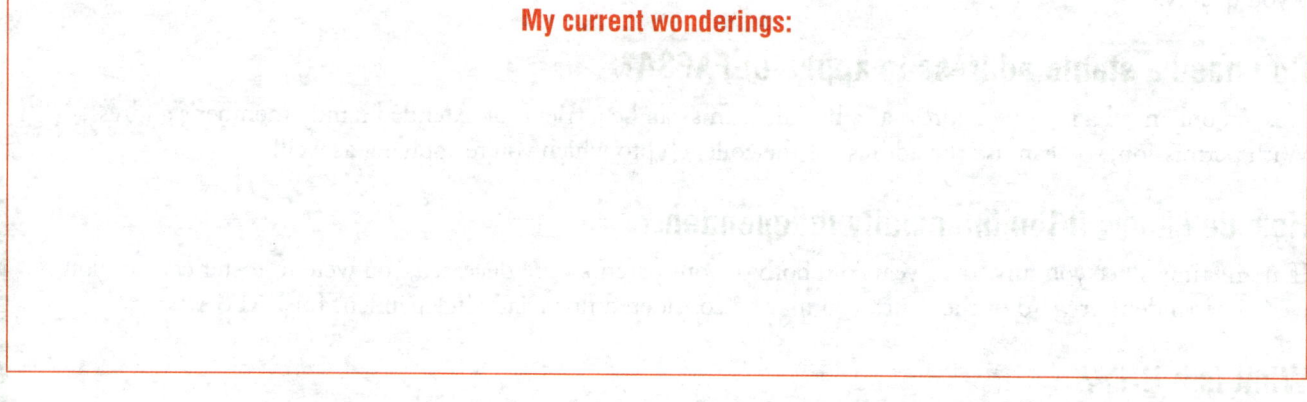

My current wonderings:

Resources for Students in Foster Care and Students Who Are Homeless

Transition Centers

This is a place that is geared towards serving the needs of older current and aged-out foster youth. Every transition center offers different services, however generally they can help with things that include but are not limited to: housing assistance, education and employment assistance, counseling, and transportation help. Search "transition centers near me" and/or ask your case manager to find the transition centers closest to you.

Vocational Rehabilitation Services [Voc Rehab]

This a state-run program for people with various work-related disabilities (and illness) to meet educational and career goals. Generally, they can help with transportation, accommodations for work, tuition, and more. You can often start the process with getting help from them from your junior or senior year of high school.

211   www.211.org

This is a service that helps connect you to local educational, employment, and emergency resources.

Students Who Are Parents

You may benefit from the resources on this sheet if you have a child or are currently expecting a child.

FAQ

How can I take classes if my schedule is busy?
Consider taking online and late-night classes. Some schools even offer classes that are part in person and part online.

What does "all you can learn tuition" mean?
These are colleges and universities that let you pay a flat rate to take (usually online) classes for a certain period of time (usually around four to six months). In this period, usually you can take as many classes as you'd like. Some even let you take the final exam for that class to get automatic credit, which is a major timesaver if you already know the material for that class! Search "all you can learn tuition" for more details.

How can I handle childcare if I take in-person classes?
Some schools offer on-campus childcare programs, and some of these programs even offer discounted rates. This is a great option for when you need to go to class and want to be close to your child, or can't drop them off with someone else.

Will I have less support from my school if I enroll part time?
Some colleges have web pages specifically for students who are studying part-time. Financial aid can be impacted if you become a part time student.

What is emergency financial aid?
Emergency financial aid is usually a grant or short-term loan that is used to help students whose education is in jeopardy by a financial situation out of your control. Ask the financial aid office at your schools of choice if they offer this type of aid.

Are there scholarships available specifically to me?
Some institutions and organizations offer grants and scholarships made specifically for parents, yes!

My current wonderings:

Resources for Students Who Are Parents

Achieving The Dream
This is a growing network of community colleges across the US that are committed to helping their students.

YoungLives
YoungLives is a branch of a big network called YoungLife, a faith-based youth organization. On participating campuses, they provide a lot of support to young parents including mentors who are parents living in the same community/region.

Students with Learning Disabilities

If you have a disability that interferes with your ability to do math, write, read, or even a condition that may affect your memory, organization, and/or time planning, you may benefit from this sheet.

FAQ

How can I form a studying routine that's most helpful to me?
Find a studying schedule that works best for you. Many people enjoy the Pomodoro Technique, where you work for a set number of minutes and then take a break for a set number of minutes, doing this until you are done. There are other techniques that you can use to reach studying and other goals such as "timeboxing," and "the X effect," too. You can find information on those on a web search.

How can I take advantage of the disability accommodations office?
Learn what accommodations are available to all students, and which are beneficial to your disability and learning style. The office can also connect you to support and social groups for disabled students as well as job help at some schools! In college, the process of getting accommodations is started and led by you. The school isn't required to talk to you about getting help if they believe you may need it.

If I received accommodations in high school, does that mean I can automatically get them college?
No. You have to go through the accommodations process all over again, where the college will determine what accommodations you are allowed, but you can transfer a 504.

Are there classes for people with learning disabilities?
While there are developmental classes that help students strengthen their abilities in certain subjects to be able to perform at the college-level, as far as college courses, everyone attends the same classes.

Do I have to disclose my disability on my college application?
No, you don't have to. It may be a nice option to if it helps explain irregularities on your student record.

Do IEPs exist in college?
No, they do not. You may get a 504 Plan through your university's disability accommodations office.

My current wonderings:

www.educationopensdoors.org

Resources for Students with Learning Disabilities

College Steps   www.collegesteps.org
This is a non-profit organization that supports college students with learning disabilities.

The Common Application   www.commonapp.org
This website allows you to fill out one application form for over 700 colleges. It also alerts you when certain due dates are coming up.

Bookshare   www.bookshare.org
This is a virtual library with over half a million books (including some textbooks) available to you at your disposal. This is free to students with qualifying disabilities, and $50 a year to people who qualify but are not students.

Job Accommodation Network: JAN   www.askjan.org
This is a website that you can browse and a hotline that you can call with questions regarding workplace accommodations and the Americans with Disabilities Act (ADA).

Your State's Department of Rehabilitation Services
They help with paying for college, things you'll need to live on campus, connecting you to medical programs, etc.

Bridges from School to Work Program   www.bridgestowork.org
This program helps young adults in major US cities find entry level jobs. They must have had an IEP in public school. This can be helpful for finding a part time job while in school.

Students Who Are Undocumented

You may benefit from this sheet if your immigration application was denied, you entered the US without inspection, or your immigration status has expired.

FAQ

What scholarships are available to undocumented students?

There are organizations and schools that have private scholarships made for undocumented students. Check out the resources section of this page to find some of them. Many schools offer their own scholarships as well, and some states offer financial aid to undocumented students through their state based financial aid application.

Can I be accepted to any university if I am undocumented or if I don't have a social security number?

Each school has their own policy on admitting students who don't have a social security number. You can call the admissions department to ask them of their policy and/or talk to organizations for undocumented youth pursuing higher education.

Do I need DACA to apply for college?

No, you do not.

If I've lived in my state for a long time, will I be able to have in-state tuition?

Most states will charge undocumented students out-of-state tuition prices no matter how long they've lived in the state, however there are some states (including but not limited to Florida, Texas, New York and California) which have laws that allow undocumented students who meet certain criteria to be given in-state tuition prices.

Can I fill out a FAFSA application if I'm a U.S. citizen but my parents are not?

Yes, you may. Be sure to mark the box that indicates that your parents are not U.S. citizens. Your parents will still be required to sign the application form to verify its authenticity. Enter your parent's social security numbers as 000-000-0000. Leaving that area empty or reporting incorrect information may impact your FAFSA acceptance.

If I am undocumented or a DACA recipient, can I get federal financial aid?

No. You may be eligible for state and/or school-based financial aid! Most states and colleges use information collected on the FAFSA to determine whether you are eligible for aid.

What are some things that I might want to look for when it comes to school location?

Location, cost, and student population diversity are often important factors for undocumented students. Location can be important because immigration laws vary all across the country. Cost can be important if financial aid is needed to fund their education. Diversity on and around campus can be important if you don't have the opportunity to travel. Being around people you're comfortable with is important.

Is there a way that I can get reduced-fee or free legal services for immigration help for being a student?

Some universities offer free and low cost legal services for undocumented students on campus. States with a higher immigrant population are more likely to have these offices in their bigger schools. You can look up the site of each school you're interested to see if they offer that.

Resources for Students Who Are Undocumented

United We Dream   www.unitedwedream.org
This is a youth led immigrant organization. They list many resources on their website.

TheDream.US
This organization helps give DACA students scholarships.

National Immigration Law Center   www.nilc.org
This organization is dedicated to immigrant rights, and has a FAQ sheet for DACA students, along with tips for filing tax returns and getting driver's licenses.

Immigrants Rising   immigrantsrising.org
This organization supports young undocumented people's educational and career goals. On their "resources" pages, they have a list of scholarships that don't request proof of permanent residency or U.S. citizenship.

Immigration Equality   www.immigrationequality.org
This organization is for LGBTQ+ immigrants' rights.

My Undocumented Life   www.mydocumentedlife.org
This is an organization that helps undocumented immigrants find up-to-date information and resources.

Students Who Are Economically Disadvantaged

You may benefit from this sheet if you qualify for free or reduced lunch, or any form of public assistance (Medicaid, Social Security Income, Temporary Assistance for Needy Families, etc).

FAQ

Is it hard to get a scholarship?

There are many types of scholarships, each with unique requirements. Scholarships can range from ones that have academic, community service, "first in family," writing, and more themes. Some are easier to get, and others take quite a bit of time to prepare for!

You can find scholarships through web searches, private organizations, high schools, and more. Sometimes employers will help pay for school if what you're studying is relevant to the job as well.

I'm having trouble filling out my FAFSA. Can I get help with that?

If you have trouble with filling out your FAFSA, a school guidance counselor can help you. There are also "full walkthrough" videos to help explain the FAFSA online. Search "Form Your Future" to find a guide that can help answer your questions as well.

I can't afford the application fees for all of the institutions that I want to apply to. What do I do?

Contact the colleges that you're interested in, as some of them will waive the fee for your application. Some schools will even waive the fee if you have exceptional academics or make an in person visit to the college! If you are an income-eligible student who takes an SAT or SAT subject test in a district or state program during high school and receive a waiver, you can choose from over 2,000 colleges to apply to at no cost!

What can I do if living on campus is too expensive?

The office of Student Housing Services at your school of choice often has information about off-campus living options and resources for students who are under financial distress. You can also use your financial aid dollars towards campus living. Also look into leadership roles at the school that offer more affordable (and sometimes free) housing and meal plans.

Do campuses have food pantries?

Some do! More and more schools are beginning to start campus food pantries. These pantries are limited in how they can help, so other options (like the Supplemental Nutrition Assistance Program, for example) should be sought out as well.

Is there a way that I can work on campus?

Most colleges have work study programs. These are a bit different than a typical job since you're working for the school. These jobs are usually accommodating to your class schedule and academic needs! The office of Career Services can help you find work. Also, as the internet becomes more and more a part of people's daily lives, more opportunities to work online (from your dorm) are becoming available! With an option like this, you are less likely to have to pay for transportation and other work expenses.

If I live off campus, can I get help with paying for internet?

Internet companies are beginning to offer discounted internet and house phone rates for people who are on government programs like Medicaid, SSI, food stamps, etc. Through calling 211 or visiting **211.org**, you can also be connected with local resources that help with basic living expenses.

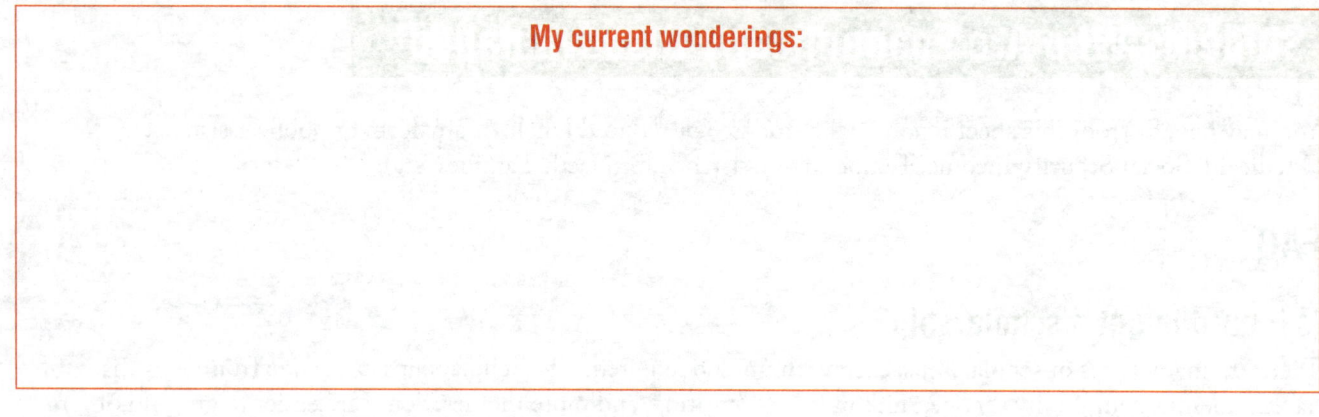

My current wonderings:

Resources for Students Who Are Economically Disadvantaged

211   www.211.org
This site can connect you to local resources that include but aren't limited to: health clinics, food, housing help, and employment.

Form Your Future   www.formyourfuture.org
This website has a guide that helps you fill out your FAFSA.

FinAid   www.finaid.org/calculators
The "calculators" section of this site has a financial aid award letter comparison tool. It also has other calculators that are helpful when trying to budget for college.

eCampusTours   www.ecampustours.com
This website allows you to do a tour of a campus without having to physically go there. There are over 1,000 colleges showcased on this site.

The Common Application   www.commonapp.org
This site allows you to apply for more than one school at a time. About half of the schools that allow you to apply in this manner do not have an application fee.

Students Preparing for Nontraditional Training and Employment

You may benefit from this sheet if you are considering gaining a certification through a trade school before a college degree or instead of a college degree.

FAQ

What is a trade school?
Trade school is also known as: technical, vocational, and/or career schools! They can be public and private, though many are for-profit businesses. These programs are typically 2 years or less. Certification programs are also available at community colleges.

Is financial aid available for schools that aren't colleges or universities?
Not all colleges and career schools participate in federal student aid programs, however many do! It's important to check. Private scholarships are also available.

What does it mean to be an accredited institution?
A school becomes accredited when it meets the minimum standards that are established by a private agency. The United States government doesn't regulate schools, but the website of the U.S. Department of Education does list the agencies that they believe are credible. Accreditors can be regional or national. It's important to note that in some cases, regionally accredited schools won't accept transfer credits from a nationally accredited school. This happens because the academic standards and courses are different.

What are some benefits of trade schools? How is it beneficial?
Trade schools are options for people who want to get the training that they need in order to start their new career in a shorter amount of time than it takes to get a degree. These programs often cost less as well. Some people enjoy trade schools because they teach people exactly what they need to know to do their jobs, and they don't usually have to take courses that are unrelated to their certification. Some people even use trade schools as stepping stones for going to college as with their certificates, they can earn more money and be better equipped to pay for college expenses and other needs.

How do I know if going to a trade school will be a cost-effective option for me?
Something to consider may be figuring out how many years of salary after you get your first job related to the certificate it will take to earn back the money that it cost you to complete the program. Figuring out how big of a need there is in the workforce for people with that particular skill is important as well. Use local employment data by searching "employment data for _____ jobs."

Are there online trade schools?
Yes! They exist. Do an online search for "trade schools online" or "online vocational schools" to find some examples. Adding your state name to the search (but not in quotation marks) can also be helpful.

What type of programs do trade schools offer?
You can find programs like: plumbing, home inspection, solar energy technology, aviation maintenance, licensed vocational nurse [LVN], paralegal, automotive mechanic, medical coding and billing, business management, accounting, child development, and so many more.

www.educationopensdoors.org

My current wonderings:

Resources for Students Preparing for Nontraditional Training and Employment

The US Department of Education's Database of Accredited Postsecondary Institutions and Programs   www.ope.ed.gov/dapip

This is the list of postsecondary educational agencies that the US Department of Education believes are credible.

Students with Limited English Proficiency

You may benefit from this sheet if English is not your native language and you're currently learning it.

FAQ

Can I take the SAT and/or ACT test in my native language?

As of today, both exams are only given in English. It may be beneficial to take the PSAT or PreACT to evaluate which components of the test you need extra support to prepare for. Consider which components of the test highlight your strengths. The SAT includes a verbal and writing component as well as a math section. On the other hand, the ACT includes subject tests which may correlate more closely to your classes in school.

Does the SAT and/or ACT provide accommodations for English language learners?

Accommodations for English language learners include: more testing time, a bilingual word-for-word dictionary, a translation of the testing instructions in your native language, and testing in a different location. These accommodations are not automatically given, and must be requested early as it can take several weeks for accommodations to get approved.

How can I stay up on note taking in classes?

Partner up with another student if possible. It's a great way to share and compare notes, and prepare for upcoming tests. With programs and apps made specifically for the exchange of notes, collaborating with classmates has become easier than before.

How do I know if a college I'm looking into will be supportive for me as I learn English?

Seek out a school that has an "English language support program" (sometimes called a "bridge program"). These campus programs are there to help students whose native language isn't English in their studies. Look into college preparation programs in your area, too. They can set you up with a timeline on when to do things as well as share a network of people who can help you apply for college.

Will I have to take any extra exams in order to get accepted into a college?

Some colleges may require students with limited English proficiency to take the TOEFL (Test of English as a Foreign Language) exam or a similar one before admission. If you know what colleges you're interested in, look into that ahead of time so you can find resources and prepare yourself for the exam.

What is instant decision day?

This is a day where an event is held-- often at high schools or local venues, that allow college admission officers and students to meet. At the end of each meeting, the college has the option to give you an offer of admission! This is different than the regular process of applying for a college and having to wait weeks or months to get a response. Search "instant decision day" to determine if this is an option for you.

Is it possible to get help writing my college essay?

Yes! Contact an English teacher to ask for feedback after you're done writing the first draft of your essay. There are also guides available online specifically for English language learners who would like help writing their essays. Search "ELL writing guide."

While you're in college, you may also like to take advantage of writing centers on college campuses.

My current wonderings:

Resources for Students with Limited English Proficiency

The Common Application   www.commonapp.org

You can apply to over 700 colleges all with the same college application. This website also supplies more in-depth resources for Spanish speakers.

YouTube

The vocabulary used in higher education courses is often very different than that used in public school. There are a lot of ELL professors online who have video lessons specifically for people who want to learn "college vocabulary."

Libraries

Not only do many of them offer ELL classes, but they also have audio courses for learning English that you can borrow.

Students Who Identify as LGBTQ+

You may benefit from this handout if you identify as part of the LGBTQ+ community.

FAQ

Do all colleges have student led LGBTQ+ groups?
No, but many do. Browse college websites and ask staff and students at schools you're interested in about the resources that are made available to LGBTQ+ students on campus.

Are there anti-discrimination rules in place at every university?
Each school's code of conduct varies, so it's a good idea to look them up online before applying. View their inclusion statements and anti-discrimination policies. Also, see their previous reactions to incidents on campus. An understanding of anti-discrimination laws in the states where you are considering continuing your education could inform your ultimate decision.

Is it possible to get gender-inclusive housing at college?
Yes, many colleges have housing where you can choose to have a roommate of any gender. Many colleges offer gender neutral bathrooms as well.

Will I still be able to study abroad if I'm LGBTQ+?
Of course! Depending on the country you're interested in, there may be specific issues related to housing and documentation that need to be addressed.

Is my identity as LGBTQ+ confidential?
Yes, it is up to you! Talk to the college's LGBTQ+ services/center or get in contact with current LGBTQ+ students to ask about the protocol on how information is shared on campus or with their families in regard to desired confidentiality.

Is it possible that I can get counseling services from my college's health center that are inclusive of my identity?
For many colleges, yes. If you are on a parent/guardian's health insurance plan, keep in mind that your records may be accessible to parents. After turning 18, usually you can call the insurance company and request that your records be private (only available to you).

My current wonderings:

Resources for Students Who Identify as LGBTQ+

Campus Pride Index   www.campusprideindex.org
This is a national listing of LGBTQ+ friendly colleges. They have a list of over 1,000 colleges with nondiscrimination policies regarding gender identity and expression!

Point Foundation   www.pointfoundation.org
This foundation gives scholarships to LGBTQ+ students.

Athlete Ally   www.AthleteAlly.org
This organization aims to end anti-gay and anti-trans discrimination in sports.

National Center for Transgender Equality   www.transequality.org
This organization has information on trans rights on many topics including school, healthcare, and more.

Consortium of Higher Education LGBT Resource Professionals   www.LGBTCampus.org
In the "resources" section of their website, they have a directory of colleges that have LGBTQ+ campus centers.

The Trevor Project   www.thetrevorproject.org
This organization helps connect LGBTQ+ youth to resources, and is able to help aid in crisis intervention.

Planned Parenthood   www.plannedparenthood.org
This nonprofit organization provides sexual and reproductive health services that are inclusive to LGBTQ+ people. This includes helping with service referrals, support groups, education and hormone replacement therapy.

Students with Physical Disabilities

You may be a student with a physical disability if you have a health condition that affects your physical functioning, the ability to move freely with ease, your fine motor skills (hands), and/or energy.

FAQ

What scholarships are available to students with physical disabilities?

There are a multitude of scholarships (both private and public) available to and specifically for disabled students. Some of these scholarships are made by different disability organizations, and others can be found through online searches.

How will I access medical care when living on campus?

Depending on your situation, public insurance like Medicaid may be available to you, and in some circumstances you may have the option of staying on your parents' insurance plan until the age of 26. Many colleges also have plans specifically for the students going to their schools as well. Some people have one insurance, and some have more than one.

If I need attendant care, how will I get that?

Most people who get attendant care get it through Medicaid waivers. This can give you the ability to hire your own attendants often through agencies although sometimes you may conduct your own search as well.

Are students accepting? How do professors react?

Every school is different, however looking up a school's website to see if they have any student-led clubs for those with disabilities, as well as looking to see how much info and what info is on their site in respect to their disability accommodations office can help you a lot in choosing a school where you will thrive the most.

What do I do if my professor refuses my accommodations request?

If you have a 504 Plan through your university's disability / accommodations office and your professor refuses to allow the accommodations that the disability office has permitted, this would most likely violate the American with Disabilities Act (ADA) and Section 504 of the Rehabilitation Act. If the accommodations office has confirmed the need for the accommodations, the school must comply. Contact the accommodations office if this happens.

Do I have to tell my professor about my disability?

No! You are under no legal obligation to do so. You can choose to meet with your professor to explain how the accommodations you've been granted are useful to you and answer any questions that they have and you feel comfortable answering.

Can my high school 504 plan follow me to college?

While there are no IEPs in college, Section 504 (504 plans) covers your needs if the school you're attending receives public funds. Colleges have their own eligibility criteria in order for you to qualify to haven a 504 plan, so it's necessary to contact their disability / accommodations office ahead of time to establish disability and figure out which accommodations you may be allowed.

What type of paperwork do I need to get accommodations?

If you need accommodations, it's important to bring recent disability documentation to the accommodations office. The documentation should not be older than 5 years. 2 years or more recent is best. (Every college is different in their requirements.) Strong documentation that shows evidence of the limitations you have that can affect how you do schoolwork is necessary. If you're having trouble figuring out which documents will be helpful, ask yourself what aspects of potential assignments will be difficult for you due to your disability. Then find documentation that shows why those aspects of the assignments would be more difficult for you.

What does "FERPA" stand for?
It stands for: Family Educational Rights and Privacy Act. It's a federal law that protects the privacy of your student records! Generally speaking, FERPA gives you the right to access all of your educational records before giving consent for it to be accessed by someone else (including your parents). You have the right to ask your school to correct any records you believe are inaccurate or misleading, too.

What if I have major food allergies?
The office of accommodations / disability services will be who coordinates accommodations for major food allergies! (Celiac disease, etc). If you are on a special [medical] food plan, contact disability services to see how they accommodate food plans.

Are people with human immunodeficiency virus or acquired immunodeficiency syndrome covered by the ADA?
Yes! Federal laws protect people with these conditions, both symptomatic and asymptomatic, are protected. Section 504 protects these individuals as well!

What should I look out for if I use a mobility device?
If you use a mobility device, the size of the campus and where things are located in proximity of each other are things that should be looked into before committing to a school. Weather patterns (rain and snow, in particular) during school seasons and areas of the campus that are inaccessible (and may have/require alternate paths) are all things that should be considered before committing to a college.

Do private universities have to comply with Section 504 laws?
If that private school receives public funding (which most do), yes.

Do private universities have to comply with ADA laws?
Generally, Title II of the ADA covers vocational schools, universities and community colleges that are publicly funded and Title III of the ADA covers privately funded schools.

My current wonderings:

Resources for Students with Physical Disabilities

Your State's Department of Rehabilitation Services
They can help with paying for college, trade schools, things you'll need to live on campus, connecting you to medical programs, etc.

Bridges from School to Work Program   www.bridgestowork.org
This program helps young adults in major US cities find entry level jobs. They must have had an IEP in public school. This can be helpful for finding a part time job while in school.

Bookshare   www.bookshare.org
This is a virtual library with over half a million books (including some textbooks) available to you at your disposal. This is free to students with qualifying disabilities, and $50 a year to people who qualify but are not students.

Job Accommodation Network: JAN   www.askjan.org
This is a website that you can browse and a hotline that you can call with questions regarding workplace accommodations and the Americans with Disabilities Act (ADA).

Vocabulary

DIRECTIONS:

1. DEFINE each word using the glossary in this book or a dictionary.
2. ANSWER the questions listed below for each word.

Vocabulary Word	Definition	Have you ever heard/seen this word before?	Explain how you have heard this word used before. If you've never heard or seen it, what other word (in any language) does it look like to you?
		Y N	
		Y N	
		Y N	
		Y N	
		Y N	
		Y N	
		Y N	
		Y N	

Additional words to complete on notebook paper: _____
_____

Glossary of Terms

Academic Advisor/Guidance Counselor
A person at your school who will help you pick the right courses for your graduation plan and provide support on your path to postsecondary education.

Acceptance/Admission
An offer to attend a school or program you applied to.

ACT (American College Test)
A standardized test designed to measure a student's level of content knowledge before granting admission. Also see SAT (Scholastic Aptitude Test).

Admissions Committee
A group of people who review submitted applications and make decisions on acceptance or denial.

Alma Mater
A phrase used to describe the school from which one graduated.

Alumni/Alumnus/Alumnae
People who have graduated from a school or program.

AP (Advanced Placement)
AP classes are advanced coursework with a weighted GPA, that give college credits based upon exam scores.

Application
The documents a student submits to the school(s) they want to attend.

Associate's Degree
This degree is granted after completing at least 60 credit hours, usually about two years of college.

Attendance Zone
The boundaries a city has established for which neighborhoods attend which schools.

Bachelor's Degree
A four-year degree from a college; usually requires at least 120 credit hours. This is what people usually mean when they talk about a "college degree."

Binding Application
Binding admission means that the applicant has to attend the school they applied to if their application is accepted.

Budget
A practice of balancing your income and expenses by determining how much of your income you want/need to allocate for specific things and creating a log to track progress.

Business Casual
The most common business dress code in a professional setting. Pants without denim, close toed shoes, and a nice shirt are recommended.

Business Professional
The most formal professional attire, usually a dark colored suit.

Candidates Reply Date Agreement (CRDA)
An agreement several colleges follow that gives applicants a deadline to accept or decline offers of admission.

Career
A commitment to a field or job within a field for an extended time.

Career Aptitude Test
A test that narrows down a major or career choice that aligns to your interests, abilities, and skills.

Capped Major
Some majors are "capped," meaning the school will only admit a certain number of students into the program each year because so many students desire that major.

Certification
Certifications provide specialized training in a particular skill or trade. Certifications are gained at all levels of education.

Character Strength
An internal positive quality a person has and can share with others.

Class Rank
A number that reflects your GPA compared to the rest of your class. It is listed as a number or as a percentile.

CLEP (College Level Examination Program)
A CLEP test can be taken to award college credit for classes without actually taking them, if a student scores high enough.

COA (Cost of Attendance)
The estimated cost of completing one full year at a college or in a program. For college, it includes tuition, room and board (housing and food), student fees, books and supplies, and sometimes transportation costs.

Co-Ed
A school, facility, or program that includes all gender identities.

College
An institution where students study to earn a degree and/or certificate after high school.

College Admission Requirements
The set of criteria needed for a student to apply to college.

Common Application (The Common App)
An undergraduate college admission application that students may use to apply to several participating schools at once.

Community

Write your own definition:

_____

_____

_____

Community College
An institution where students earn degrees and/or certificates. Tuition discounts are often given to students in the local community.

Community Service
Experiences you have sharing your time and strengths with your community as a volunteer (without pay).

Commuter Student
A student who lives off-campus and travels to school for classes.

Compound Interest (Banking Setting)
Earned interest on the total amount of money in the account, including past interest earned.

Course Audit
If a person has an interest in learning more on a topic, but doesn't want to have the class become a part of their GPA, they can audit a course with approval from the instructor.

Course Drop and Add Date
Students are generally allowed to drop or add courses to their semester schedules up to a specific date in the semester. Classes dropped before the drop date do not become a part of a student's GPA.

Course Credit
See **Credit Hour**.

Course Fee
The tuition a student pays per credit hour for a class.

Course Numbers
Numbers assigned to courses in college; the higher the number the more advanced the class.

Cover Letter
A one-page letter summarizing your skills, past experiences, goals, and how they align with the organization or company you are applying to.

Credit Hour
The number of credits given for a course, which is then used to determine GPA.

CSS (College Scholarship Service) Profile
A financial aid application provided by the College Board in the U.S. It is similar to the FAFSA, but is not free to complete.

Cumulative GPA
Calculates your grade point average (GPA) from all classes to date.

DACA Students (Deferred Action for Childhood Arrivals)
Undocumented youth granted DACA are protected from deportation for two years, subject to renewal, and provided with a work permit. In almost every state, DACAmented students can apply for a driver's license. For more information on eligibility and resources to apply for DACA, search United We Dream and DREAM Educational Empowerment Program.

Deferred Admission
Permission from a college where you have been accepted to postpone enrolling in the college. The postponement is usually up to one year.

Degree
Degrees are what students get for completing a program of study at a college or university. There are three basic types of degrees: Associate's, Bachelor's, Master's and Doctoral Degrees.

Degree Requirements
The required courses or projects required for completion of a degree program. They may include a number of credit hours and a minimum GPA, among other specifics.

Deposit
A deposit is money placed in a bank account, usually to gain interest.

Diploma
A diploma is a document which shows that a person has finished all requirements for graduation from high school, a certificate, or a degree program.

Dissertation
A dissertation is a requirement for a Doctoral Degree. The lengthy essay is based upon scholarly research, and it must be an original contribution to the field.

Doctoral Degree
A doctoral degree, also known as a PhD or doctorate, is the most advanced degree that can be earned. This is why people who have a PhD are often called doctors even if they don't work in a hospital or clinic.

Dormitory
Dormitories or residence halls are buildings on college campuses where students live.

Dual Credit Classes
A dual credit class is a college level class taken by a high school student. A dual credit class gives credit towards high school graduation as well as towards a future degree or certificate program.

Early Action (EA)
An option to submit your college applications before the regular deadlines to increase your chances of admission; early action applications are not binding.

Early Admission
An option to submit your college applications before the regular deadlines to increase your chances of admission. Early admission deadlines are usually between October and November.

Early College High School
A high school partnered with a college that is designed for students to receive both a high school diploma and an Associate's degree at the same time.

Early Decision (ED)
An option to apply to your first-choice college before the regular deadline to increase your chances of admission. Early decision applications are binding.

Employment
A time when a person is paid for work, also known as a part of the work force.

Enrollment
This is the process of selecting classes each semester in college. It may also include paying fees/tuition.

Enrollment Status
A full-time or part-time enrollment status depends on the number of credit hours a student is taking in a semester. 12 or more is full-time enrollment, less than 12 is part-time enrollment.

Extracurricular Activities
Non-classroom activities that students can get involved in at school or in their community.

Expected Family Contribution (EFC)
A part of the FAFSA where a student shares the expected amount of money that their family will contribute towards their education. The EFC is subtracted from a college's COA (Cost of Attendance) to determine how much financial aid a student will receive.

Expenses
Money spent on personal needs and desires (housing, food, transportation, etc.).

FAFSA (Free Application for Federal Student Aid)
The FAFSA is an application for financial aid, including loans, grants, college work study, and other federal and state programs. It is often required before a student can be considered for many scholarships.

Federal Pell Grant
A grant given to students from the federal government based upon financial need. Students must complete the FAFSA to be eligible for the Pell Grant.

Final
A culminating test, paper, or project assessing your knowledge gained throughout the semester.

Financial Aid
Money students use to cover college expenses. Aid comes in the form of grants, scholarships, loans, and work-study.

First Generation College Student
A student whose parent(s) or legal guardian(s) have not completed an undergraduate degree program.

First Impression
An opportunity to present our best qualities when we first meet someone or are in an environment that is unfamiliar. First impressions are formed in the first 3 seconds of meeting a new person.

Fraternities/Sororities
Fraternities and sororities are social organizations at some colleges that are made up of like-minded people.

Freshman
A student in their first year of high school or college.

GA
Stands for "Graduate Assistant." See **TA (Teaching Assistant)**.

Gen Ed
Stands for a "General Education" course, which are courses all students must take, regardless of major.

GPA (Grade Point Average)
GPA is the sum of a student's grades, divided by the number of credit hours to get an average.

Graduate School
A degree program for students who want to study a subject area in further depth beyond their undergraduate degree. Graduate degrees are master's, doctoral, and professional degrees.

Grants
Financial aid that does not require repayment.

High School Application Requirements
The specific requirements needed to gain admission to a magnet or private high school, which can include a minimum GPA, strong recommendations, advanced coursework, etc.

High School Graduation Requirements
The set of criteria students must complete in order to graduate from high school. Note, these are not always the same as college admission requirements.

Humanities Courses
Humanities courses are classes covering subjects such as literature, philosophy, and the fine arts. Most undergraduate degrees require a minimum number of humanities credit hours.

Hydration
The process of drinking enough water for one's body to achieve a balance and function properly.

Income
Money gained through employment and investment returns.

Informational Interview
An interview conducted to collect information about a job, career field, industry or company. An informational interview is not a job interview.

In-State Tuition
A reduced tuition rate for students who attend college in the same state they live.

Interest (Banking Setting)
A deposit into your account from the bank based upon the amount of money you have deposited into the account.

IB (International Baccalaureate)
IB is a twelve-year curriculum that focuses on a worldview perspective of education. Only select schools are IB schools. The high school program is called the Diploma Program (DP) and is completed during the final 2 years of high school.

Internship
An internship is a temporary job (usually 2-3 months) that allows experience in a work environment for a specific career. Internships can help narrow down a career choice.

Interview
A formal meeting in which one or more persons question, consult, or evaluate another person for a potential job or acceptance to a school.

Interviewee
An interviewee is a person who is being interviewed, or is being asked questions.

Interviewer
An interviewer is a person in an interview setting who is asking questions to the interviewee.

In-State Tuition
A student who meets state residency requirements pays a discounted tuition at a college in the same state.

Junior
A student in their third year of high school or college.

Junior College
See Community College.

Laboratory
Most science courses have a required separate lab course to be taken the same semester. In lab, students conduct experiments and do the hands-on practice of the class.

Lecture
Traditional class sessions with a professor teaching the course to students, often in lecture format.

Loan
Financial aid that must be repaid, usually with interest added.

Lower Division Courses
These courses, usually 100 or 200 level, are the first classes you take in college (usually as a freshman or sophomore). Most are prerequisites for advanced courses.

Major
A student's concentrated field of study in an undergraduate degree program.

Master's Degree
A graduate degree that usually requires two or more years of study after completing a bachelor's degree. A master's degree program usually culminates with a thesis.

Mid-Term Exams (Midterms)
During the middle of each semester, instructors may give mid-term exams that test students on the material covered during the first half of the term.

Mindset
A way of thinking.

Minor
A student's secondary field of study. A minor usually consists of 5-8 courses, which is less than half of the courses required for a major.

Mock Interview
A mock interview is a practice interview.

NCAA
The NCAA is an organization that oversees athletic program participation, guidelines, and eligibility for competition at over 1,000 colleges and universities, with roughly 500,000 student athletes participating.

Networking
Networking is building relationships both personally and professionally. Relationship building is meeting people, interacting with them, and developing connections.

NMSQT
The NMSQT is the National Merit Scholarship Qualifying Test, taken in high school which can lead to scholarship money.

Online courses
Classes held through an inline portal rather than in person or in a classroom.

Out-of-State Tuition
Tuition rate that students pay if they choose to attend a public college that is not in their home state. Private college tuition does not vary based upon state residency.

Pass/Fail Courses
Courses that do not assign grades and are not calculated into a students GPA are called Pass/Fail courses. Transcripts have a "P" for Pass or a "U" for unsatisfactory.

Percentile
Percentiles are a way of communicating class rank as a percentage. For example, a student in the top 50% of their class means that the student's GPA is ranked the same or better than 50% of the students in their class.

Personal Statement
A type of application essay that is explicitly about the applicant's uniqueness, achievements, and desire to be a part of the program.

Petition
A petition is the name for both the process and the form a student fills out to request consideration of special circumstances. For example, if a student is denied admission to the college of their choice, they may petition for admission based on exceptional circumstances.

Postgraduate
See "graduate school." A student who pursues an advanced degree after earning a bachelor's degree.

Postsecondary
Any school after high school. Also see College.

Prerequisite
A course that must be taken prior to enrollment in another course.

Priority Date or Deadline
The date by which your application — whether it's for college admission, student housing or financial aid — must be received by a college to be considered.

Private College/University
A school that is not funded with public dollars and instead relies on donations, tuition, and fees.

Professionalism
Professionalism is exhibiting acceptable qualities or behaviors connected to the expectations of the setting. Qualities describe the character, disposition, or nature of a person.

Public College/University
A state funded college or university.

RA (Resident Advisor)
An upper-class student (junior or senior) living in a freshman dorm as a peer counselor and hall supervisor.

Reading Days
Also known as "dead days," is a time at the end of each semester before final exams that regular classes are not held so students can study and attend review sessions.

Recommendation Letter
A letter written by someone who can highlight your skills, accomplishments, leadership experience, academic successes, extracurricular involvement, ambition, and goals as a part of the school and scholarship application process.

Reference
Someone who can comment on your personal character, work ethic, or past work experiences, usually as a part of the job application process.

Registrar
The registrar's office is responsible for the maintenance of all academic records. Records can include: class enrollment, athletic eligibility, honor roll eligibility, academic probation and verification completed of degree requirements for graduation.

Regular Admission
This is the type of admission that most schools offer. There is a set deadline by which an applicant has to submit their application.

Résumé
A document that highlights a person's education, work and academic experiences, honors, community involvement, skills.

Rolling admission
A type of admission that allows schools to accept students throughout the year.

Room and Board
The cost for living on campus and participating in the campus dining plan.

SAP (Satisfactory Academic Progress)
SAP is a standard for minimum GPA and credit hour completion students must achieve each semester in order to maintain their financial aid under federally supported programs.

SAR (Student Aid Report)
A summary of responses filed on one's FAFSA. It is sent to the student and colleges/universities the student listed on their FAFSA.

SAT (Scholastic Aptitude Test)
A standardized test designed to measure a student's level of content knowledge before granting admission. Also see ACT (American College Test).

Scholarship
Financial aid that does not require repayment.

Semester
A half-year term in a school or college, typically lasting fifteen to eighteen weeks.

Semester GPA
Your grade point average (GPA) for a single semester.

Senior
A student in their last year of high school or college.

Social/Emotional Counselor
A counselor who promotes skills and practices to help students make decisions, build relationships, develop coping skills to process difficult emotions, and mature through self-awareness.

Soft Skills
Skills that are practiced over time, and often are a reflection of how you exist in your day to day – communication, leadership, problem-solving, creativity, collaboration, etc.

Sophomore
A student in their second year of high school or college.

Student Activity Fee
A fee that is separate from your tuition. These fees fund student organizations, activities, and other services provided on campus.

Study Group
A group of people who meet as often as necessary to help each other with schoolwork, prepare for tests, share information, and discuss knowledge gained in class.

Subsidized Loans
Subsidized loans do not build interest for at least the first half of one's college education. They are called subsidized loans because the government "subsidizes" (or pays back) any interest that builds for a time.

Summer Session
A summer term of classes, lasting approximately six weeks.

Syllabus/Syllabi
An outline of the important information about a course. Written by the professor or instructor, it usually includes important dates, assignments, expectations and policies specific to that course.

TA (Teaching Assistant)
A graduate or undergraduate student who works with a professor for research and student support; they also sometimes teach classes on behalf of the professor.

Thesis
An extensive research paper written on a specific topic as a part of a student's degree requirements. They are usually presented to a committee of professors for review.

Trade School
Trade schools, also called vocational or technical schools, are schools that teach a set of specific skills and knowledge related to a particular job or career field for students pursing a certification.

Transcript
An academic record showing courses taken, grades received, academic status and honors received.

Transcripts (Official)
See Transcript. Official transcripts are stamped and sealed by the school.

Transcripts (Unofficial)
See Transcript. An unofficial transcript is a complete academic history that is a print out of all of your classes and credits that is not sealed.

Transfer of Credits
If a student chooses to change colleges, they must request a transfer of credits for classes taken to count as a part of degree requirements at their new college.

Trimester
At schools that use the trimester system the school year is divided into three trimesters. Often called: fall trimester, winter trimester and spring trimester.

Tuition
Tuition is the amount paid for each credit hour of enrollment.

Undergraduate
A student who is pursuing an Associate's or Bachelor's degree.

Unemployment
Unemployment is when a person within the workforce is without paid work.

University
A university is composed of undergraduate, graduate, and professional colleges which offers degree programs to students.

Undocumented Students
Students who lack lawful residency or visiting status in the country they live in.

Unsubsidized Loans
A federally funded loan that is not based on financial need. Interest builds as soon as one begins college.

Upper Division Courses
Classes designed for students within a specific course of study that usually have prerequisite courses and are taken in the second half of a student's college career.

Variety (Food)
The practice of eating several different types of food to absorb different vitamins and minerals into one's body.

Verification
Verification occurs when a student's FAFSA is either by random selection or due to an issue with their application. It means additional information in required for acquiring financial aid.

Waiting List
An admission status where students are not fully admitted, but have also not been declined. Admission may require additional coursework, or simply time for the university to determine availability of space based upon how many other admissions offers are accepted.

Whole Foods
Foods that exist in their natural state and have not been processed.

Withdrawal
See **Course Drop and Add Date**. If withdrawing from the school, must follow established procedures for doing so to ensure they do not continue to pay tuition.

Work Study
This program provides college students with part-time jobs to help pay for school. There are two different kinds of work study: Federal Work Study (run by the government) and non-Federal Work Study (usually run by the college a student attends).

Review Game

PART 1

DIRECTIONS: Using the answer bank, write in ONE answer choice in each of the boxes of your game board. Note, they will not all fit.

Answer Bank

Networking	FAFSA	GPA	Bachelor's Degree	College
Guidance Counselor	Tuition	Junior	Recommendation Letter	Scholarships
Sophomore	ACT/SAT	Loans	Soft Skills	Résumé
Percentile	Semester	Major	Credit Hours	Minor
		Extracurricular Activities		

Game Board

PART 2

DIRECTIONS: Starting at the top of the list, read the questions below. Write the answer to the question using the answer bank on the previous page. If you have that answer choice listed on your game board, color in the box until you have all of the squares colored in.

GOING FURTHER

Upon determining the correct answer to each question, find the reference for the information in the book and write the page number next to the question.

Question	Page Number
_____ are a type of financial aid that does not have to be paid back.	_____
A _____ is someone who ensures you're taking the right courses for your graduation plan and supports your journey to postsecondary education.	_____
Sports, fine arts, and enrichment opportunities are examples of _____.	_____
These are standardized tests used for college admission: _____	_____
This type of undergraduate degree is usually 4 years long: _____	_____
_____ is the sum of your grades divided by your total credit hours.	_____
Awards, Honors, Skills, Community Involvement, Work and Academic Experiences as well as Education can be found on this document: _____	_____
_____ is another word for relationship building.	_____
The application that must be completed in order to be eligible for federal financial aid is called the _____.	_____
On a résumé, your experiences should be listed in _____ order.	_____
My grandmother is supportive of my education goals in every way, but cannot write a _____ for me; instead a teacher or coach needs to.	_____
The amount of money students pay for classes in a semester is called _____.	_____
A place where students study to earn a degree and/or certificate after HS: _____	_____
A second year student in a high school or college: _____	_____
Along with your grades, this number is used to calculate your GPA: _____	_____
Communication, leadership, problem-solving, creativity, collaboration are all examples of _____.	_____

Transition to College Timeline

DIRECTIONS: After getting accepted to college, there are still a lot of steps to complete before attending your first college class. This Guidebook is full of resources for you to use in that transition. Go back through this guidebook and identify 10 worksheets that will be helpful to you and place a bookmark on those pages. Utilize this timeline as a guide.

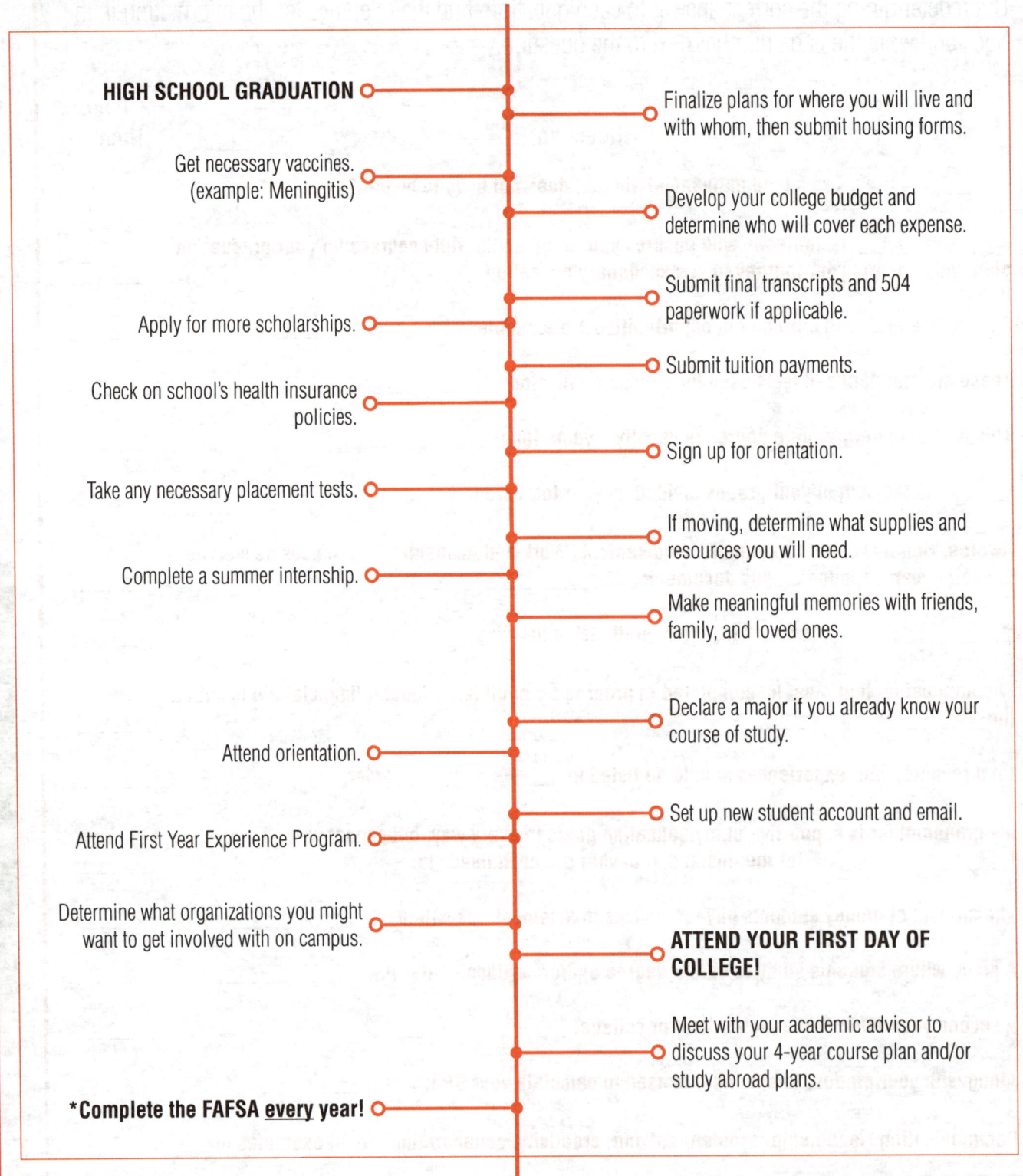

- **HIGH SCHOOL GRADUATION**
- Finalize plans for where you will live and with whom, then submit housing forms.
- Get necessary vaccines. (example: Meningitis)
- Develop your college budget and determine who will cover each expense.
- Submit final transcripts and 504 paperwork if applicable.
- Apply for more scholarships.
- Submit tuition payments.
- Check on school's health insurance policies.
- Sign up for orientation.
- Take any necessary placement tests.
- If moving, determine what supplies and resources you will need.
- Complete a summer internship.
- Make meaningful memories with friends, family, and loved ones.
- Declare a major if you already know your course of study.
- Attend orientation.
- Set up new student account and email.
- Attend First Year Experience Program.
- Determine what organizations you might want to get involved with on campus.
- **ATTEND YOUR FIRST DAY OF COLLEGE!**
- Meet with your academic advisor to discuss your 4-year course plan and/or study abroad plans.
- ***Complete the FAFSA <u>every</u> year!**

© 2019 Education Opens Doors, Inc.

NAME _____

NAME _____

NAME _____

NAME _____

NAME _____

NAME _____

NAME _____

NAME _____

NAME _____

NAME _____

NAME _____

NAME _____

NAME _____

NAME _____

NAME _____

NAME _____

NAME _____

NAME _____

NAME _____

NAME _____

NAME _____

CERTIFICATE OF COMPLETION

_____

YOUR NAME

IS READY TO PURSUE AN INFORMED AND GOAL-FILLED FUTURE!

_____

YOUR TEACHER

&

CERTIFIED BY:

_____

THE EDUCATION OPENS DOORS TEAM

You've completed the Education Opens Doors Student Guidebook, congratulations!

We hope it has helped inform your goal filled future. At the beginning of the book, we shared a message with you. Here it is again. Don't forget to take this book home with you as a resource for you and your family!

Message to Students

Your future isn't written yet. What will your story say?

You are capable of extraordinary accomplishments and truly changing the world. This manual is one tool you can use on your journey to make the world a more incredible place.

Below is some advice from the creators:

- Surround yourself with a positive circle of support.
- Know that you have the right to live a choice filled life.
- Use the resources available to you.
- Speak up for yourself.
- Explore all of your options.
- Ask questions.
- Keep this manual and use it as a guide!

The journey starts with you! Now is the time to explore the pathways that will lead to your ideal future.

All our best,

The Education Opens Doors team
www.educationopensdoors.org

Follow us for updates: @educationopensdoors